RESPONSES

Responses

Musical essays and reviews

David Cairns

Alfred A. Knopf
New York   1973

Library of Congress Cataloging in Publication Data

Cairns, David.
    Responses: musical essays and reviews.

    1. Music—Addresses, essays, lectures.
I. Title.
ML60.C14A3   1973   780   72–10599
ISBN 0–394–48520–3

First American Edition

TO ROSIE

Contents

Contents

IV Miscellaneous Essays and Reviews

Acknowledgments

I am indebted to the editors of the *Spectator*, the *New Statesman*, the *Financial Times* and the *Observer* for permission to reprint, or extract from, concert and opera reviews which appeared in their journals. In going through them I have tidied up a few awkwardnesses and obscurities in the writing and restored a number of passages which were cut at the time for lack of space and which seem to me necessary to the shape or balance of the argument. In addition, in the case of three of the essays published here, I have rewritten and greatly expanded what were originally much shorter pieces: they are the essays on *Idomeneo* and the Diabelli Variations, which began as sleeve notes to the Philips recordings of those works, and the study of the relationship between *Les Troyens* and the *Aeneid*, which is based on a paper read to the Royal Musical Association in 1969 and subsequently printed in the Association's Proceedings. Finally, I would like to thank Mr Richard Temple Savage who kindly copied the dozen or so music examples reproduced in the book.

Introduction

About half of what appears here has been in print before; but the whole book can be said to be a product of my time as a music critic. Naturally I have an interest in believing that the time was not wasted, and that among what I wrote are things worth reprinting; and although I have tried to devise the book in such a way that it hangs on a stronger thread than that of random impressions and purely personal taste, I cannot claim that it embodies any systematic philosophy of criticism. Even if I wanted to I would have none to propose. I share the view of a modern writer that criticism 'has about it neither rigour nor proof'; it can only be 'passionate private experience seeking to persuade'.* But being a critic has left me with one conviction which has become almost a creed, that it is better in every way to admire than to find fault (though not necessarily easier). I believe it is the business of critics as well as music-lovers to respond. This book has been put together in that spirit. The essays and articles on particular works and composers are my responses—my tribute, and my attempt to describe and analyse the echoes they arouse in me. In the same spirit I have included some pieces, new and old, which set out to evoke the special qualities of some of the performers who have meant most to me in my musical life—adding a few anti-heroes for the sake of spice.

By 'response' I do not of course mean that one should admire uncritically. Mere appreciation is the last thing that

* George Steiner, *The Death of Tragedy*.

is advocated. Rather, it is a positive approach to what is there, starting from the working hypothesis that the composer knows best. I believe great composers do not let us down, if we trust them; experience, when we allow it, teaches us that whole-hearted, committed belief is not only a more rewarding but a far more real state than the questioning half-acceptance which often precedes it. What is involved is not merely an act of faith, though it may begin with it. The works justify the faith.

Therefore I have tried to 'season my admiration with an attent ear', to contemplate my household gods not as a blind worshipper but judiciously and to test them at every turn. If I cannot see the imperfections which some of them are said to contain, it is not for want of diligent looking. It is a matter of the angle of vision. The difference in approach may not after all be very large, but the results can be most beneficial—such as the conclusion I have been forced to that *Fidelio*, that arch-hybrid, is a coherent masterpiece of dramatic construction. Such claims are not, I hope, advanced lightly. I am 'seeking to persuade'; and one can only do that when one has a strong personal experience to communicate and good reasons to give for it.

'Nothing is real until it is experienced': Keats' remark is valid for criticism as well as for life. It is because I am aware that my experience of contemporary music has not gone very far, and not with any conscious gesture of reaction, that most of this book is taken up with the music of the past. I feel I have more to say about it because generally speaking I know it better. No invidious distinctions are intended. Though the highest achievements of Western music seem to me to come from the half-century from 1779 to 1828, I am not therefore on the side of the past against the present. The history of a masterpiece is in any case not a static thing. The great works of the past are continually part of the present; we have them, and we contribute to them our own responses. Perhaps it is against the spirit of the times and the irresistible movement of contemporary culture to want to go on believing in the concept of the work of art—its existence (which no one can argue away), its greatness, its necessity, the genius and discipline required to create it; but, despite all that is said and done to prove that Art is dead, I can see no inherent reason why it should not go on being added to. Certainly it takes a tough and resilient nature to withstand the triple pressures of the horrors of the modern world, the ever-present oppressive accumulation of history, and the breakdown of an agreed common language, and to turn them to positive account; but it is not impossible. The museum to which many of our keenest minds contemptuously compare the collected art of Western civilization, and which they would like to raze to the ground in the name of a new social order, should rather be seen as a university, constantly expanding its curriculum, and open to all. Where the art comes from, when it was made, has ceased to matter. Music, at least, resists enrolment under any banners, reactionary or revolutionary. At its greatest it does not belong to the age and ideology which produced it, but transcends all temporary association with their failures or injustices. It is not for any system, but only for life. The organization of society may tend to restrict it to a limited class, but it is itself non-exclusive. The great works of music, from whatever time, are common possessions. They help us to live; they should and can belong to everybody. The critic's main task is to help to bring this about, by writing about them.

The only question is, how: how to communicate one's experience of music? Can words ever be other than deeply irrelevant to what a composer, or a fine performer of his music, actually does? Some of the greatest music is the most recalcitrant. A work such as Bach's organ Fantasia in C minor seems to ponder the mysteries of the universe; but that is really all there is to be said—and what is achieved by saying that? For this reason the book is weighted towards opera: dramatic music submits less grudgingly to being written about (though here again anything like a philosophy of opera criticism seems to me out of the question; there are no laws in so volatile and essentially pragmatic a medium). In general I have tried to arrive at a language part analytical, part evocative, more descriptive than technical but freely mixing both elements, with which to express what I feel. All attempts to put music into words are ultimately doomed. The best one can hope is to send the reader back to the original. If that happens, something has been gained.

London, 1972

Part I

Operas

Fidelio

The world can almost be divided into those for whom *Fidelio* is a flawed work by a composer of genius wrestling with an uncongenial art form and those for whom it is among the supreme masterpieces in any medium. Of all the issues about which musical opinion disagrees, few stimulate more divergent beliefs and none, it seems to me, better illustrates the truth that in such cases the rival points of view are not mere opposite sides of the coin, but that the man who loves and therefore accepts the work of art knows much more about it than the man who thinks he can see quite clearly what is wrong with it. Their positions are not comparable; the difference in their respective knowledge is a difference in kind.

To love *Fidelio* means, of course, committing oneself to the highest possible estimate of its greatness. It is simply, in Peacock's words, 'the absolute perfection of dramatic music'. The work becomes a touchstone, a force to forge and break friendships, a possession to grapple to one's soul with hoops of steel. Yet the *Fidelio* dispute is not—as is sometimes assumed—a question of faith against reason, sober judgment opposed only by a passionate suspension of it. Faith has its reasons too. Critics of the work are, however, given to representing the issue in such terms. They see clear-headed good sense on one side and, on the other, nothing more rational than the immoderate enthusiasm which, granted its subject and its composer, the work regrettably but understandably tends to breed. To them, the stumbling-blocks in the way of accepting it are such as only the extreme zeal of the convert can wish away. Tovey was informed that it 'showed "paralysis of mind" to speak of *Fidelio* as if it were a good opera'. In his recent book *Beethoven: the Last Decade*, Martin Cooper, after citing the work as an example of 'Beethoven's imagination investing commonplace literary material with real sublimity', observes that we should not allow the composer's personality to 'blind us to the facts'. The 'facts' are that it demonstrates all too clearly Beethoven's lack of experience of opera, not merely in the enormous labour it cost him and the reworking it underwent over a period of nearly ten years, but also in the mixture of genres to which he resorted in his uncertainty. The resulting confusion is hardly less damaging in the more concise final version, and it detracts from the work's virtues and weakens its credibility. No one doubts the sincerity or the force of the feelings that went into it; but it is blindness, and nothing less, not to admit that Beethoven failed to embody them in a coherent theatrical shape. An opera which begins as a *Singspiel*, then turns into a heroic melodrama, only to end as a cantata, cannot seriously be put forward as a convincing example of dramatic form. *Fidelio* is a hybrid—a magnificent hybrid, if you like, but a hybrid all the same. That it is by Beethoven does not make this any less true.

The trouble with such arguments is that they leave the heart of the matter untouched; they end before the arguments of the other side have started—that is, short of the experience that is the beginning of enlightenment. To look at *Fidelio* in terms of various conventions is to confuse form with formula (a distinction which, as Boito observed, was obvious to the clear-thinking Romans, 'who made the second word the diminutive of the first'). The facts about a work of art are what the artist does with his material.

Nor is emotion the monopoly of one side. Emotion is behind the discriminating stance of the sceptic quite as much as it is behind the all-or-nothing fervour of the enthusiast. The difference is that in the former instance it is negative emotion—embarrassment, resentment even, at the uncomplicated intensity of naked emotion in *Fidelio*, mixed with and disguised as disapproval of its untidy overlapping of categories. In any case, it is a muddled and deluded view of criticism that supposes detachment to be superior to 'uncritical' acceptance as a position from which to assess a work of art. Positive emotion releases the understanding. The music-lover who accepts *Fidelio* is not averting his eyes from weaknesses which are perfectly evident to an unbiased perception. He is aware of the features that another dislikes, but he sees them differently, as part of the profound category-defying truthfulness of a work that is not an example of any dramatic form but its own. The point about genres and styles is the kind of objection that seems very cogent when you stand outside the world of *Fidelio*, gazing in. Once you have become an inhabitant it ceases to have any meaning as an objection, any ability to 'trouble the mind's eye'. Far from ignoring the point, you recognize it as one of the chief elements in the work's unique power over the imagination.

The power of *Fidelio* lies beyond the obvious appeal of the combination of a simple but riveting plot with the characteristic loftiness-cum-physical excitement of Beethoven's music. It was admirably summed up by Peacock, writing at the time of the work's first performances in London:

[*Fidelio*] combines the profoundest harmony with melody that speaks to the soul. It carries to a pitch scarcely conceivable the true musical expression of the strongest passions and the gentlest emotions, in all their shades and contrasts. The playfulness of youthful hope, the heroism of devoted love, the rage of the tyrant, the despair of the captive, the bursting of the sunshine of liberty upon the gloom of the dungeon, which are the great outlines of the feelings successively developed in this opera, are portrayed in music not merely with truth of expression as that term might be applied to other works, but with a force and reality that makes music an intelligible language, possessing an illimitable power of pouring forth thought in sound.*

* *The Examiner*, 27 May 1832. Reprinted in *Thomas Love Peacock: Memoirs of Shelley and other Essays and Reviews*, ed. Howard Mills, London, 1970.

It may well be that this power would not have been so great without the enormous effort that the work cost Beethoven—if that is not a truism. Such effort was common with him; his music seems to derive its special urgency of utterance partly from the convulsions of its coming into the world. In *Fidelio*, however, the convulsions were fiercer and more protracted than usual. 'Of all my children, this was born in greatest labour,' Beethoven told Schindler. His struggles with *Fidelio* have been used to prove his unsuitability to opera. They are evidence, rather, of the hold of this particular operatic subject over his mind. The struggle to learn the craft of writing for the stage—the art of uniting musical structure and dramatic movement—was nothing to the struggle to master and mould the feelings that the subject stirred up in him. What made *Fidelio* so difficult for Beethoven was the combination of an unfamiliar medium with a theme that expressed his most passionately held beliefs, answered his deepest longings, and mirrored his most private sufferings in a setting of the eternal suffering of the race. Tyranny, freedom, injustice, brotherhood, the noble wife (an ideal that was so vivid to him just because it was unrealizable in his life), and the solitary man immured within walls or in the prison of deafness—these explain its fascination for him and the obstinate search for the definitive form. It is as though, to compose a work worthy of such a theme, Beethoven must submit to an ordeal comparable to that of Florestan and Leonore, must on his own plane of creative endeavour live through the same night of toil and torment, descending to the same abyss of despair, yet upheld by the same faith in ultimate victory; it could not be achieved less dearly.

There were other, external, factors of course. The commissioning of a revival, in 1814, and the revision of the text that Friedrich Treitschke carried out for it, were vital contributions to victory. In the revised libretto the action is tightened up; what was diffuse and indecisive becomes clear and to the point; everything now serves the central business of the drama. But it was Beethoven who stipulated the revision. He chose Treitschke and, as Treitschke's account shows, he was closely involved in its progress. Beethoven, for instance, insisted on a new ending to the first act; and the solution finally decided on—the return of the prisoners to the cells and their hymn of farewell to the light of day, which forms an ideal link with the Dungeon Scene—was the joint work of poet and composer. Beethoven knew now what was required. He could identify the elements—those due to the influence of French opera especially—which in 1804 and 1805 had tended to deflect the dramatic impact of his score. The clear-sighted ruthlessness of the musical revisions that produced the final form of *Fidelio* represents a feat of artistic discipline with few equals in the history of music. To watch him, at first hesitantly and sometimes crudely (in 1806), then with heroic nerve and surgical precision, ply the steel upon himself and take the knife to the often superb but over-luxuriant inventions of the first version, is an awe-inspiring sight. The cuts range from a single bar in the Canon Quartet, through innumerable small but significant compressions, to the shortening of Leonore's aria by a third and 'O namenlose Freude' by nearly a half. Beautiful elaboration and conventional repetition alike are stripped away.

Hardly less important are the reductions to the orchestral texture—most notably of all in the Dungeon Scene—which give the 1814 version its austere exalted sound, the wide-spaced, deep-founded sonority that resounds in one's mind at the mention of *Fidelio*. The original version is, by comparison, a romantic score—a luxury such a work could not allow itself. Differences are epitomized by the trombones: liberally employed in 1805, but in 1814—if we except the overture—used strictly as a special colour (almost always in association with the idea of Florestan's grave), and playing in only 64 bars of the whole opera, 50 of them in the Grave-digging Duet. Finally, the music that Beethoven composed in 1814 to replace rewritten or discarded scenes: Leonore's recitative 'Abscheulicher', the B flat final ensemble of Act 1 with the 40-odd bars preceding it, Florestan's vision of Leonore, the first section of the final scene with the Minister's address, and the concluding Presto—all of it music conceived in the highest spirit of the first inspiration, but marked by the tautness and concentration of musical and dramatic invention that were frequently missing before— complete a revision so drastic as to make a virtually new work. These additions do not merely substitute the compelling and the dramatic for the banal and the unmotivated; they round off the design in just the places where it had been deficient. The final result, generally and in detail, vindicates Beethoven's judgment; the devastating directness of *Fidelio* as we know it is the work of 1814. It had taken him twelve years, three versions, four overtures and pages of sketchbook, to reach his goal. But he had reached it at last.

The contrast between the final version's sureness and the original version's diffuseness of intention is evident from the outset in their respective treatment of the opening scenes. In the 1805 version the transition from *Singspiel* atmosphere to epic drama may justly be criticized as clumsy and unconvincing. The background is harped on excessively; we keep returning to it just when we think we have left it behind. The great issue looms into view only to be swallowed up in further domesticity, and the Marzelline/Fidelio subplot is allowed to become an uncomfortably and irrelevantly prominent motive in the dramatic development.* Now, in the shorter, conciser and reordered version of 1814, the transition is precisely gauged; realism and dramatic tension are held in balance; the Marzelline subplot is emphasized

---

* This has not prevented the rise of a heresy—in the name of formula and in the best tradition of modern *Urtext*-obsession—according to which the order of the opening scenes has a unity in the fuller original version that was sacrificed in the revision. It is even argued that the original *Fidelio* as a whole should be treated as a valid alternative version, if indeed it is not to be preferred as being more truly Beethovenian.

To quote the Duke of Wellington, if you believe that you will believe anything.

just enough to offset the mighty events that are soon to
sweep it aside. In this form, the drama's gradual emergence
from its domestic background becomes a dynamic, positive
element—one of the things which help to give *Fidelio* its
psychological power and truth to life. The pacing is now
exactly right; the everyday setting is neither obtruded nor
too abruptly abandoned. Immediately after the Quartet,
which has sounded a deeper note than any yet heard in the
work, Rocco sings his 'Gold' aria (in the 1806 revision it
had been removed), and homely touches continue to throw
the high drama into relief, such as Rocco's invoking the
king's birthday and the fine spring morning as excuses for
letting the prisoners walk in the garden.

Beethoven's first act (originally two acts) now moves in a
carefully controlled progression from the sprightly teasing
Duet to the sublimity of the hushed orchestral music on
which the curtain falls. The point must be emphasized; it
is not only in the great business of the dungeon scene that
Beethoven is at his height, but also in the long preparation
for it. The slow increase of tension and rise in emotional
pressure so work on us that, in the final bars of the act, the
simplest four-note phrase on cellos and basses, descending
from tonic to dominant and answered by solo clarinet—
music heard earlier in the movement, during an ominous
aside between Pizarro and Rocco—becomes charged with a
mysterious pity (a *locus classicus* of Beethoven's ability to set
up profound reverberations by the most commonplace
means). The huge expansion of feeling by which the music
has attained this power grows with the drama's approach to
its centre. Every step of the way to Florestan's cell is
marked. As events draw Leonore inexorably towards the
object of her quest, so the musical language deepens and
intensifies. The broadening of the melodic line in the opening
Duet as Jacquino goes to attend to the knocking at the
postern gate and Marzelline is left alone to think undis-
tractedly of Fidelio; the warmth that spreads over the score
as divided violas and cellos steal in over pizzicato basses at

the beginning of the Quartet in response to Rocco's 'Meinst du ich kann dir nicht ins Herz sehen?' ('Do you think I can't read what's in your heart?')—a ravishing sound and at the same time a moving touch of irony, the music hinting at issues more momentous than Rocco dreams of (and the first of many such enrichments of colour and texture achieved by separating basses from cellos); in the Trio, the heroic leap of phrase which catches Leonore's exultation at Rocco's agreeing to her working with him in the cells—the first decisive step towards her goal—and the surge of anguish that comes with the turn into the minor and the steep ascent to a high A flat at the word 'Leiden' ('suffering'—a word that Leonore will recall, an age later, when she holds Florestan in her arms). In the same movement, the unearthly sound of double basses playing above cellos in the desolate key of E flat minor and the plaintive phrase for oboes and bassoons that pierces the dark texture of the strings as Leonore longs for an end to her griefs; the ferocity of Pizarro's 'Ha! welch' ein Augenblick', a scream of fear and hatred that lifts the aria far above the conventional villainy of the words; the grimly laconic gestures of the succeeding Duet; Leonore's horror and sense of outrage, which by an effort of will she masters and turns to fruitful ends, as the recitative's violent emotions relax and broaden into the aria, a prayer for hope which becomes an affirmation of faith and charity—by these slow, sure degrees Beethoven's plan unfolds. Leonore's aria is followed by the unlocking of the prison doors, on her suggestion, and a moment later by the sight of men like shadows feeling their way into the light, the music stirring to life with the slowness of cramped limbs stretching in the forgotten warmth of the sun.* The juxtaposition of Leonore's radiant declaration of belief in her mission and this quiet, almost motionless, introductory music acts both on a specific and on a general level, confronting her with the reality she has come to find and telling

---

* The effect is enhanced if the producer makes a slight pause between the last line of dialogue and the first bar of music.

us a central truth about the work—that its subject is not one particular prisoner but all prisoners.

On the same high tide of emotion the music of the following scene sweeps us into the tumult of feelings unleashed in Leonore by the news that the Governor has given permission for Fidelio to help Rocco in the cells, and that their work, which is to begin at once, will involve digging the grave of an unnamed prisoner who may well be Florestan. A breathless allegro, in which the flame of Leonore's hope now burns bright, now flares and gutters like a candle in the wind, is succeeded by an uneasy andante, full of shifting harmonies, passing dissonances and displaced accents. And so, by way of Pizarro's fury at discovering that the prisoners have been let out—music in which his whirling, obsessive semiquaver phrase heard in the earlier aria and duet is again prominent—to the great hymn that closes the act in clouds of glory. This final ensemble does everything that the previous version did not. It makes a grandly dignified formal conclusion whose exalted and generalized character prefigures the ode to liberty and love that will end the opera; it gives us, in the benediction of its final bars, a glimpse of the *Vorsicht*, the providence watching over all; and it takes the action up to the supreme point to which it has been moving throughout the act, yet leaves it poised in suspense over the solitary figure who has come to dominate the drama, though as yet unseen.

We see him from the beginning of the second act. Beethoven's grasp, which has not faltered through the long first act, now tightens. From now on the work has us by the throat. Berlioz's comment on the dungeons Quartet is applicable to the whole scene: we can hardly tell what is happening to us, we are seized and swept along by the torrential force of emotion that music and action, merged indistinguishably, together generate—to such an extent is the composer identified with the situation. But it is precisely Beethoven's once despised dramaturgical sense that gives this scene, in the definitive form, its overpowering force. The variations of pace, texture and colour, the shafts of light that penetrate the darkness, the momentary relaxations of tension; the ferocious insistence, and at the same time the freedom and flexibility, of the rhythms; the dramatic impact of speech following and preceding music, or alternating with it in that trickiest of devices, Melodrama, and, in the Quartet, breaking in on it with electrifying effect (an 1814 addition); the expression of human passion and endurance screwed up to the highest conceivable pitch; the sense of events hurtling forward out of human control yet at the same time inevitably, as though obedient to some inscrutable power—this is no *tour de force* of 'personality' but the art of music-drama at its most masterly. The sequence and timing of movements are so calculated as to give the climax, when it comes, the maximum explosive energy. From the chained, half-starved Florestan's statement of faith, his delirium and collapse, we are led without a break first to the Melodrama, with its extraordinary depiction of chill, tomblike darkness and its poignant fragments of music previously heard, and then to the gravedigging Duet—gloomy, cavernous music, towards the end rising to heroic vehemence, before sinking back to end in a mutter. By contrast, the Trio makes a glowing point of light in the surrounding gloom; the music's heavenly breadth of melody and warmth of texture (cellos and basses again separate) are all the more moving for being heard in the light of Leonore's discovery, made in the intervening dialogue, that the prisoner is Florestan; and from the point of view of the scene's dramatic construction, it creates an essential interval of calm before the storm.

Upon this calm the spoken dialogue obtrudes with brutal realism. The Trio is followed by Rocco's signal, the arrival of Pizarro and the Quartet. This Quartet, as Berlioz has said, defies analysis: we know only that there is nothing like it in music. But—to mention one detail—note how, at Leonore's cry 'Kill his wife first!', the rhythm staggers and the impetus of the music is checked, as Florestan and Leonore stare at each other and no sound comes from the

orchestra except a kind of stammer from the woodwind:
even Leonore has forgotten what is happening; for a few
bars time is suspended—before she turns again to face
Pizarro and the music plunges forward with redoubled
force. The psychological truth of that moment alone would
show Beethoven a master of opera. But the whole scene
does that. Not a move is made or a note placed without
compelling cause. The redundancies and imperfections
of the original version have been expunged and corrected—
the declamation of the Quartet revised and made more
telling, the Duet and Trio pruned of repetitions which weak-
ened them, the over-elaborate motivic development, thick
textures and copious tremolando of the introduction to the
act cut back and trombones and contrabassoon removed
altogether (the latter instrument being now confined to
three numbers in the opera, the Quartet, the Gravedigging
Duet, and the energetic, slightly pompous March which
announces the arrival of Pizarro in Act 1).

In keeping with the same psychological veracity, the
following scene between Florestan and Leonore brings no
reduction of tension. Though dissonance is largely banished
in favour of a translucent concord, musical and dramatic
expression are still stretched to breaking point. How otherwise? The tension of spirit needed to do what Leonore has
done is too great to be relaxed now, at the very moment when
she has saved Florestan yet can barely grasp the fact. Once
again Beethoven judged correctly when he removed the
recitative which originally intervened before the Duet,
moving though it is: Leonore collapsing at last under the
strain of her superhuman efforts (and her chagrin at having
allowed Rocco to take the pistol from her), Florestan unable
to go to her aid because still chained. The recitative, with its
poignant oboe obbligato, is in itself a fine conception. But to
pass directly from Quartet to Duet by way of a few sentences
of spoken dialogue showed a deeper understanding of
dramatic reality. The frantic joy of the sustained high As
which blaze out at the end of the Quartet is now carried

straight over into the Duet, the musical texture's scorching intensity refined still further for the expression of a happiness almost too great for human speech. Who but Beethoven could have found music for it (music whose development from first germ to final form was appropriately long drawn out, the main theme appearing as early as 1803, in the unfinished opera *Vestas Feuer*)? In its panting, headlong movement, its infinite tenderness, its ardours and sudden hesitations, it captures the whole indescribable moment; music becomes 'intelligible language' at the point where language ceases. The Duet evokes Leonore and Florestan with almost unbearable vividness—the involuntary glance and gesture as well as the inexpressible joy, the 'namenlose Freude' that floods through them. They touch each other, whisper each other's name, scarcely able to believe that it is true. Once, they look back; and at the phrase 'nach unenbaren Leiden' Beethoven creates a beautiful image of prolonged suffering by a simple repetition of the bass note C, one dissonance resolving onto another. But everything is forgotten in the ecstasy of communion—everything except each other and gratitude for the merciful providence of God.*

After this, what should Beethoven do but what he does? The drama, in its final form, can only continue upwards to the expression of a love which transcends the particular and embraces humanity: it has been the theme of the whole work. 'Whoever he is'—even if he is not her husband, and her quest has been in vain—Leonore must save this man. Her pity wells up and flows towards him, long before she can be sure that he is Florestan. It leads her, in the second half of the dungeon Duet, to a sublime resolve: 'I will loose your chains, unhappy man, I will surely set you free.' The melancholy curve of the vocal line, now a fourth higher, more forcefully accented and free of its wailing oboe counter-

---

* The 'recapitulation' of the *unenbaren Leiden* phrase in the fuller form of the original version was one of several unanswerable arguments for shortening the Duet. The main work of revision belongs to 1806, but important improvements in the melodic line were made in 1814.

point, takes on a new vigour, then moves into C major and, with the orchestral texture suddenly radiant with high woodwind chords sounding a heroic rhythm, rises in a great sweep of phrase to a pitch of exaltation. This crucial idea, implanted in the drama at its most apparently hopeless point—the preparing of the prisoner's grave—flowers in the final scene into a C major hymn to all mankind. The intensely human drama of Leonore and Florestan is subsumed in a vision of universal brotherhood, the representative suffering man is set free and the truth discovered in the depths of the prison, at the point of death, shouted from the rooftops. But until the final blazing statement, when individual identity melts and the voices themselves become pure instruments in the holy all-consuming radiance of sound, the scene is concerned with ordinary, specific human beings: the opera must come back to earth before it ascends into universality.*

Now at last the tensions of the last two hours can be relaxed. (The 1814 change of scene from Florestan's cell, where the original dénouement took place, to the castle esplanade, is a necessary part of the process.) With imaginative genius Beethoven returns to the tone of the opening scenes of the opera. The music is once more touched with the homely and the mundane—the everyday reality out of which the drama grew, and which may anywhere and at any time be the setting for exceptional manifestations of courage, love and the refusal to tolerate injustice. There is a jolly march, the crowd waves, the spring breeze flutters the bunting, Rocco does his not very impressive best to explain himself, Marzelline hides her head on Jacquino's protective shoulder, the Minister, having been about to make Rocco unlock Florestan's chains, turns and hands the key to Leonore (thus fulfilling her prophecy in the dungeon: 'Ich löse deine Ketten'), and a hush descends, heads are bared,

---

* It has also to deal with Pizarro. Universal brotherhood does not in this case include the tyrant, who is led away to suitable punishment. There were limits even to Beethoven's radical way with operatic convention.

for a moment everyone is still, acknowledging a power beyond life and man's reckoning.

Is all this naïve? One might as well ask, is the plot implausible? As it happens, it follows an incident of the Revolution, still recent when Beethoven composed his score; but even if it did not, the question would be irrelevant. The music, in conjunction with the words, gives the stage events a plausibility, and the sentiments behind them a truth that, when the work is experienced in a good performance or relived in the memory, make everything else seem unreal. In the same way, though there may not have been many women in history capable of doing what Leonore does, Beethoven leaves no doubt that she is one of them. Far from being an idealized figure, the personifications of the perfect wife and the spirit of divine justice rolled into one, she is painfully alive. The music shows her constantly on the verge of breaking point. Often her heroism falters. We hear it, for example, in the allegro molto of the finale of Act 1, where eagerness gives way to a terrible bleakness at the thought that it may be her task to dig Florestan's grave, and again in the succeeding andante, where the calm, resolute dignity of her replies—so strikingly contrasted with the shifty Rocco's apologetic remarks—breaks down and she weeps at her own plight as well as at her husband's. The woman behind the heroic mask is never forgotten. Listen, in the gravedigging scene, to the sheer weariness of her music and to the way this sense returns to the vocal line, after the brief moment of exultation, dragging once more the plaintive oboe counterpoint—only, vocal line and oboe counterpoint are now one, wailing the melancholy minor sixths together. Or listen to the unexpected D flat amid all the cheerful F major bustle at the end of the Trio in Act 1, and the pain it conveys. Leonore's courage may be exceptional but it is never less than intensely human; it would not move us so deeply if we were not made aware of what it costs her in spirit and physical endurance.

The 'naïvety' of such strokes of expressive characterization are not those of an operatic primitive. It is a measure
of Beethoven's power that he can overwhelm us by the
simplest things: as in the final bars of Act 1 (already referred to), or in the momentary clouding of the pianissimo 'O
namen-, namenlose Freude' by the repetition of the phrase
in the minor, as for an instant Leonore and Florestan touch
again on their past sufferings, or in the prodigious *coup de
théâtre* by which Leonore's pointing the pistol at Pizarro
seems actually to produce the trumpet call which rings out
faint but clear from the tower hundreds of feet above her
(here Leonore is the avenging angel in person). But it is the
power of a composer who can afford to be simple because
he is sure of himself and master of his means. *Fidelio* is a
subtly and precisely imagined score. The work is almost as
rich in characteristic orchestral felicities as *Figaro* or *Così**
—to mention a few, the sound of bassoon and pizzicato
violins and violas at the end of the prisoners' chorus; in
the second act Trio, the scurrying violas and baleful clarinet
(as the wary Rocco shies away from the thought of giving
the prisoner food in defiance of orders); or, in the final
ensemble of Act 1, the martial trumpets, shining woodwind
and pizzicato strings dissolving into a dull throb of drums
and, a few bars from the end, the heart-stopping moment
when the stress and striving are silenced and then, for two
long beats, all sounds cease except a sustained octave F on
violins and violas.

Such felicities are no mere effects, however irresistible.
They speak of Beethoven's insight into human feelings as
well as of his skill in orchestration. Instrumental colour is a
hardly less essential or refined means of dramatic expression
for Beethoven than for Mozart. It is the scoring of the
March, for instance—in particular the inhuman sound of the

---

* A score which Beethoven was not above being influenced by, despite his
puritanical disapproval of its moral tone—as the shared key, horn sonority,
imperious arpeggios, huge downward leap from a major third, and noble,
heartfelt sentiments of Leonore's aria and Fiordiligi's 'Per pietà' demonstrate.

contrabassoon pumping away in the bass and the strange accentuation resulting from the timpani's being limited to two notes, tonic and dominant—that gives this outwardly jaunty music its tense, menacing air. In the Duet for Pizarro and Rocco, the instrumentation articulates and emphasizes the dramatic meaning at every turn, from the peremptory string and horn octaves of the opening, the violin phrases that sting like a lash, the writhing string unisons, and the yet more sinister stillness of divided cellos and basses and low sustained wind chords (as Rocco pictures the dying man, so soon to be put out of his misery), to the sudden roar of trombones that strikes across their whispered colloquy and the strident horn-writing of the conclusion. The conversation between Pizarro and Rocco in the finale to Act 1, in which the Governor upbraids Rocco for letting the prisoners out and the old gaoler replies that it is the king's birthday and, in any case, 'let him reserve his wrath for the one down there who is shortly to die', is masterly in its use of contrasting string textures; the transition from the sunny geniality of Rocco's first words to the grim meaning-fulness of his aside to Pizarro is accomplished with a smooth-ness that strikes a chill. There is something hideous in the ease with which Rocco takes on Pizarro's idiom—so that Pizarro's reply can only be set to the same pattern of stabbing offbeat accents followed by a rattling chain of semiquavers over a strutting bass, though made more dangerous still by slightly more emphatic accentuation and the transferring of the semiquavers from second violins to darker violas. Note, too, the dreadful suavity that comes over the strings at the phrase 'Hier will ich stille Ruhe haben'—a suavity whose context makes it quite distinct from Rocco's similar music a few lines earlier.

Beethoven's strokes of colour can, as we have seen, be of the utmost simplicity. The most stunning example is the effect of the trumpet call which, entering in the flat sub-mediant key of B flat, arrests the furious impetus of the D major Quartet at its height. There is the broadest possible contrast of colour earlier in the Quartet, when Florestan's proud retort to Pizarro is heralded by a brilliant flourish of horns, trumpets and drums—a sound that glows like a shining sword in the darkness. But equally typical are the little touches that, fine though they are, can alter the whole character of the music and shift it momentarily in a new direction. An example—again from the Quartet—is the double bass entry on the fourth beat of the bar, forming with oboe and clarinet the major triad of A, at Leonore's 'I have sworn to bring comfort to him'. It is a tiny detail, lasting a couple of seconds; but the effect of this entry *before* the bar-line, after three emphatic downbeat Gs, and this brief assertion of a stable key in the surrounding diminished seventh harmony, is out of all proportion to its size. The appearance of a totally different colour, rhythm and harmony in the midst of wild turbulence gives us a sudden fleeting sense of a power deeper than human vengeance. It is one of the many unforgettable moments—impossible, unnecessary, to put into words—when *Fidelio* 'speaks to the soul'.*

Beethoven's variety of scoring in *Fidelio* is a study in itself. In three-quarters of the work a combination of instruments is used that is unique to each particular number. Thus, for the ecstatic Duet 'O namenlose Freude', where the sound must be of fierce intensity, clarinets are omitted from the woodwind band (for the only time in the work), and in the more lyrical passages cellos and basses are given separate parts, so that the cellos can sing in the upper register in great arcs of melody while the basses maintain the steady rhythmic pulsation. The introduction to the Dungeon Scene, in its final form, takes some of its special colour from being the only music in the work scored for horns and timpani without trumpets or trombones; the use of the timpani as a solo, not a tutti, instrument, and of two pairs of

---

* Like many of the most graphic touches in the Quartet, this is a product of 1814. In the 1805 and 1806 versions the diminished seventh harmony and downbeat rhythm are maintained throughout these bars.

horns spanning three octaves, helps to evoke a precise physical atmosphere, a sense of darkness and cold, vaulted space that is as vivid and complete as anything in Wagner or Berlioz. Note how the fragments of woodwind melody which rise like human cries out of the gloom (as though forced out by the rasping strokes of the violins on the G string), are given to two or three different instruments at a time, playing the same notes in different registers. *Fidelio* is full of these expressive doublings, an octave or two octaves apart, and always where grief flows deepest. The characteristically plangent sound they make is one of the score's distinguishing features. Another is the grainy richness and energy of the lower register that results from the frequent separation of cello and bass parts, to which reference has been made. Of course it is impossible to sum up in one phrase a score in which constantly varying colour is integral to the dramatic expression, but this combination of harsh gleam at the top of the compass and dark glow at the bottom epitomizes the sonority that we hear when we think of *Fidelio*. It is more than an atmosphere: it is an image of human suffering in a context of divine providence. The message of the work is incarnate in the sound.

Like all great operas *Fidelio* creates its own world. Because it is *sui generis*, we may at first resist it and, instead of attending, ask questions which in our unresponsive state seem very searching. Later, we wonder how we could have been so obtuse. For, when known, it transcends denominations. The intensity of Beethoven's vision is such that everything drawn within its fiery orbit loses separate identity and becomes assimilated into the nature of the work. To label the origin of this or that element ceases to be relevant; all are part of *Fidelio*. Every formula of *opéra comique* that it lays its hands on—spoken dialogue, *mélodrame*, the moralistic view of life, 'good' and 'evil' orchestral effects—is exploited in an entirely individual and personal way. Even its use of travesty, the woman dressed as a man, is absolutely fresh, so that a burlesque convention becomes an essential part of the dramatic reality. No doubt it was Beethoven's naïvety and the uninhibitedness of his emotional responses that made these things possible; he simply did not see the objection to mixing genres or to using dialogue opera, with its division into separate 'numbers', as a vehicle for the loftiest ideas, and he proceeded with the same disregard of categories as in his symphonies. But the process by which the emotional responses become art and the vision is worked out in musical and dramatic terms is anything but naïve. If the result is much more than a work of art (in the narrow sense of the phrase), it *is* a work of art, as I have tried to argue. Perhaps only Beethoven could have brought off such a feat. He did bring it off, and that is all that concerns us. *Fidelio*, in its final form, is a dramatic masterpiece which with the freedom of mastery uses whatever it needs, to say what it has to say. The message 'speaks to the soul' because it is embodied in coherent operatic form; the work is true to its own laws. They are the only ones that matter. To realize this, and accept those laws, is to possess a key to one of art's great exemplars and enrichments of human existence.

Falstaff

Falstaff has traditionally been thought of as a 'musician's opera', a work whose essence is too delicate and elusive, and by implication too restricted, ever to appeal to the general opera-going public. To suspect that this is no longer so may be no more than a naïve desire to share one's admiration with as many people as possible, combined with a genuine inability to understand how anyone could fail to see that *Falstaff* is one of the most wonderful things that ever happened to music. The moment I encountered it, at the Cambridge Theatre in 1949 with Stabile in the title role— from that first galvanizing bar, with its silent downbeat followed by a crashing C major chord and a dismissive arpeggio of insolent assurance and well-being—I knew that I had made a personal discovery of an importance comparable to that of my first glimpse, a year or two earlier at the piano of a high-church clergyman of confirmed Wagnerian persuasion, of that other, ampler and broader C major world of *Die Meistersinger*. It used to be a favourite anti-Wagnerian gambit to point out that the whole of Verdi's opera could be comfortably contained in Wagner's third act. This made *Falstaff* in some way superior to *Meistersinger*, but it also carried the suggestion that *Falstaff* was a more rarefied pleasure, by definition reserved for the few, its brevity, swiftness, subtlety of touch and conspicuous lack of most of the qualities popularly associated with Verdi being such that it must necessarily pass most people by.

I do not believe it is mere wishful thinking to see that as a phase in the work's history which is now over. Record companies do not record an opera as often as they record *Falstaff* out of pure love of art. Opera houses are institutions which reflect opinion as well as helping to mould it; if *Falstaff* figures increasingly in their repertoires, it is not for educational reasons. The public does not stand still. It is capable of learning. So is criticism. The conclusions that each has been coming to about the nature of *Falstaff* are parallel and complementary. The public no longer finds that the work goes too fast for it; it has caught up. It has begun to realize that melody is not synonymous with aria and that, so far from there being no tunes in *Falstaff*, the tunes never stop; the work lacks only those contrasting passages of tunelessness which in early Verdi allow you to remark on the abundance of tunes. On its side, criticism has come to recognize that there is nothing uncharacteristic about *Falstaff*. Verdi's final achievement of a flexible style, close-knit but totally free—a style with which he could, so to speak, do everything melodically—was neither a confession of failing inspiration nor a repudiation of his past. In part, as with the later Haydn, it was simply a matter of greater skill—a harmonic and contrapuntal mastery that enabled him to give full, uninterrupted scope to his natural powers, to be most thoroughly himself. *Falstaff* is melodically the richest of all Verdi's scores. There is no paradox in that, and no contradiction in its also being the most integrated and through-composed, the most sophisticated in terms of motivic allusion and cross-reference.

It used to be fashionable to trace Verdi's later style directly to the example of Wagner (Stravinsky, in one of his phases, described *Falstaff* as 'poisoned by music-drama'). But the Wagnerian influence, so far as it existed, was general, not specific, and thoroughly Verdian in its application; it only reinforced a tendency that is natural in composers as their command of their métier and their sense of dramatic continuity and irony increase. The Italian tradition is not wholly inconsistent with cleverness; and to identify the fine threads whose interweavings go to make the texture of

Verdi's score—to observe, for example, all the recurrences of the rhythm

heard in the first bar of the work, or to follow the varied adventures of the ubiquitous triplet figure

and its derivatives, from its appearance at the end of the opening scene to its final return, as an infinitely sly and knowing counter-subject to the fugue which ends the opera—is only to deepen one's appreciation of the melodic invention that *Falstaff* stimulated in the 77-year-old composer. Verdi did not abandon his normal style; he refined and strengthened it. There may not be a great deal of precedent in the earlier operas for the humour, the light-fingered wit, the irony, the sheer high spirits of *Falstaff*, but what there is—in *Un Ballo in maschera*, for instance, in *Rigoletto*, or in *Otello* (the brilliant ensemble for Iago, Cassio and Otello in Act 3 is in the ripest '*Falstaff* style')—is enough to show that even in this respect the work does not mark a totally new departure in Verdi's career. Equally, those gun-shot chords, those roars of trombone and timpani as Falstaff hymns the expanding frontiers of the kingdom of his paunch or breaks off his denunciation of Bardolph and Pistol to cry for sack, have been heard before. The musical idiom that Verdi needed for the work, a style at once massive and light on its feet, fruity and mercurial—the nimbleness of Falstaff in flight from the eleven men in buckram, 'larding the lean earth as he walks along'—was ready to hand. Conventional Verdian hallmarks—the expansiveness of phrase, the powerful rhythmic emphasis, the sledgehammer blows of the brass—are found here in profusion. It is the context that gives them a fresh character.

Ford's lament to Falstaff as he describes his vain lavishing of gift upon gift on the impervious Alice is reminiscent of the great melodic span of Elisabetta's music in the first act of *Don Carlo*—'Arcan terror m'avea nel cor . . . amata io son.' The situation makes it comic; the style is not essentially different. The nearest Verdi comes to dissociating himself from the composer he had been is by the implied self-criticism with which he pokes fun at his own mannerisms—as in the parody of his 'sinister' music, complete with shuddering tremolo, clarinets in the low register and writhing chromatic bass, in Alice's mock-solemn description of Herne the Hunter. In *Falstaff* all aspects of Verdi's art have their fulfilment and redemption, and Italian opera completes the reform-from-within which its critics, from Berlioz and Wagner to Bernard Shaw, had declared impossible—a growing-up and attainment of reality symbolized by the emancipation of that hoariest of operatic ploys, the striking of midnight, which, while inspiring a musical and dramatic effect of true enchantment, is represented not by the six starveling strokes that had done duty in Italian opera till then but by the full resounding twelve.

The distance travelled between *Nabucco* and *Falstaff* is as far as any travelled by an artist. Verdi got there by his own exertions, it goes without saying; and he was still Verdi at the end of it, in strength and in character. More truly himself than he had been able to be before the collaboration with Boito. The significance of Boito's advent cannot be over-emphasized. It was not only that it induced Verdi, after long hesitation, to come out of virtual retirement and compose for the stage again. Until then he had been, with all his achievements—and nothing said here is said with any wish to belittle the Verdi of *Ernani*, *Trovatore* and *Don Carlo*—incomplete: in Shaw's words, 'a man possessing more power than he knew how to use, or indeed was permitted to use by the old operatic forms imposed on him by circumstances'. Boito changed that. It would be a crude simplification to call him Verdi's artistic conscience and the provider of the taste that Verdi lacked; Verdi was conscious of his own limitations and had always striven to remedy them.

But contact with a mind and personality of Boito's suppleness, breadth, cultivation and fine ardour could not but be a liberating experience for him. Until then he had dealt with librettists (one of whom, Piave, he had, unsuccessfully but in all sincerity, recommended for an important chair in literature). Now he had a poet working with him, one who revered his genius but who also understood it, and understood how to handle it, and who loved Shakespeare as passionately as he. Boito provided Verdi with the first indispensable means of composing Shakespearean opera, as opposed to opera based on Shakespeare. The texts of *Otello* and *Falstaff* are masterpieces of their kind. They fulfil every major requirement of a first-rate opera book: they are skilfully made and beautifully written, they extract the essence of a great drama and make it accessible to the composer in a form suitable for his purposes, and they are the starting-point for consummate dramatic music.

It is arguable that even Boito could not make a perfect libretto out of *Othello*—that, even allowing for music's greater suggestive power, the necessary compression of Shakespeare's first two acts into one, though most expertly done, slightly but significantly upsets the balance of the drama. The libretto of *Falstaff* is, however, without flaw. Here Boito fulfilled to perfection the task as he expressed it in a letter to Verdi:

> to sketch the characters in a few strokes, to weave the plot, to extract all the juice from that enormous Shakespearean orange, without letting the useless pips slip into the little glass, to write with colour and clarity and brevity, to delineate the musical plan of the scene, so that there results an organic unity that is a *piece of music* yet is not, to make the joyous comedy live from beginning to end, to make it live with a natural and communicative gaiety . . .*

The grafting of the Falstaff of *Henry IV* onto the plot of *The Merry Wives* to achieve an authentic portrait of 'Seerr Jon' in a setting of comedy—a mould for Shakespearean

---

* Quoted in Frank Walker's *The Man Verdi*, Dent, 1962.

music-drama such as an opera on *The Merry Wives* alone could not be—is a work of art in itself as well as the cause of art in another. Strangely enough, the result has not been universally admired. Even the language has been found fault with, though on what grounds is not clear. (Vaughan Williams' 'medicated Shakespeare' is a good phrase, but has not the remotest application to a text which for the most part renders its original word for word into very choice Italian.) A more common objection is that the action virtually comes to an end with Falstaff's immersion in the Thames at the conclusion of Act 2; the rest is mere mechanics, a variation on what we have seen already. The objection is plausible; but it does not go very far. The music should tell us otherwise, even if we had missed the point of the action. It is characteristic of the deepening and subtilizing of Verdi's art which followed from his association with Boito that this final act, in response to the fresh turn in the drama, should move into a new dimension of poetic enchantment and human awareness. Like the Fandango and Barbarina's cavatina in *Figaro*, Verdi's evocation of the slow onset of darkness in the penultimate scene of *Falstaff* prepares for the magical atmosphere of a bosky summer night, full of moonlight and pools of shadow, which pervades the final phase of the intrigue.*

But even without the music, the objection will not stand scrutiny. On the most superficial level of plot construction, it ignores the fact that the conspiracy in Act 3 is not a duplication of the conspiracy in Acts 1 and 2 but differs from it in

---

* The parallels between the two operas in these final scenes are not confined to a similarity of moods. The moment when the antlered Falstaff, waiting for Mistress Ford beside Herne's Oak, likens himself to Jove disguised for love's sake in the semblance of a bull, is strikingly reminiscent of Figaro's 'Tutto è tranquillo e placido', in the great broadening out of the music as well as in the invocation of classical mythology and the momentary act of contemplation before rapid action. Later in the scene, the Minuet's serenity and sense of complication resolved recalls 'Pace, pace, mio dolce tesoro' at the comparable stage of Mozart's dénouement and, in a similar context of the unwary husband about to have his self-importance shattered, conveys the same air of deceptive innocence.

one essential respect. In the first two acts Ford, not being party to his wife's stratagems, believes that she is deceiving him. In the third act, by now disabused and aware that the merry wives are out to fool Falstaff yet again, he assumes that this time he is fully in the know, and is himself fooled into marrying his daughter to Fenton, while the favoured suitor, Dr Caius, is paired off with Bardolph, whose meteoric nose, until then concealed under layers of muslin, now illuminates the darkness of Windsor Forest to its furthest recesses. It is the bourgeois Ford, in fact, the man who was going to make the fat knight grovel, who is revealed as the true ass, and Falstaff who rises to dignity from the ruins of defeat. That is the second and deeper significance of this final act. We need this spectacle of Falstaff's humiliations in order fully to realize the superb resilience of the man. He must be shown steeped in bile, distended and turbid with Thames water, cursing his fate yet gulled once again by his incurable romanticism; he must be caparisoned like a cloven-footed beast, taunted and kicked and pinched by the superior realists of the world, the butt of everybody, so that his resurgence may be as great as his fall seemed complete. It is only in that final assertion of spirit, beginning with the great cry 'Riconosco Bardolfo!' and ending with the swelling rebuke of his triple 'Son io, son io, son io' ('I am not only witty in myself, but the cause that wit is in other men'), that he towers over his tormentors and vindicates to us the central article of Falstaffian faith: that if the world is unable to see him as he sees himself, then so much the worse for the world. Not till the last scene, in short, does the drama reach its consummation; the work ends with the final ensemble and not before.

Boito said, near the end of his life, that he asked no more than 'to be the faithful servant of Verdi, and of that other, born on the Avon'. Though himself a composer of great talent and once high ambitions, he saw that his glory lay in this: that he had brought the two men together. The composer of *Falstaff* has become a Shakespearean artist. He has Shakespeare's combination of empathy and detachment, his constantly surprising lyrical energy, his ease and felicity of utterance, his memorability, his sense of the charm of unpremeditated love, his taste for elaborate fooling, his appetite for the variety and absurdity of life, his relish of the joyous intricacies of comedy, his feeling for balance, his awareness of the mysteries behind reality. Does this pitch Verdi's claims too high? Writers on music are given to exalting their favourite works beyond reason, wantonly invoking comparisons with *King Lear*, the *Divine Comedy* or the *Oresteia*. There are after all very few operas whose music can soberly be said to achieve a near-equivalence, in beauty, subtlety, and richness of imagery, of Shakespeare's language; and most of them are by Mozart. I do not think more than one of them is by Verdi, and that one is *Falstaff*. *Otello* is a glorious work, but it is, except intermittently, a noble operatic tragedy *after* Shakespeare. In composing *Falstaff*, Verdi had the benefit not only of a relatively easier task but also of the release of creative energy that can come from the completion of a gruelling one. *Falstaff* recreates Shakespearean comedy in the medium of music, by means of a style grown cunning with years of experience without any loss of its youthful fires, which burn as brightly as ever but with more concentrated heat.

The characters in *Falstaff*, to borrow another remark of Boito's, 'all bask in the sunshine of that Olympian old age'. As with the characters in those other two great operatic comedies, *Figaro* and *Meistersinger*, they are sharply delineated yet share a recognizable family language, the common idiom of their world. It is not Falstaff alone whose final cadences have a tendency to sit down massively on the supertonic and survey life while letting the tonic wait its time. So have Mistress Ford's, as when she dwells lovingly on the word 'gioia' in 'Gaie comare di Windsor'; so, as though in mockery, does Mistress Quickly's, when she makes deep obeisance to Falstaff at the Garter Inn ('Reverenza');

and thus too Mistress Ford, designating the hostess for
the role of witch at the revels in Windsor Forest. But
you never quite know who is mocking whom; and, as in
Mozart, the orchestra mocks them all.

The braying motif which represents ridicule and all
manner of discomfiture including cuckoldry, first appears
in a sweetly demure guise in the letter-reading scene,
comes nearer to its true self when Bardolph warns Ford of
the danger that he may sprout a pair of horns, and reappears
in all its derision as Falstaff is about to tell the thunder-
struck husband of his assignation 'dalle due alle tre'. Ford
himself makes use of it to bewail the pathetic failure of his
wooing. In the third act, it is punningly referred to when
Falstaff, alone at Herne's Oak with a pair of antlers strapped
to his head, justifies to himself the length that love has
forced him to go to; here it takes on an almost majestic air,
a dignified acceptance of the world's follies. Later in the
same scene it roars out with reckless ardour as Falstaff
accosts Alice with serious intent to board; but in the scene
by the Thames it expresses the depths of Falstaff's indignity
and indignation:

And the moment of his admission before the whole company
that he is a double-damned ass is the occasion for its most
bitter and disgusted manifestation:

Yet, in the end, as the fortissimo flourish before the final
fugue informs us, no one is exempt; everybody is included:
'Tutto nel mondo è burla.'

It is natural, again, that Ford should borrow the triplet motif, which he associates with Falstaff's monstrous 'dalle due alle tre', for his appalled recognition that he is that proverbially most ridiculous thing, a jealous husband. One could also argue that musically speaking Alice is 'aware' of the motif and that her use of it in her love scene with Falstaff—'O soave Sir John'—is therefore well within the category of conscious deception. Yet there is surely a wistful note behind the play-acting, a hint that Alice's respectable but lively mind is half-falling under his sway; and when, a moment later, we find her echoing the very phrase to which Falstaff, in the opening scene of the opera, boasted of the beauty of Ford's wife ('sua moglie è bella'), we know that she has succumbed and is picturing herself as the 'Lady' of Falstaff's fantasies.

This suggestion of layers of ambiguity and passion beneath the comic action is typical. It is typical too of Falstaff's power over his reluctant fellow-citizens that the music to which he salutes the bounty of Master Brook and the stream of life-giving liquor that he brings with him— 'Bene accolta sia la fontana'—should recur in the mouth of Ford when 'Signor Fontana' urges Sir John to spend his gold freely on his behalf. The whole idiom and language of the score spreads outwards from Falstaff himself. 'In quest' addome c'è un migliaio di lingue'—his belly is a sweet thunder of multitudinous tongues crying his name— 'Falstaff immenso! Enorme Falstaff!' That glorious modulation from Ford's gingerly A major to the C major of 'Caro Signor Fontana' epitomizes Falstaff's genius, his 'forgetive' warmth, his power to transfigure arid fact.

When Boito told the still hesitant Verdi that 'there is only one way to end your career better than with *Otello*, and that is to end it with *Falstaff*,' he spoke perhaps more truly than he knew (though, shrewd psychologist that he was, the likelihood is that he knew). Verdi needed Falstaff. He needed him, to rid his system of Iago and the evil that could produce the Credo's dreadful nullity and the bloated imaginings of 'Era la notte'; to restore his balance. Mistress Quickly's 'Reverenza' purifies the grim unisons of the Credo; and the grief of the Willow Song is exorcized by Nanetta's gleeful call to the woodland spirits who are her girlhood friends from Windsor. Shakespeare's Falstaff (in Professor Kott's slightly disapproving phrase) 'scoffs at history'; and Verdi's is his true descendant. The work was Verdi's purgation, his return to life. He celebrated it with the most exquisite evocation of young love at its most care-free and enchanted that any composer of any age has ever produced. The love of Fenton and Nanetta, which Verdi 'sprinkled' over the opera, as Boito planned that he should, is an old man's statement of belief not in the certainty of happiness but in its continued possibility. Yet if we could choose one moment from the inexhaustible delights of the score to represent the work, it should be the quiet C major chord that spreads over the orchestra as Thames water is banished and wine extends its beneficent warmth through Falstaff's body and soul, while he says, with an irresistible sense of the fitness of things, 'buono'. That 'good' is life's illogical, eternal answer to death and all the horrors that flesh and spirit are heir to.

The Midsummer Marriage

Recognition of Michael Tippett as a major composer dates from a surprisingly short time ago. Until as recently as the late 1960s, he was generally felt to be too eccentric a figure to be taken quite seriously: a sincere, even at times an inspired voice, but too far from any kind of mainstream development, and too often apparently uncertain of what he was doing, to be accepted as a composer of central importance by any of the representative opinions of the day; a flawed visionary, he hardly knew how he stumbled on his admittedly radiant inventions, and was apt to stammer in communicating his visions to the world. If he is now looked up to as an artist with something vital to say about the problems of human life in this century, a contemporary who 'speaks as a seer', it is not he that has changed but our attitude to him. Tippett's music has simply grown more familiar. Orchestras are learning to play it; and critical judgment—which can never remember to allow for the distorting effect of inadequate performance on new music—has shifted accordingly. Tippett has become something of a master: a master who remains disconcertingly unpredictable but whom we have learned to love. Perhaps, too, the conception of what constitutes contemporary music, of what is possible for composers in the second half of the 20th century, has begun to ease and grow more inclusive.

The part played in all this by *The Midsummer Marriage* has been both crucial and symptomatic. In particular the complete recording, conducted by Colin Davis, which appeared in 1970, came with the force of revelation to many people—

some who till then had barely heard of the opera—and made them vividly aware of a composer of outwardly traditional but profoundly original genius and of a work whose profusion of superb melodic utterance and absolutely fresh handling of tonal harmony almost obliged the history of music in our time to be rewritten. Yet this same work had been a byword for the mixture of inspiration and muddle that was held to characterize the music of Tippett—a composer who because of certain obstinate limitations of technique could only 'limp towards the light'. The vision that he was struggling to express in his opera had not, it was objected, been worked out in theatrical terms; the score was typically overloaded with notes, and as for the libretto, he should never have tried to write it himself, his mind was a welter of abstract ideas and his taste in words altogether too unreliable.

Such conclusions were thoroughly natural, given the need to be seen to evaluate a work before one has had time to absorb it. The unusual character and treatment of the drama, the accident of two productions which contrived to be equally unilluminating in quite different ways, the tendency of opera-goers, like the peers in *Iolanthe*, to leave their brains outside, the composer's propensity for philosophizing about art in essays which sometimes required to be read more than once in order to be understood, and the music's formidable demands on its performers—these diverse factors combined with the cornucopian richness of the score to implant the idea of *The Midsummer Marriage* as a lovely jungle of invention, full of beauties but undisciplined, overgrown and, finally, impracticable. It was magnificent but it was not opera.

In practice, whether or to what extent an opera works on the stage is much more a matter of chance—the chance of a particular production reacting on the chemistry of the individual sensibility—than we like to admit. Contrary to the assumption which lies behind so much writing and thinking about opera, there are no fixed and definable laws by which it can be stated that this music is genuinely operatic, that is not. The ultimate test is in the experience of each opera-goer. We can decide a piece is unoperatic, then decisively change our minds in the light of subsequent discovery. Very often it is the music by itself that convinces us of a dramatic validity which no stage setting that we have yet seen has succeeded in translating into visible shape. Tippett's drama can indeed be described, and apprehended, in such a way as to seem incurably untheatrical: an allegory of human fulfilment through sublimation and self-knowledge, a modern suburban *Magic Flute* told in terms of Jungian psychology, with the masculine and feminine principles, *animus* and *anima*, dressed up as characters out of Bernard Shaw (an industrialist, a mechanic, a secretary, a young rebel, even a 'He-Ancient' and 'She-Ancient'), the action shuttling between the natural and the supernatural, and the libretto a riot of symbols from Greek, Celtic, Christian and Hindu mythologies.

All this is quite true so far as it goes. Its refutation, or rather its positive acceptance, lies not in words but in music, not by argument but by experience; the justification of the work is in the minds of those for whom it is a most potent reality. This is not so naïve as it may sound. To make the music of *The Midsummer Marriage* one's own is not simply to be so in love with it that for its sake one would tolerate any inadequacy on the part of the libretto. It is not to deny that Tippett's dramaturgy may occasionally falter or that here and there in his choice of language he has misjudged the effect that a word or phrase will have when sung. Nor is it merely to accept that this is the libretto the composer set, that these words opened the floodgates of his musical imagination, and without them there would be no *Midsummer Marriage*; nor even that the music's beauty makes the effort of understanding the libretto thoroughly worth while—profoundly as well as obviously true though that is. Rather, it is to discover that, as so often, the music has taken possession of the libretto, has become it, to the point where it is no longer possible to consider the libretto separately, for it has ceased to have a separate existence: the composer is the dramatist; the score that the words generated incarnates the drama, and through it the drama is manifested and understood.

The means by which such a process of absorption operates in a symbolic music-drama is difficult to describe. If the music is strong enough—if it impresses itself sufficiently on our imaginations—it imposes its own dramatic world within which everything is clear; but the significance may well transcend words. Music fills out the hints of the text and gives vibrant life to its bald statements, setting them resonating so that they strike answering chords in us. It endows the concepts of the text with reality and form, suggests the deeper, often contradictory meaning that lies below the surface, telescopes time, compresses experience. In short, it makes explicit. But it may do so in a way that cannot be, and does not need to be, exactly accounted for. In the ordeal scene of *The Magic Flute* the power of music, through the particular pattern of trombone chords and irregular drumbeats accompanying the serene but highly charged melody of the flute, achieves in a few bars a sense of far-reaching human development, of prolonged strain endured and turned to good, that is unmistakable but also indescribable. Sometimes we may have no clear idea what actually 'happens' in terms of outward action: for example, at the end of *The Ring*, where, as Ernest Newman remarks, Wagner was able by means of music 'to convey to the *feeling* of the listener what the poet in him found impossible to express in words'.

As a matter of fact the action of Tippett's opera is far less obscure than is commonly alleged. Though the ideas behind it may be many-layered, the imagery through which they are conveyed is for the most part directly comprehensible by a Western audience. The difficulties largely vanish if we accept the work's dramatic premises: that the 'unreal' dimension of the spirit, like the ancient temple in the woodland clearing, is 'much nearer than expected' and can be

entered at any time; that the characters' imaginings can take
concrete form and become the action; and that what we
witness is a vision of spiritual growth and harmony, a symbolic marriage game played out in a setting at once timeless
and of today. The old stones become buildings again,
peopled by antique priests and their acolytes and alive with
ritual movement; truth, worldly power, youth, age, are
personified; nature takes anthropomorphic form; human
dancers act out the conflicts and reconciliations of the psyche.
The whole thing is a dream, with a dream's fluidity and
vividness. In one sense nothing happens. When Mark and
Jenifer meet in the wood in the final scene and with their
friends descend the hill to start a new life, no time has elapsed
since the opera began: it is still Midsummer morning, as in
the opening scene (though a Midsummer morning whose
light shines with a clarity not encountered before in the
opera). But being a dream it is full of significant events,
obedient to their own inner logic. *The Midsummer Marriage*
is obscure only if we try too soon to pin down and particu-
larize, to ask why, to assume confusion before we have given
ourselves a chance to experience otherwise, to label with
specific terms—soul and body, will and senses, intellect and
instinct, heaven and hell—what is deliberately not specified.
If on the contrary we let it work on us and explain itself in its
chosen way, we are given the freedom of a world of heightened reality which enriches and illuminates our existence.
We participate in a celebration of wholeness, a vision of
divided man healed by the power of sympathetic magic and
restored to a life as abundant as the burgeoning wood seen
at the high point of the natural year. We may not be able to
express it exactly, but we do not have to: the music has
already done so.

To attempt what Tippett attempted in his first opera—the
re-writing of the traditional comedy of the obstacles to a
marriage in the language of dreams, the staging of a
sustained and complex metaphor—required a Wagnerian

confidence in the power of his music. The confidence was not misplaced. The music of *The Midsummer Marriage* is prodigious in its force and its wealth of imagery. A flood of lyrical invention rarely equalled in 20th-century art surges through it. But it is controlled: the technique is equal to the inspiration. The first, and lasting, response is delight at the sense of spontaneous creation, at the freshness and sweep of its invention; the second and complementary recognition is of the certainty with which the ideas are handled and shaped. Familiarity with the work only deepens admiration for Tippett's skill. At every turn one discovers attributes of a mastery that he was once said to lack: a cunning felicity of touch, a rich but disciplined orchestral imagination, which keep the endlessly proliferating counterpoints and glowing textures free from congestion, a sure feeling for dramatic pace, a sense of architecture whereby the work moves in a series of great arches, with a balanced tension of energy and stillness. The vision has been seen and grasped entire, and the music embodies it as a whole and in all its diversities and ambiguities.

Tippett did not achieve this mastery without a struggle. He is one of those artists, like Beethoven or Berlioz, who have to toil and sweat to acquire the talent their genius demands. But the marks of the struggle are nowhere visible except—and there, as it were, by design—in the long aria of Madame Sosostris, where the composer steps for a moment outside the action and re-lives the agonies of artistic birth. For all its elaboration the score seems to move without external impulse, to bud and blossom and explode into leaf as naturally as the rich midsummer fecundity it so triumphantly evokes. To account for it we are driven to call on the 'collective unconscious' of which Tippett has written in describing the genesis of his opera, and to borrow Stravinsky's dictum about the composition of the *Sacre*: Tippett was the vessel through which *The Midsummer Marriage* passed.

I doubt if Tippett chose its harmonic idiom—an idiom which makes it the most tonal of all his major works, not excepting *A Child of our Time*, the Concerto for double string orchestra and the Piano Concerto. It came out that way because it had to. The *Midsummer Marriage* style was, in a sense, the inevitable outcome of the work's dramatic conception of reconciliation and unity-in-abundance. But it was inevitable only given Tippett's freedom and audacity of spirit, his position in time and place, and the extraordinary mixture of innocence and receptiveness in his nature. A kind of saving naïvety enabled him to do what no one else could have done or would have dared to do, and what he himself could do only once. Probably no one but an English musician of his generation, brought up in a predominantly Germanic tradition but also steeped in Purcell and the Elizabethan and Jacobean madrigalists and lutenists, and at the same time relatively isolated from contemporary developments on the continent, would have conceived of composing such a score. Yet how unlike so much English music it is, in its uninhibitedness, its large ideas and bold execution, its almost complete avoidance of the manufactured ensemble and the facile sequence. *The Midsummer Marriage* is an unexpected illustration of Stravinsky's dictum that tradition is made, not inherited. It is the product of three-and-a-half centuries of music and a work of overwhelming originality. Like Walther's song, as Hans Sachs recalled it on St John's Eve, it is both old and new, the past reborn for the tormented present.

Here and there, especially in Act 3, we find allusions to familiar masterpieces or epochs of musical history: Bach's chorales in the serene, multitudinous orchestral music that punctuates and finally submerges the concluding chorus, *Figaro* humorously borrowed for the ringing of the temple doorbell, a strong Gibichung atmosphere in the horn triplets descending in sixths over a timpani roll as the chorus go off to meet Madame Sosostris, and a parody of the Ninth Symphony in the 12/8 march in B flat shortly afterwards; perhaps, too, at the opening of Act 2, a pagan echo of the celestial chatter of woodwind at the end of the Missa

Solemnis. But the familiarity we are aware of is mostly of a different sort. Where have we heard this music before? We can hardly believe it has not always been part of our consciousness. When we listen to Mark's first aria we wonder how such tunes could have waited till now to be invented. At the climax of Sosostris' great statement—'I am what has been, is and shall be'—the words answer our sense of amazement that such glory can have remained hidden so long. It is as though Tippett, while composing the work, was attuned to archetypal sounds always in existence but unheard before; as though he had had access to some secret natural force, by virtue of an instinctive power largely lost in modern civilization. Out of his deep but peculiarly unfettered relationship with the past he created a new song and a new dance for the renewal of the human spirit.

Like the concord it celebrates, the predominant consonance of the opera's musical idiom is a dynamic quality, the product of fruitful tension. There is no suspicion of monotony, slackness or routine in it. Any such danger was dispelled from the start, first and most obviously by the fertility of Tippett's thematic invention—melody, large-spanned, passionate, richly decorative but powerfully moulded, soars out in ungrudging profusion—and then by three things hardly less important and not properly separable from it: his characteristic and prodigious rhythmic vitality, the freshness of his harmonic invention, and his superbly assured and imaginative use of the traditional symphony orchestra. Rhythm, virile and flexible, adapting itself equally to the ecstatic and the conversational, elaborately wrought, subtly stressed, but irresistible in impulse, carries the music forward on strong currents, and provides a sinewy bass for the luxuriant harmonic texture. This texture is in turn constantly enriched by a systematic use of superimposed fourths which, though Tippett was to abandon it before long, amounted to a new extension of diatonicism. (Melodically, too, the interval of the descending fourth acts as a kind of unifying leitmotiv throughout the work, culminating in the great chain of B flat—F—C—G—D stretching from high trumpet to bass trombone just before the climax of the final Ritual Dance.)

But the use of fourths is only a part-explanation of the freedom of Tippett's handling of tonal harmony and the freshness that results from it. We are so conditioned to see music in evolutionary terms, as a movement away from tonality, and to equate progress with dissonance, that we cannot help expecting works written, however sincerely, in tonal idioms to be fundamentally retrogressive, if not evasive and undervitalized. Generally speaking they may be; for most serious composers atonality has long been both a historical and a personal necessity. But for Tippett, who has rightly been called 'one of the few great non-neurotic musical masters of the past hundred years',* it has never been, and least of all when his imagination was immersed in the composition of his first opera. *The Midsummer Marriage* is no more old-fashioned in the age of Boulez and Berio than *The First Circle* is old-fashioned in the age of Robbe-Grillet; there is no law eternal or temporary that decrees otherwise—though the obstacles to writing such works today are no doubt considerable. In Tippett's hands the old harmonic devices become rejuvenated, for the simple reason that for him they had not lost their force. The six-four chords in Mark's aria, the dominant seventh that steals into the fourth-laden texture after the first 'Sleep, sleep' in the Jack/Bella Duet, the grand modulations at the climax of Madame Sosostris' scena, sound like fresh inventions because Tippett himself was able to feel them so.

Just as he reinterprets diatonicism in response to the composition's spiritual and dramatic demands, so he uses the late-Romantic orchestra without inhibition as an absolutely personal medium of his thought. The sounds of this orchestrally resplendent score are not so much startling in themselves as marvellously apt and evocative. Tippett's instrumentation is the faithful expression of the poetic idea,

* Bernard Jacobson, in *Stereo Review*, July 1971.

whether that idea is the cold blue radiance of Jenifer's immortal imaginings, the fierce dry heat and pounding hoof-beats of Mark's Dionysiac pride, Bella playfully flourishing her powder-puff, King Fisher's boardroom blend of suavity and bluster, the black veils stirring round the hidden, disturbing truth, the incandescence of 'carnal love trans-figured as divine consuming love' at the blazing climax of the fourth Ritual Dance, or the stillness that succeeds the fading of the vision. The music is just as much at home in its down-to-earth conversations as in its visionary flights. Tippett found the lightest of hands with which to draw his Papageno and Papagena. And how masterly is his musical distillation of the passage of the hours, from summer dawn to midday, through the vibrant heat and the shadow-pools of afternoon to milky night and the chill mists of a new dawn! Once again a simplicity in the highest sense naïve enabled him to find images for bird, beast and fish, tree and stream, hawk and hare, sunrise, moonlight and cockcrow, which strike us, the moment we hear them, as so obviously right that we cannot imagine how they could be otherwise, how they could ever not have been.

Yet the sense of archetypal inevitability that shines through the music of *The Midsummer Marriage* must not be allowed to blind us to the sophistication with which all this rich variety of musical event is controlled in the interests of coherence and dramatic shape. Tippett never indulges his creative facility. Even the long monologue of Madame Sosostris, in which he seems to stand apart and speak *in propria persona* of the burdens and exaltations of the artist's hieratic calling, performs at the same time a necessary function in a drama of the indivisibility and inescapability of Truth (run away from it or manipulate it though we will). Truth, for King Fisher, is what it is expedient to tell the shareholders and, in his personal life, what he wishes to believe: in terms of the dramatic resolution, what he must be brought face to face with. Truth stands for the difficult but fruitful process of learning about ourselves in order that we may grow into fullness of life—though the solemnity of explanations of this sort conveys an impression of didacticism that is quite foreign to the work's enormous zest.

Similarly, Tippett is at constant pains to relate the natural setting to the psychological drama. The Ritual Dances in Act 2, in which the setting becomes the foreground, are no mere brilliant diversion (indeed the use of the once-conventional middle-act ballet for organic purposes is one more example of the work's revivifying of tradition). They contain many different, simultaneous meanings; music-drama is the art which makes such simultaneity of meanings possible while rendering their explanation superfluous. We may try to interpret them in various ways: simply in terms of the diurnal cycle of which man's life remains indissolubly part, or in terms of 'female' instinct hunting down 'male' logic; in terms of the aggressiveness that should be recognized as an element in the most vital and harmonious human relationship, or rather as a stage, a necessary recognition, in the development towards such a relationship (for the three dances of pursuit are subsumed, in Act 3, in the final dance of 'the Voluntary Human Sacrifice'); or in terms of the painful demands of life, from which we try to escape and which seek the death of our old unregenerate self so that a new self may be born. Such interpretations, each of them valid so far as it goes, stop short of the music's overwhelming sense of natural power. Nature in *The Midsummer Marriage* is an integral part of the opera—both a metaphor of the central argument and an active agent in it. The wood in which the action takes place is at once a naturalistic wood, a symbol of natural energy at its most abundant, and a magic place full of hidden presences from which no one is immune. (Jack and Bella cosily picturing their married existence are themselves unconsciously responding to them—as the recurrence of a variant of the woodland's numinous horn-chords at each entranced pause in the conversation quietly reminds us.) And the pure, purged light of the Midsummer sunrise that floods the hilltop clearing as the orchestra brings the opera to an end gives intense actuality—again as words could not do—to the vision of lives reborn and beginning again in a new understanding.

The Midsummer Marriage exemplifies Keats' remark that 'what the imagination seizes as Beauty must be truth'. Its particular truth is one that has not found many great artists in the past hundred years able to proclaim it. The work is an ode to joy, an exclamation of belief in the continued possibility of human life, and in the power of art and in its gaiety —Yeats' 'gaiety transfiguring all that dread'. It is an improbable work for the mid-20th century to have produced. Perhaps only an imagination so deeply compounded of innocence and toughness could have done so, at such a point in the tragic history of the human race. For there is nothing archaic, escapist, unreal about Tippett's vision. Like the blessed man in the Psalms he has used the wilderness for a well. 'I would know my shadow and my light': the words of the narrator in *A Child of Our Time*—the work out of whose final prayer for renewal *The Midsummer Marriage* grew—stand for the purpose and the achievement of Tippett's opera. The dread is not evaded but faced and experienced and overcome; the joy is won by the sweat of the spirit out of a knowledge of suffering and an acceptance of the inevitability and the necessity of painful change. 'All things fall and are built again,' sing the chorus at the end, echoing Yeats' line from the same poem. If Tippett's imagination has since tended to move away from the opera's confident assertions (and at the same time to abandon its thematicism and lyrical expansiveness), if the sense of an era in tumultuous transition, which the opera acknowledged and celebrated, is now more harshly felt in the style and content of his music and if he has been forced to more guarded, stoical conclusions, the work itself is not the less substantially there, nor its truth any less eagerly to be embraced. *The Midsummer Marriage* exists. It speaks to

our needs, fulfilling the high and unchanged function of the
artist to create

> images of the past, shapes of the future; images of vigour for a
> decadent period, images of calm for one too violent, images of
> reconciliation for a world torn by divisions and, in an age of
> mediocrity and shattered dreams, images of abounding, generous,
> exuberant beauty.*

* Michael Tippett, *One Pair of Eyes*, BBC 2, February 1972.

Die Meistersinger

When every possible argument has been raised against it, *Die Meistersinger* remains one of the supreme achievements of post-Renaissance art and one of the delights of a music-lover's existence. We may concede that at the end everything makes a little too smoothly for righteousness, with the immense dramatic machinery, in Joseph Kerman's words, 'purring to its calculated close'. We may feel, as Wagner himself felt before Cosima persuaded him out of his doubts, that Hans Sachs is made to address us once too often, and that the drama's original direction comes near being lost in the public adulation of the all-wise Meister with whom Wagner came increasingly to identify himself. We may regret that the more elaborate final version of the Prize Song sacrifices some of the charm of Walther's first inspiration in the interests of variety. We may even find a touch of sadistic, if not fascist, bullying in the manner in which Beckmesser is put down: does the orchestra not exult a little too triumphantly in his impending downfall, in that savage parody of the serenade/cudgelling motif with which it depicts him hurrying out of Sachs' workshop, followed by the level gaze of the Cobbler? We may, finally, complain that even here, in what is supposed to be a comedy, Wagner is inordinate and insatiable in his demands on us, that the whole thing is simply too long for normal human endurance. But all objections fade in the presence of the work's extraordinary beauty and mastery, its poetic power and completeness. In a good performance it does not even seem long; on the contrary, no work is less tiring, more uplifting to the mind and the senses. Every faculty is refreshed by contact with it.

This is partly because of the nature of the subject (operatically most uncommon) that Wagner has chosen to bring to life in music—a community of people seen and felt going about their daily existence from one ordinary, absorbing incident to another; but it is also because of something which is part of the same illusion of actual life being lived before our eyes, and without which the illusion would fail—the sense of spontaneous creation which runs through the work. In a score as vast and complex, as ingeniously worked and intricate with cross-references as any he wrote, Wagner never once overlays his material, never clogs the purely musical flow. It is all music; there is none of that resort to formula or bluff that in *Tristan* and *The Ring* sometimes takes the place of invention. Yet hardly a bar does not have its exact motivic reason and justification. Everything is remembered and accounted for. The little turn of phrase to which David answers Walther's question 'What is a Mastersong?' will reappear with perfect punctuality three hours later as Eva pronounces a baptismal blessing on the newborn child of genius and tradition.*

* a figure that echoes the love motif in *Die Walküre*.

The great hive of motivic activity that is the score of *Die Meistersinger* is summed up in the endless proliferations of the melodic cell formed by the intervals of descending fourth and rising minor third, first heard, played by the solo viola, in the fourth bar of the opening scene:

No character or event is untouched by its influence. (The 'birth of a Mastersong' motive, just mentioned, includes it.) We meet it in the second phrase of 'Am stillen Herd', at the beginning of the *Fliedermonolog*, in the theme to which Sachs explains to Walther the value of conventions in art, in the persistent horn figure at the start of David's recital of the modes, and in the little violin phrase which teasingly punctuates the exchange between Sachs and Beckmesser when the latter produces the stolen poem from his pocket. Beckmesser's serenade makes great if vulgar play with it. It is prominent in the related music of the cudgelling which the Marker receives from the outraged apprentice and, given to the bassoon—an instrument whose half-droll, half-magical character is ideally suited to the purpose—it is the last music we hear in the second act before the curtain falls with the final chord.* It is of course present in the Prize Song. Beckmesser's own attempt at a prize song includes it, in a flattened form (as his main motif is a minor-key variant of Walther's). The same germ produces the *Johannistag* motif, and innumerable melodic figures, central and incidental. A detailed investigation would show the score honeycombed with it.

The family likeness between themes is important in three respects. First, it is Wagner's means of suggesting the

* Or *should* fall with the final chord. In practice, despite Wagner's precise instruction 'genau mit dem letzten Takt', it almost always falls in the preceding bar, with inevitably fatal effect.

coherent, particular world of his opera; it contributes to the specific *Meistersinger* idiom and symbolizes the organic community of Nurembergers united in work and play. Secondly, it has the dramatic function of making the Prize Song, when it at last appears, the consummation of everything previously heard and thus the living symbol of traditional wisdom born anew. (It has been said that Wagner takes an enormous risk and 'stakes the fate of his work' on his ability to invent a great tune that will convince the audience that it is in truth a 'Prize Song'. But in a sense he does not have to invent it: since the action began the music has been ceaselessly creating and developing melodies and fragments of melodies in preparation for the tune, so that when the moment comes to produce it he has only, like Elgar, to pluck it from the air around him—by now enriched with the accumulated associations of two-and-a-quarter acts.) Thirdly, the close interrelationship of his themes enables Wagner to move with complete freedom between them, to weave them into a symphonic web which, with all its complexity of internal allusion, is totally without any sense of contrivance. The motifs in *The Ring* can be shown to be just as significantly interrelated. But, their range of style and harmonic language being so much wider, it is not always possible for Wagner, with all his skill, to avoid artificiality and heavy-handedness in their manipulation. There are occasions when one is forced to admit the cruel justice of Debussy's comparison between leitmotiv technique and a lunatic at a party who, every time he speaks to you, presents you with his visiting card. In *Meistersinger*, on the contrary, with its narrower and more homogeneous idiom, the overriding impression is of a composer giving himself unpremeditatedly to the sheer pleasure of music-making, revelling almost carelessly in the richness of his fancy, unable to restrain his impulse to decorate the huge design with yet more loving and delicate craftsmanship even when, like a medieval stonemason, he knows it will not be noticed. Like his hero, 'Nun sang er, wie er musst'.

He sang as he had to. One explanation of the effortless abundance of *Die Meistersinger* lies in its date. Its place in the chronology of Wagner's career is crucial. The heroic labours of the last ten or twelve years—the uncompleted *Ring*, the ruthless dedication of his will to a totally new concept and system of opera, the emotional strains of *Tristan* and the audacious and exhausting journey it had taken him into the harmonic future—demanded a reaction. With an instinct of self-preservation and renewal no less sure than moved Verdi to compose *Falstaff* after *Otello*, he took up again the idea of a comedy on the old Nuremberg guilds that he had sketched nearly twenty years earlier. If the result was a work larger in scale than anything he had yet written, the reason was simply that he had so much to say about it. His art was by nature comprehensive and the pace of his musical processes leisurely and cumulative, and to re-create 16th-century Germany in a manner that the Wagner of the 1860s considered fitting required unlimited space. But the expansiveness of the score is, also and above all, witness to the flood of invention that the subject released in him.

In *Die Meistersinger* Wagner gave his psyche a rest and celebrated his temporary liberation from his life's mission. The return to solid historical fact was a holiday from the dark ambiguities of mythology, just as the return to diatonic harmony was a respite from chromaticism. Instead of having to create his own tradition and then explain it to his audience, he had one already existing and known to call on, one that was unambiguous, based firmly in time and place, yet rich in suggestion and deeply rooted in his own consciousness. We do not have to reject the mythologizing Wagner of *The Ring*, *Tristan* and *Parsifal* to understand the relief that the composition of *Meistersinger* must have meant. Even politically speaking, the evocation of an idealized German past, with its vision of a secure and harmonious social order, must have been a profoundly welcome escape from the disillusionments of the present, the burdens of revolutionary thought in the years after 1848. He had earned himself this freedom and he threw himself unrestrainedly into the enjoyment of it.

Yet it would be quite wrong to see the work as in any important sense untypical of Wagner, as a backwater in his career or a repudiation of the artistic values he stood for. When people talk about a 'different' Wagner, who allows himself to write charming tunes and genial harmonies and to give full play to the gift of humour hinted at in *Rheingold* and *Siegfried*, they merely express a predilection for the kind of work which *Meistersinger* represents. It is that that is different, not the manner of treating it. In composing such a work Wagner may apparently have turned about and reverted to the devices of the tradition he believed he had been sent to destroy: ensembles, choral finales, formal songs, old-style overture, ballet and, in place of the knotty alliterative verse of the Nibelung dramas, a more conventional poetic style; yet he remained faithful to the logic of his fundamental principles. The subject answered a deep musical and emotional need at that moment in his life, a need for stability, relaxation, the touch of familiar things. Given that fact, it demanded from Wagner precisely the treatment that he gave it. Just as in *Tristan* the dramatist forced the musician to compose in an unprecedentedly dissonant style which is not resolved until the final chord, when Isolde and Tristan find their union in death, so in *Meistersinger* the character of the drama imposed its own natural musical idiom. The idiom is in origin that of German folk-song (in his use of which Wagner observes the golden rule of folk-song settings, that their harmonization should be basically diatonic; none of Hanslick's pronouncements is dafter than the one in which he speaks of the '*Meistersinger* style' and German folk-music as antithetical). But there was nothing retrogressive about the composition of such a work by the man who had just written *Tristan*. Though chromaticism is used to enrich and no longer to disrupt tonality—as the shock effect of that brief quotation from *Tristan* in Act 3 of *Die Meistersinger* powerfully reminds us—it is, harmonically, no less rich and original a score. The traditional forms are integrated into the general symphonic argument with a skill which shows the music-dramatist at the full stretch of his powers, while the mastery of large-scale construction goes beyond even what Wagner had achieved before. In the quintessentially Wagnerian arts of thematic transformation, transition, development of long musical periods out of fragments of melody, and evocation of mood (whether psychological or of natural surroundings), Wagner never surpassed what he did here; and in sustained vitality and felicity of musical invention he never equalled it.

One thinks of the metamorphosis of Sachs' song about Adam and Eve—rough, emphatic music with an edge of bitterness—into the radiant wonder of the prelude to Act 3; the enchantment that comes over the cudgelling music—itself in part an ironic development of Beckmesser's serenade—as the moon rises over the deserted streets at the end of Act 2; the feeling of a hot June night out of doors in a town, conveyed by so many touches: the multiple orchestral trills and the gaiety, shot through with sadness, of the apprentices' voices at the beginning of Act 2, the murmur of horns and tremolo strings—summer evening fragrance made audible—as Sachs catches the scent of the elder tree, the constant horn sonority, the twang of Beckmesser's lute in the alley. One thinks of the transition from Sachs' jubilant exit, ringing with the proud splendours of the Prize Song and the Nuremberg motif, to Beckmesser's furtive entry and the sudden glow in the strings as his eye alights on the manuscript of the Walther's poem and the music of the Prize Song steals in, accompanied by suspicious twinges on the violas; or, from earlier in the same act, the burgeoning of the *Johannistag* melody out of the 'glow-worm' music (another magical transformation of the cud-gelling motif); the breathtaking beauty of the long melody that floats out from the spellbound strings in the stillness following the first blast of the Nightwatchman's horn; the tender, subtle cross-currents in the dialogues between Sachs and Eva; the melodic lines sprouting and springing into a

great branching arch of counterpoint to welcome the assem-
bly of the masters in Act 1; the exquisite woodwind embroidery of David's Baptist song and the leap of excitement
in the violins as he realizes that it is his master's birthday;
the wealth of vivacious and humorous comment lavished
on the accompaniment to the recital of the modes or the
Tailors' guild-song; the splendour and utter rightness of the
great chorale into which the overture sails with a sense of
calm inevitability and which, with its expressive inter-
jections by the orchestra, at once establishes the character
of the work and a good deal of its musical material as well as
the dramatic situation at the rise of the curtain: Walther's
impatient ardour, Eva's gleeful innocence as she peeps from
behind her prayer-book, and the voice of the community
united in traditional ritual. But to illustrate all the compositional riches of the work is both impossible and
unnecessary. They are landmarks in the experience of
unnumbered operagoers.

In turning back once more to the German historical past for
his source and inspiration Wagner, as we have seen, was
doing nothing that was alien to him. It was part of his
inheritance, though with characteristic thoroughness he
steeped himself in Protestant chorale and the elaborate rules
of the Mastersingers' guild as a preparation for writing the
work. Once embarked, however, absolutist that he was, he
instinctively saw his task and opportunity as nothing less
than a gigantic summing-up of the German musical tradition. The score of *Die Meistersinger* is like a great river into
which all the main tributary streams of German style and
technique flow: chorale, fugue, march, ländler, strophic
lied, united in that all-embracing symphonic development
which is the ultimate demonstration of the creative art. The
work is thus more than a picture of one time and place in
Germany's past: it is a tribute to German civilization at its
sturdiest and, through it, to an epoch of European consciousness that was drawing to an end as Wagner celebrated

it. And beyond that, it is a hymn to the life of civilized Western man, his sense of order, his accumulated wisdom, his self-awareness, his dreams and longings, his capacity for happiness, and the sudden impulses of self-destructive rage that seize him, making him—as Sachs sings—'deaf to his own cry of pain'. At the same time what gives the work its enduring fascination, and what makes these larger issues live and move us, is that it *is* a picture of one time and place, a community rooted in historical reality, evoked with the mixture of patient cunning and imaginative ruthlessness that are part of the secret of Wagner's greatness. The picture is idealized but, as the music embodies it, it rings true. It is a picture of mankind and nature in accord, human beings at peace with their world. This is what is meant by the goodness of *Die Meistersinger*. It is something that lies far deeper than the slightly contrived consummation of the final tableau or the taunting of an ill-natured official, deeper too than the portrait of Sachs or the truths about art and the artist, central though they are to the work—the sense of life working out right: that sense which Puck expresses in his homely incantation 'On the ground/Sleep sound', as he charms the demon of discord from Lysander's eye, and which in the opera culminates in the scene where Sachs accepts his sadness and then turns to the friendly duties that await him, while the chorale with which the whole work began peels out its joyous message.

In composing *Die Meistersinger* Wagner ostensibly turned his back on his mythologizing self; yet he created a myth as potent as in any of his music-dramas. *Die Meistersinger* domesticates the golden age; it brings it down to familiar earth and makes it at home, across the street and in the fields, so that we recognize its face and, for the length of this long but inexhaustibly refreshing work, live it and make it our own.

Idomeneo

To know *Idomeneo* is to discover one of the marvels of dramatic music; yet it is only now, two centuries after its composition, that the work's greatness is beginning to be truly appreciated. The beauty of individual numbers has never been denied (one of them, the seductively languorous chorus 'Placido è il mar', going so far as to become a favourite with Victorian glee-clubs), but a supposedly moribund form has made it easy prey to pejorative generalizations and the German passion for 'performing editions'. History has been against it. As Daniel Heartz remarks,* such a work could have no place in the 19th century's stereotyped conception of the elegant, limited 18th. And in the first half of the 20th, though Mozart came to be recognized as the universal genius he is, it was largely on the strength of his comic operas, compared with which the grand and tragic style developed in *Idomeneo* and the contemporary Kyrie in D minor may well seem at first a trifle stiff. *Idomeneo* simply did not fit in with the new discovery of Mozart the dramatist of the human comedy. It was so different that criticism could cope with it only by travestying it. Even now many quite enlightened Mozart-lovers think of it as a noble fossil. For them, there are the 'Big Five'—*Entführung*, *Figaro*, *Don Giovanni*, *Così*, and *The Magic Flute*—and there is *Idomeneo*, which is not the same thing at all. The work's low status in Germany and Austria, the home of Mozart culture, is reflected in the extraordinary fact that it is not

* 'The Genesis of Mozart's *Idomeneo*', in *Mozart-Jahrbuch*, 1967–8: a landmark in modern understanding of the work.

generally available as Mozart wrote it, but only in garbled form. The indignities practised on it in Paumgartner's edition show that Salzburg has learnt nothing since the day when Mozart shook off the dust of its stifling provincialism.*

All this was made possible by the attitude of mind which categorizes works of art and then reacts to them accordingly. *Idomeneo* was an *opera seria*—a genre associated with rigid musical forms, abstract two-dimensional characters, and conventionally heroic conflicts and resolutions; a dying genre which not even Mozart could bring to life, whatever pains he might take with it and whatever the charming and even powerful things he might create while doing so. *Idomeneo* was a particularly obvious subject for this labelling process because, except in *La clemenza di Tito*, Mozart never returned to the kind of operatic writing it represents, but instead applied his dramatic genius to *opera buffa* and its German counterpart. His next stage work, *Die Entführung aus dem Serail*, written about a year later, could hardly have been more different or, superficially, more concerned with the living world of real feelings and recognizable people, whereas *Idomeneo* was imprisoned within a petrified convention; and though *Entführung* is dramatically the less satisfactory of the two, its position as the first great *Singspiel* and the ancestor of so many well-loved operas and operatic characters ensured it a degree of respect rarely granted, until now, to *Idomeneo*. It followed that *Idomeneo*, with all its beauties, could not be a living dramatic entity. Even for so

---

* Among other things, Paumgartner removes Idomeneo's first aria, allocates Elettra's characteristically large-spanned arioso 'Soavi zeffiri' to the 'two Cretan maidens', whom we heard earlier ushering in the reign of perpetual concord in thirds and sixths to the accompaniment of pretty flourishes on oboes and bassoons, and rearranges a large part of Act 3 so that the carefully devised sequence of scenes is destroyed and one of the most magical changes of mood in music, the conclusion of 'O voto tremendo', disappears without trace. Among many optional cuts indicated is one of nine bars in the Quartet, a movement so beautiful, and beautifully proportioned, that one might have thought it would humble the most meddlesome Kapellmeister, even without Mozart's own testimony that 'If I knew of a single note that ought to be altered in this Quartet, I would alter it at once.'

fervent an admirer as Edward Dent, who did so much to advance the cause of the work, it was a museum piece, to be revived only 'on some special occasion . . . which we shall attend in a spirit of pilgrimage'.

As it happened, Dent's faith in the work's 'profound and noble sincerity' was soon to be vindicated to an extent that he can hardly have expected. In 1947, the year in which the revised edition of his *Mozart's Operas* was published, *Idomeneo* was put on at Oxford by Jack Westrup, and not long afterwards Glyndebourne gave their famous series of performances (with Sena Jurinac as Ilia). The effect of these events on musical opinion in this country was profound. Within a decade, at Sadler's Wells, *Idomeneo* had been taken into the repertory and finally revealed as a vital dramatic work in its own right, capable of holding the modern stage and attracting the general operatic public.

It only shows how unwise it is to label works, especially works written in a medium as complex and chancy as opera, before you really know them. *Idomeneo* was certainly not the same thing as *Figaro*, *The Magic Flute* and the rest, but did that oblige it to be inferior? Quite apart from the fact that *opera seria*, so far from dying in the last quarter of the 18th century, lived on well into the 19th (if indeed it has ever died), how much is achieved by describing *Idomeneo* as one? What exactly is meant by the term in this actual instance? Less, it turns out, than was supposed. In the first place, the strong French influence which the work reveals requires us immediately to modify the description; the values and techniques of *tragédie lyrique* constantly colour those of *opera seria* and in the last act end by almost displacing them. Secondly, the test with any musical form is what it becomes in the hands of the particular composer. It is above all a test we must not forget when the composer is Mozart. With Mozart, the genre is what he makes of it. Of all the great masters he was the least consciously bothered by questions of how and what sort, and the most instinctively attuned to assimilate what was already to hand (which is not the same thing as saying that he did not think about what he did, or that he is not, paradoxically, the most protean of composers). Judged by the criteria of Wagnerism which for long dominated ideas about opera, *Idomeneo* belonged to a genre hopelessly limited and in need of reform. We can concede a point to the old generalizations: given the genre's usual limitations, the results are remarkable. In *Idomeneo* we watch Mozart making of it very largely what he wants. No work more strikingly demonstrates his ability to take a convention and put it to his own transcendent purposes. Far from being inhibited by it, he uses it to create music which rarely falters in its dramatic impetus and which is not surpassed in grandeur and intensity by any of the later masterpieces.

To some extent the marvel is explicable by the circumstances which brought the work into existence. The commission to compose an opera for the Munich carnival of 1781 gave Mozart just the chance he had been waiting for. Emotionally and artistically he had grown up. It was as though, with the experiences of his mother's death and his unhappy passion for Aloysia Weber, he had learnt suffering and pity. The tremendous adolescent exuberance and physical, almost sexual, energy of the Salzburg masses had matured into something no less vital but richer, darker, more profound; the new note heard at intervals during the previous few years (in the E flat Piano Concerto, for example, or the Sinfonia Concertante, K.364) was ready for sustained expression. Conscious of these powers, he felt increasingly frustrated by the lack of opportunity for exerting them in Salzburg, which to its other disadvantages added the crucial drawback of not possessing an opera. Munich, on the contrary, had one of the finest in Europe, the Mannheim company, which had lately moved there with the Palatine Elector's court. Mozart had first encountered it three years earlier, in Mannheim, and knew what it was capable of. Its orchestra had created new standards and new possibilities by the force, delicacy, dynamic range and expressive richness and variety of its playing. The company contained some first-rate dramatic talents, and a stage director and a designer, Pierre le Grand and Lorenzo Quaglio, who were intelligent artists and at the same time acknowledged masters of scenic effect. The intellectual atmosphere of Carl Theodor's court, which rivalled Frederick II's in discriminating and dedicated cultivation of all the arts, and where Voltaire was an honoured guest, and Shakespeare and Greek and Roman sculpture were studied with equal enthusiasm, helped to foster an operatic environment of exceptional seriousness. An idealistic young composer writing for it would find his instinct for drama encouraged and his demands understood as in few other places.

As a further incentive to great things, there was the admired example of Gluck's French operas, with their consistent loftiness of temper and concern for expressive truth, their use of the chorus to build up a monumental style of drama and vary the musical pace and texture, and their demonstration of the dramatic possibilities inherent in the old theme of public duty and private torment. A useful lesson could also be learnt from Gluck the autocrat and single-minded artist, who let nothing and nobody come between him and the realization of the dramatic idea. To quote Heartz's summing up, 'Mannheim opera was characterized by vocal, orchestral, and choreographic virtuosity in the service of stage realism, *Sturm und Drang* intensity, and a concept of grandeur in tune with the Greek Revival.' The subject stipulated for the Carnival opera—Idomeneo's fatal vow (for which an early 18th-century French libretto, by Antoine Danchet, was to be used as model)—was well chosen; the Jephtha-like tale offered precisely the scope for varied effects and the appeal to his deepest humanity that Mozart needed. In short, it was a challenge that could hardly fail to rouse him to something exceptional.

Nonetheless the response is astonishing. Nothing quite prepares us for the achievement of a level of *dramma per musica* unheard since Monteverdi. Under the stress of the challenge, Mozart has suddenly become a mature dramatist, able to exploit the virtues and ignore the limitations of the medium and to speak a new language of unprecedented force and flexibility. From the very outset the new language proclaims itself. The first section of the opera—overture, recitative, aria—contains the essence of the *Idomeneo* style and at the same time proposes the main themes of the drama. The overture is no mere curtain-raiser but the ideal preparation for what is to follow. It is the drama in microcosm: grand but ominous music driven forward relentlessly, as though by the surge and sweep of the sea felt both as a physical presence and as the angry god Neptune, symbol of the power of malignant fate over human affairs.

Ilia's long monologue—into which the overture leads directly, from a conclusion of momentous quietness—provides even surer proof that Mozart has become a great dramatic composer: he has learnt that vital but elusive secret of good opera, a strong, supple recitative style. In its richness, freedom, formal coherence and psychological penetration the accompanied recitative in *Idomeneo* shows a decisive advance on anything that Mozart had written in his early Italian operas or had heard in contemporary *opera seria* and *tragédie lyrique*; this is already the familiar expressive idiom of 'Don Ottavio, son morta', Tamino's scene with the Speaker, and 'Welch' ein Geschick' in *Entführung*. The music that Mozart writes while acquainting us with the situation at the rise of the curtain—music now resolute, now hesitant, indignation melting before love—charts the crosscurrents and ambiguities of feeling in the captive Trojan princess with moving sympathy, establishes once and for all the nobility, purity and passion of her character, and leads by a subtle natural progression into the relatively calm statement of the aria, 'Padre, germani'.

The aria, in turn, introduces us to another quality not encountered before in Mozartian serious opera—a combined terseness and subtlety of expression. The dovetailing of recitative and aria by a simple and beautifully original adaptation of the two chords which conventionally close a recitative, the economy with which a heart overflowing with contradictory and only half-acknowledged feelings is conveyed, the harmonic freedom, the variations in the reprise and in particular the amplification and intensification of emotion at the key words 'E un Greco adorerò?' ('Am I then to love a Greek?'), the perfect shape of the whole*—these things once again announce a new Mozart.

We shall find examples in *Idomeneo* of the luxuriance of the Salzburg Mozart—a luxuriance that was to recur on a more generous scale in *Entführung* and provoke the Emperor's quizzical (and commonly misquoted) comment: 'an *extraordinary* number of notes!'—but it is rarely that it does not perform an organic function, whether directly as psychological expression or indirectly as ironic contrast, or both simultaneously. Ilia's aria in the second act, 'Se il padre perdei', is decorated with florid concertante parts written by Mozart to please the Mannheim principal flute, oboe, horn and bassoon; yet in exploiting the exceptional talents of his wind-players he makes them serve the purposes of the drama. This is typical of his whole approach to the composition of *Idomeneo*. He has created for himself the freedom to indulge his incomparable gift for evoking a dream-like contentment, in such a way that it not only does not damage the dramatic realism but enriches it. The aria marks an important point in the gradual unfolding of Ilia's personality: she no longer hates her Greek captors, and we sense that in her new mood of happiness she will soon be ready to acknowledge the reason that has brought about this change of heart—the growing love she feels for Idamante. At the same time, the effect of the music's serene and lavish beauty, in the context of Idomeneo's guilty angst, is one of irony; while, dramatically, the king's realization that Ilia is in love with his son gives a further twist to the tragedy. Mozart conveys this latter idea in the space of half a bar. Ilia leaves

* Which, however, has not prevented Paumgartner from marking an optional cut of eleven bars in his edition.

the stage; Idomeneo is alone with his thoughts. The orchestra, without a pause and in the same andante tempo, softly repeats the second theme of the aria, but in a changed colouring which by the simplest shift of harmony muddies the translucence, turning an image of felicity into an expression of dark foreboding.

This passage, brief though it is, can stand for what is new and different about the work: its intense self-consciousness (in the good sense), its resourcefulness, its compassionate understanding of the interaction and interdependence of human lives, its uncovering of the dark side of reality.

The musical phrase in question is related to the rhythmic figure which runs through the entire opera like a motto. It is worth looking at the widely differing contexts in which this motto appears. We first hear it in the overture (ninth and eleventh bars), as a wild cry on the woodwind in tune with the general character of slightly hectic grandeur. I quote its second occurrence, in the more usual triplet form:

This aspect of the motto is intensified in Elettra's first aria and the orchestral passage which links the aria to the shipwreck scene, and again at the end of Act 2 and in the last bars of Elettra's aria in Act 3. At the conclusion of the overture, where it dominates the music (being repeated on the successive notes of a downward melodic minor scale), and then shortly afterwards in 'Padre, germani', it takes on a more subdued quality of inner agitation; the two final beats are now subdivided:

When Idomeneo, at a price, has saved himself from the gods'
immediate wrath, it finds a temporary repose:

But a moment later, as conscience begins to gnaw, the restless feeling returns:

In Idomeneo's great aria in Act 2, 'Fuor del mar', the notes
are lengthened and evened out in suitably regal fashion:

At the opposite pole the motto can lend itself, in the context
of the love Duet, to a sense of bliss blossoming irresistibly:

or to a pathetic hesitation, in the scene where Idomeneo,

under extreme pressure, haltingly reveals to the people that the victim is Idamante:

Here the motto is developed, briefly but with great suggestiveness, so as to compress into a few bars the sense of an agonizing decision being taken—the stricken Idomeneo's acknowledgment of defeat and submission of his heroic will to brutal necessity. The motto's appearance, shortly afterwards, underlines the pathos of Idamante's calm surrender. But its final flowering is reserved for the last scene of all, when the king in the presence of his people hands over authority to his son. Purged at last of all anxiety, the springing phrases add grace to this noblest of recitatives—though the associations it has acquired in the course of the opera give an extra poignancy to the drama of Idomeneo's supreme renunciation.

In no other opera of Mozart's, not even in *Don Giovanni*, do thematic reminiscences play so large a part. We should not exaggerate their importance: the motto is not a leitmotiv. Nor in itself does their presence make *Idomeneo* a great work, though it is one of the reasons—the peculiarly pictorial use of orchestral colour is another—for calling it a paradoxically forward-looking work. What it does help to show is the intense seriousness with which Mozart set about his task; it is part of the whole *Idomeneo* spirit. That spirit may be summed up in two words: dramatic truth. Four or five routine arias in an opera lasting three hours (though Mozart's routine is most other people's inspiration) represent the sum of his obeisance to convention. For the rest he has, as though at a stroke, created a fresh conception of drama through music. It is a matter both of detail and of structure. The smallest touches as well as the largest effects bear witness to the overriding ascendancy of dramatic values. When Elettra repeats Idomeneo's phrase at the beginning of the Trio, melodic, harmonic and textural variations colour the music in a way that shows us the emotions of the moment through her eyes; the downward sweep of the vocal line, the momentary turn of the harmony towards a gloomy D minor, the more broken accompaniment, the chromatic twists followed by wide leaps (suggesting that neurotic fears are active even in the hour of her triumph), the aristocratic hauteur of the whole ten-bar span of melody —here is music as powerfully and subtly characteristic of Elettra as is Donna Anna's 'Lascia alla mia pena' in the Sextet in *Don Giovanni*. Kerman's aphorism, 'The composer is the dramatist', is as true of *Idomeneo* as it is of the later masterpieces.

That it was a conscious preoccupation we know from the letters which Mozart wrote his father from Munich while the opera was in rehearsal. They are full of instructions for Leopold Mozart to pass on to the librettist, Giambattista Varesco, a minor cleric on the staff of Salzburg Cathedral. Varesco, like most librettists, has had a poor press, and he was no Boito; but the task of adapting Danchet's *Idomenée* to the Italian stage was carried out for the most part competently and at moments with a certain flair. Yet Mozart clearly played a crucial part in it from the outset; and after he moved to Munich he continued, through the agency of his father, to demand important changes. These changes were all aimed at replacing stilted or prolix utterance and implausible situation by dramatic verisimilitude and individual emotion. In one letter, for example, we find Mozart insisting that the cavatina intended for Idomeneo between the two choruses at the end of Act 2 must go: as he unanswerably observes, 'Is the thunder to stop so that Raaff can sing an aria?' So the aria went, and was replaced by the grand but desperate orchestral recitative that we know—a passage which actually succeeds in heightening the tension, till it can only explode in the panic-stricken prestissimo of the final chorus, 'Corriamo, fuggiamo'.

The pianissimo conclusion of this chorus is dramatic proof of Mozart's confidence in his powers and in the seriousness of his audience. He is so sure of himself that he can afford to satisfy his instinct (which requires that the music dwindle away almost to nothing), and not bother courting applause at the end of an act whose continuity of design has almost throughout ignored the conventional demands of popular taste. Not that the pursuit of Gluckian dramatic ideals involves, for Mozart, a corresponding musical austerity— far from it. The conciseness which we find in *Idomeneo* is the result of an intense concentration. All the constituents of musical expression, the techniques of composition which Mozart had been patiently acquiring since childhood, are pressed into service. *Idomeneo* is a marvellously abundant score. Mozart's contrapuntal mastery imparts to the harmonic and instrumental texture an unprecedented energy. Symptomatic of this is the prominent part played by the violas—always a favoured instrument with Mozart, but here elevated almost to the importance we associate with it in *Figaro* or *Don Giovanni*: to mention two examples, the quiet but rasping chord which, held for two bars across the restless quaver movement of the other instruments, adds an extra colour and tension (dominant against tonic harmony) in the introduction to Elettra's first aria; and the scene, diametrically opposite in character, in which Ilia finally declares her love to Idamante, and the frustrations of two-and-a-half acts resolve. Here the violas' sustained notes, held across the bar-line against the violins' triplet movement and the regular detached quavers of the cellos and basses, are at the heart of one of the most beautiful expressions of emotional release in Mozart.

Vitality and variety of string texture had of course been characteristic of Mozart's style long before *Idomeneo*, but never before on such a scale—at one extreme the delicate enchantment of 'Idol mio', at the other the wide-spaced,

high-lying chords and furious syncopations of the shipwreck scene and, in between, the splendid sweep and
authority of the part-writing in 'Fuor del mar', evocative
both of the grandeur of Idomeneo's personality and of the
sea that has him in its power, and intensifying rather than
impeding the music's driving momentum. This is typical of
Idomeneo—textural elaboration rarely lacks a specific dramatic purpose. It is the same with the work's harmonic invention,
whether in large-scale or intimate expression: the audacious
means used in Act 2 to depict all nature in upheaval, or the
tenderness that floods over the music at the lovely modulation
from A minor to C major when Ilia speaks to Idamante of
sorrow being overcome by the unalterable constancy of her
love (where the richness of the effect is due to the F sharp in
the bass, which makes us expect G major, being immediately
contradicted by the violas' F natural). In the storm scene
in Act 2 Mozart stretches his harmonic idiom further than
in any other opera, in response to the dramatic and theatrical
situation. The terror of the populace at the storm's increasing violence is rendered by an unexpected wrench of
tonality from the dominant of C minor to B flat minor (a use
of shock modulation much more commonly associated with
Haydn or Beethoven). The chorus's frantic reiterated appeal
to the guilty man to declare his identity is set in a series of
downward steps from B flat minor to F, linked by diminished seventh chords on A sharp (B flat), G sharp and F
sharp, each chord being repeated and sustained, amid a
vibrant silence, by the full force of the woodwind band
reinforced by four horns. Before the chord of F, emphasized
for three bars, has had time to die away, the guilty man
reveals himself, and the harmony, via another seventh chord,
takes two more steps down into a blazing D major, with
trumpets and drums, held back till then, in full spate.

It is a moment of revelation, in the music as in the drama.
One is tempted to call the whole scene a landmark in
Romantic opera. The use of orchestral colour in *Idomeneo*
for dramatic and psychological effect anticipates the

experiments and discoveries of Romanticism. It goes deeper than mere musical pictures of sea and sky, wind and storm, vivid and apt though they are. The articulation of the larger dramatic structure is in part, whether consciously or not, orchestral. We see it most obviously in Act 2, where constantly varying types of sound are an integral part of the progress of the action, and the sea, symbol of a power beyond human grasp, is at first sportive and no more than quietly menacing, its strength for the most part latent ('Fuor del mar'), is then stilled to an illusory serenity, and finally roused to a rage all the more terrible for bursting suddenly out of the preceding calm. The contrast between the halcyon peace of the central scene—a beautiful evocation of Mediterranean felicity, all hazy, murmurous strings, caressing flute and gently mooing horns—and the terror of the storm choruses, with horns in four parts, shrieking piccolo and off-beat violin chords that strike like wind-lashed spray, is only the most obvious manifestation of a principle that is at work throughout the opera.

In almost every scene Mozart invents fresh colours with which to emphasize the argument and at the same time delight our ears (and what 19th- or 20th-century opera surpasses the sheer physical pleasure that *Idomeneo* gives us, from the quiet trumpet entry just before the end of the overture, or the marvellously airy sound of flute, oboe and violins in the introduction to 'Fuor del mar', to the volcanic crescendos in Elettra's final recitative or the fury of the full orchestra in the aria that follows?). Mozart's range of colour is seemingly limitless, his orchestral invention equal to each fresh turn in the drama. In the third act the feeling of numbed horror, of awe before an event whose consequences are too appalling to comprehend, that grips the people at the discovery that the victim of Idomeneo's vow is his son, gives rise to a sound unheard in music before, cold, thin, granite-like, made up of muted violins and violas and starkly unison woodwind pierced by the gleam of muted trumpets and bruised by the dull beat of muffled drums; yet this quintessence of desolation leads, with the briefest of transitions, to another dimension of sound, even more solemn in its simplicity. Strings, still *sotto voce*, joined after a few bars by oboes, play a march that is Gluckian in its quiet intensity, Handelian in its fusion of the learned and the galant, and purely Mozartian in its finality and in the peace, at once unearthly and filled with human compassion, that descends like a benediction on the music. Once again a new element in the drama—Idomeneo's acceptance of tragedy—has inspired a new colour. Personal decision has been subsumed in ceremony; and in the passage that follows, the sense of immemorial rites, mysterious yet consoling, is intensified by the luminous texture of woodwind and pizzicato strings which encircle the long phrases of the vocal line, as first the king, regal even in defeat, invokes the god he sought so eagerly to flee, and then the priests repeat the prayer in a high-pitched monotone whose accompanying harmony (diminished sevenths in a glowingly diatonic context), and orchestral colour (bassoons in thirds in the upper register, imitated in turn by the other woodwind), evokes with uncanny immediacy the feel of the ancient world, the otherness of a society dominated by ritual. Profound and brilliantly resourceful though Mozart's sense of colour is in *Idomeneo*, it is never indulged for its own sake. Throughout, a clear dramatic purpose is at work. The most spectacular pictorialism is but the outward projection of the human and suprahuman struggles which are the heart of the drama.

If Mozart in his ten remaining years of life never again approached this consistent use of colour to suggest both the outer physical universe and the inner world of psychological reality (he never had occasion to), it was much longer before opera caught up with what is perhaps *Idomeneo*'s most remarkable achievement of all—its continuity of dramatic construction. This continuity is achieved partly by motivic repetition, partly by the shaping of the libretto, but chiefly by the boldest and simplest of means, the running of one musical number into the next. Nothing else so triumphantly demonstrates Mozart's consciousness of freedom—freedom to override operatic conventions and impose the result on his audience, not to mention his performers. We have seen how, after Ilia's exit at the end of her aria, 'Se il padre perdei', in Act 2, the recitative in which Idomeneo broods on the implications of her avowals begins with a reminiscence from the aria and continues with further thematic references to the same source, darkened with doubt as the king feels the net closing round him. Rare though such a device is before the 19th century, 'Se il padre perdei' at least comes to a full stop. Extraordinary that it should be necessary to say so! Many of the arias in *Idomeneo* end not with the formal close prescribed in an age of singers' opera but with modulations or linking phrases which carry the music-drama forward without a break. In Act 1 the music flows uninterruptedly from Elettra's recitative and aria 'Estinto, Idomeneo/Tutto nel cor vi sento' to the shipwreck scene to the landing of Idomeneo, his aria, his meeting with his son, and Idamante's ensuing outburst of grief and bewilderment. Act 2 is even more closely knit. Elettra's 'Idol mio', the March, the chorus 'Placido è il mar' (enclosing an arioso for Elettra), the Trio, the storm, Idomeneo's confession of guilt (which is joined to the preceding section by the continuation of the stepwise downward movement referred to earlier), the 'Monster' chorus—the music proceeds in a virtually unbroken chain and in a masterly progress, through systematic contrast of colour, texture, key, rhythm and tempo, to its astonishing climax.

Act 3, though less consistently well wrought, takes the same principle still further. The first part of the act, concerned with the love of Ilia and Idamante, and suffused in the soft radiance associated in Mozart's music with the sharp keys of A and E, performs a function of large-scale contrast similar to that of the central part of Act 2, only deeper. As before, by an exception that has become almost the norm, the aria 'Zeffiretti lusinghieri' does not come to a full close but leads directly, with the appearance of Idamante, into the next scene, in which secco recitative, accompagnato, arioso and Duet grow into and out of one another in a seemingly inevitable flow; and, as before, the Duet is not so much finished as broken into by the arrival of Idomeneo and Elettra. The ensuing Quartet is introduced in the same spirit, by a natural progression from recitative to ensemble. This supremely beautiful movement (in which Mozart uses the momentary suspension of the action at a point of extreme tension to develop the different emotions of his characters and at the same time combine them into a unity above conflict) sounds a new note in the tragedy, a temper of transfigured suffering, and so looks forward to and prepares for the turning-point of the drama—the moment when Idomeneo, in bowing at last to his destiny, consents to the ritual slaughter of his son. I have mentioned the contrast between 'O voto tremendo' and the March to illustrate Mozart's mastery of varied orchestral colour and texture. As an example of continuity between two different scenes and dramatic moods it ranks, again, with the most miraculous in opera, music and drama combining to create something that neither could accomplish separately—the sense of extreme suffering giving way to a mysterious repose. Mozart requires only half a dozen bars. At the grim climax of the chorus the music turns, as though from exhaustion, into the major, the voices cease, the texture clears, horns sound soft arpeggios, the relentless triplet rhythm dies down, and a long consolatory melody, released on the violins, rises above the hushed orchestra. It is a transition as inevitable as it is unexpected. Gluck, the presiding influence on this part of *Idomeneo*, never united such extremes. The march that now steals in softly on the strings breathes a holy stillness that *The Magic Flute* in its different way equals but does not surpass. This is the high moment of the drama, but the scenes which follow do not betray Mozart's lofty conception. Dramatic truth and development by contrast remain the guiding principles behind the culminating sequence of numbers: the sacrifice scene, cut short by the Oracle, Elettra's demented fury, Idomeneo's last appearance as king (for which the warm colour of clarinets returns for the first time since the priests' unison chant), and the chorus of jubilation which salutes the new age.

Just because most of the third act maintains such an exalted level of dramatic construction, we feel the lapses from it. No one was more aware of it than Mozart. Even after it was too late for any further collaboration with the protesting Varesco, he continued to shorten and tighten the act, having always thought, as he told his father, that the libretto and therefore the music of this act was too long, but not presumably having been able to test and confirm his belief until the act went into full rehearsal. Once he was sure, he cut with ruthless conviction. Arbace could not very well lose his scene, intrusive though it is (as it was he was confined to two arias, though an important member of the company), but Idamante's aria 'No la morte'—'out of place' in the sacrifice scene—was removed. So was Idomeneo's 'Torna la pace', a beautiful piece but saying nothing not already said in the extended recitative that precedes it, and holding up the action just where it should move to its conclusion. Shortly before the first night—which took place on 29 January 1781, two days after his 25th birthday—Mozart actually threw out Elettra's magnificent aria 'D'Oreste, d'Aiace', in the interests of a tauter dénouement. Dramatic conciseness must take precedence over even the finest feats of characterization.

What of the characterization in *Idomeneo*? Throughout this essay I have tried to show that the work need not fear a just comparison with the comedies which for most people embody the accepted idea of Mozart opera, but that we are correspondingly bound to misjudge it if we come to it looking for the qualities that make them unique. We may well wonder how, even here, *Idomeneo* can be found deficient in the face of such a feat as Elettra's final aria; but this is an attitude still commonly encountered among critics and music-lovers. Missing the individuality and subtle ironies, the keenly observed humanity, that are the glory of the Vienna operas, they conclude that with all his undeniable achievements in *Idomeneo* Mozart failed in this one crucial instance to transcend the medium; the 'pallid heroes and heroines of antiquity', as Beecham called them, are no match for the 'real' people whom we meet and learn to relish in *Entführung*, *Figaro*, *Don Giovanni*, *Così* and *The Magic Flute*.

Perhaps not, but why expect them to be? The dramatic assumptions are heroic, not those of everyday life. If we adjust our expectations accordingly, we shall not be disappointed. The portrayal of character in *Idomeneo* continually rises above generalized emotion and conventional gesture. It is not the sharply personal characterization of *Figaro* and the rest, but on its own terms it is equally valid; we feel for these people in their griefs and joys. Rather can we say that they are recognizably Mozartian creations, warmed to life by the same penetrating and compassionate understanding, but seen in tragic, not comic situations. (Only poor Arbace, the king's faithful counsellor always at hand with a platitude, is taken straight from *opera seria* stock. For all that, he has one accompanied recitative of remarkable expressiveness.) Given these clearly defined premises, we see that Ilia and Elettra are as consistently drawn and as tellingly contrasted as Anna and Elvira in *Don Giovanni*, and that the development of Ilia from the unease and desperation of her opening recitative and aria to her serene exaltation in the Quartet and her sublimity in the sacrifice scene is, in its own way, comparable to Pamina's growth from girlhood to womanhood in *The Magic Flute*.

As for Elettra, when did Mozart use his mastery of musical means to more devastating psychological effect than in this picture of the formidable but neurotic daughter of Agamemnon and Clytemnestra? Her great scene in Act I shows melody, harmony, rhythm, orchestral colour, vocal virtuosity and musical form systematically deployed to convey abnormality on a grand scale; the traditional rage aria is transformed into something extraordinary, and unique to her. The voice part alternating great upward leaps of a tenth with piteous semitonal fragments; the pounding, obsessive arpeggios of the accompaniment; the frequent superimposition of 3/4 time on 4/4 to produce violent syncopations; the baleful orchestration, strangely hollow despite the presence of four horns; the atmosphere of harmonic instability, prefigured in the recitative, with its writhing chromatics, intensified in the introduction to the aria (where the key into which the recitative resolves, A minor, is not the tonic but serves instead as a long dominant pedal across which dissonance flits like the spasms of a tortured mind), and reaching its climax at the reprise in a sudden descent into C minor, the key of the storm music into which the conclusion of the aria rushes with headlong impetus—these things combine to lay bare Elettra's soul and, at the end, with a stroke worthy of the Romantics, to merge its darkness symbolically and actually with the raging of the elements. Similar means are used for the even more explosive outburst in Act 3, where Elettra, now alone in her own tormented world, deprived even of the illusion of hope, is whipped into despairing fury as though by the serpents which the words conventionally and the music most unconventionally invoke.

Yet the picture would be incomplete without the lyrical major-key scenes that Elettra is given in Act 2—the aria 'Idol mio', and the arioso 'Soavi zeffiri' enclosed within the chorus 'Placido è il mar' and written in the large-spanned, soaring style that is a feature of the unfinished *Singspiel Zaide*, composed a year earlier. Mozart is not usually given credit for this fresh example of his humanity-cum-psychological realism; but who is to say that these pieces are not 'in character', that this melting mood is not a true aspect of Elettra's complex, unhappy nature, and that she should not dream her dreams and hug her precious illusions for a brief moment? She will lose them soon enough. The music says as much, not only by the immediate context in which it is placed, but also in itself: beautiful though it is, it is touched with the obsessiveness, the withdrawal from reality, that rages openly in the great D minor and C minor arias.

Alongside Ilia's growing maturity and depth of feeling and Elettra's near-madness we may place the characterization of Idomeneo, the ruler trapped in the consequences of his own rashness. His music, which is endowed with a consistent elevation of tone, suggests unmistakably the combination of grandeur and impulsiveness, regal authority and sympathetic insight into the feelings of others, that is the cause of his plight. Here is no routine *opera seria* monarch paying lip service to conflicts between duty and inclination that are as unreal as he is. Mozart's imagination, aroused by what is timeless in the story, has ignored the rest and seized on the possibilities offered for living dramatic expression. From the moment of his first appearance on the scene— remorse already beginning to poison the immense relief of still being alive—Idomeneo's predicament is painfully real. And, as with Ilia, the music shows us his feelings changing with the development of the tragic action. The superb 'Fuor del mar', with typically Mozartian genius, uses the convention of the obligatory bravura aria (of which it is a splendid example) for consummately realized dramatic ends: the aria, at once majestic and fevered, becomes a mirror of the king's state of mind at this mid-point of the drama—guilt-ridden but defiantly regal, a classical hero on the run but not yet brought to his knees by resentful destiny. By the end of the second act, like Oedipus he is 'dans le piège'. And as the noose tightens we feel Mozart's pity for him growing. The intensification of Idomeneo's love—as though against his will—for the son whom he has discovered only to lose culminates in a wonderfully tender passage in E flat major in the sacrifice scene: 'Figlio, o caro figlio, perdona'. At the same time his final submission to fate is all the more moving for being the act of a man who throughout has been characterized as unyieldingly proud and stubborn to the point of recklessness.

Beside Idomeneo, or indeed Ilia and Elettra, Idamante may seem a disappointingly lay figure, even within the clearly accepted limits of heroic characterization, and it is undeniable that he expresses himself less personally than the others; undeniable too that his first aria, though always dignified in utterance, is long-winded, and that though his music often rises to a poignant eloquence, it does so in a much more generalized way. The role was written for a castrato (an obsolescent tradition that Mozart was to rid himself of when he revised the work for private performance five years later), but the impression persists even when we hear it sung by a tenor. Yet I think it is wrong to conclude that Idamante is another failure on Mozart's part (Arbace we have already noted) to transcend his medium. Looked at in a different way, may it not be, on the contrary, one more example of his genius for turning convention to good account? The very plainness, the almost abstract nobility of Idamante's portrayal has, I believe, a dramatic function. It is not only that, in Dent's words, '. . . the self-control, the childlike simplicity and directness of Idamante [are] to save the tragedy from its dreadful completion'. If Idamante is a type—the type of heroic, selfless young idealism—it may be because he is meant to be: he is the representative of the new civilization whose dawn is inaugurated at the end of the opera. In retelling the age-old fable of the fatal vow Mozart and Varesco kept fairly close to their immediate source for the first two acts, but their dénouement is drastically different. In their hands the story becomes a deliberate and noble expression of the Enlightenment. Danchet's Idamante dies, cut down by his father's sword. In the opera he lives, marries Ilia, and reigns over a revived and contented Crete. The happy ending is no mere convenient evasion of all that has gone before, a solving of the tragedy at a flick of the *deus ex machina*, but a positive assertion of the power of tolerance, reason, and love. Idomeneo, representative of the old

order, victim of the old decrees, yields place to his son, the
new man who sets his captives free and conquers superstition.

It is Mozart, of course, who makes this resolution convincing. Without him it could not but seem a betrayal of the
tragic vision of the rest of the opera. Music can combine and
dissolve categories which in spoken drama are mutually
exclusive, just as it can give life and shape to Platonic ideas
which otherwise would remain abstractions; and no music
more than Mozart's. In this, his first great opera, his
imaginative insight encompasses an astonishing range of
human experience: love, joy, physical and spiritual contentment, stoicism, heroic resolution; the ecstasy of self-
sacrifice, the horrors of schizophrenia, the agonizing dilemma of a ruler trapped in the consequences of his actions;
mass hysteria, panic in face of an unknown scourge, turning
to awe before the yet more terrible reality; the strange
peace that can follow intense grief, the infinite tenderness of
a father's last farewell to his son. *Idomeneo*, finally, moves us
because it holds out the possibility of human nobility in a
context of unblinking psychological truth. Here, it may be,
as well as in the richness and mastery of musical and
dramatic expression that I have tried to analyse, lies its
appeal to us, caught like Idomeneo between two eras, left
on our own with no gods to pray to, and salvation from
destruction to be sought only in man.

Humanity may need, as never before, the sanity, the profound life-renewing laughter of Mozart's comedies, to
prevent it from taking itself too seriously. But it needs, too,
that handful of special masterpieces whose qualities of
courage, hope, compassion, and above all honesty of vision
make them its natural parables and sacred texts, from which
it may learn to see the truth about itself, to 'know its shadow
and its light'. *Idomeneo* is one of those works. Perhaps Dent
was right: it should never be taken for granted, but always
'attended in a spirit of pilgrimage'. It is a secular Passion,
with power to chasten and uplift a distracted age.

Gloriana

Considering the qualities of Benjamin Britten's *Gloriana* and the place that belongs to such a work in the national operatic repertory, its early afflictions are in retrospect hard to condone. You feel that even a Coronation audience should have been able to respond with a better grace and a little more alacrity. Instead, the work came as near to being a fiasco as is possible in the temperate climate in which public art exists in this age. The fiasco was explained at the time, and even excused, on the grounds of the unsuitability of the work's subject to the particular occasion; an opera on the decline (complete with abortive love affair) and death of the first Elizabeth was hardly the right offering to celebrate the crowning of the second.

It is undeniable that, despite the elements of pageantry that it contains, *Gloriana* springs from an imaginative as opposed to a lifelessly conventional, official view of England's history; the sense of her past, largely lost in modern England, is alive in it. This sense enabled Britten to compose a genuine historical opera, a work in the tradition of *Don Carlo* and *Boris Godunov*; but such a work was bound to be above the flat unraisèd spirits of a gala Covent Garden first night, which could only disapprove of the little it perceived. It is also true that although the extravagant fashion in which Britten's admirers tended to discuss his genius was perfectly understandable (how thrilling it must have been to realize that a born opera-composer had at long last risen among us!), such displays of adulation were calculated to create a reserve of animosity against him. *Billy Budd*, two years before *Gloriana*, had not been generally liked, and the detection of what were darkly identified as homosexual undertones in it fed the antagonism. But the particular nastiness of the *Gloriana* episode lay in the unholy alliance that was forged between traditional British philistinism, in one of its most reactionary periods, and forces within the musical profession activated by prejudices of a scarcely superior kind. In opposing state-subsidized opera and Britten as the pampered symbol of it, traditional British philistinism was only acting according to its sad lights. The musical forces had no such extenuation. Administrators still resentful of the incontestable public success of *Peter Grimes* and critics blind to their true responsibilities joined hands with gossip columnists and members of the social set who considered *Gloriana* an insult to the Sovereign. The consequence was a mob, in Fielding's definition of 'persons without virtue or sense in all stations', and the feeling of this mob was that it was high time Britten was taken down a peg.

The eclipse of *Gloriana* (apart from the Choral Dances in Act 2, which were allowed to be charming, and became well known in the form of a separate suite) lasted for ten years; not until 1963 did a concert performance, given at the Festival Hall under Bryan Fairfax, startle us into an awareness of the riches lying forgotten or unguessed at in Britten's last large-scale, and in scope most ambitious, opera. Three years later Sadler's Wells decisively demonstrated the work's dramatic skill and theatrical effectiveness. *Gloriana* was revealed as a ripe example of the composer's craftsmanship and invention, his gift for hitting on the simple phrase that sums up a particular mood or situation, and his natural feeling for dramatic gesture on the grand scale; the wonder was that, even with all the various factors that were against it, it should not have been more widely appreciated in the first place.

From the opening bars of the work we are plunged bodily into the thick of things, into the re-created Elizabethan world and the pith and marrow of the argument. The thrust and glitter of these first pages, whose leaping rhythms, exultant counterpoint and brilliant trumpet writing vividly project the reality of the nearby tilting ground and the angry energy of Essex, forced to hear a description of his rival Mountjoy's triumph, typify the uninhibitedness of Britten's response to the challenge of evoking the most glamorous and hackneyed period in our history. It is a re-creation, not an imitation. But with characteristic boldness he has not so much steered clear of the pitfalls of pastiche and false sentiment that lie in the path of such an undertaking, as simply jumped over them. The copious songs and dances and the whole Elizabethan ambience of William Plomer's admirable libretto have only inspired him to a more audaciously original use of concord and the common chord. (Britten's Spring Symphony contains parallel instances of the stimulus which that ambience exerts on him.) Only someone steeped in the art of the period, in which music as well as poetry burst out in sudden astonishing profusion, someone to whom its life as it has come down to us is part of his imaginative life, could use Elizabethan music as Britten does in *Gloriana*, as an expression of his own creative personality.

The music played by the stage band in the scene at the Palace of Whitehall is the sole case of pastiche in the score. (In this it is distinct both from the brief but tragic Pavane which introduces the scene, and which is Elizabethan music reinterpreted in modern terms, and from the lute song 'Happy were he', in which a quotation from Wilbye is at once absorbed into the musical development.) But the pastiche has a specific function. This is one of the lessons that Britten has learnt from Verdi. Its purpose is to provide a mainly neutral instrumental background to the court intrigues and personal conflicts which come to a head in the latter part of the scene. The music's very neutralness contributes to the dramatic tension, in a context of suspense and expectation (*cf.* the final scene of *Un Ballo in maschera*). How disquieting and even sinister, for instance, is the

Morris Dancer's trivial, mocking saltarello, placed as it is. The period flavour, ingeniously recaptured in the music's evocative colour of flute and tabor, constant dance momentum, endless repetitions and general air of extravert cheerfulness, is turned to quite different dramatic ends.

At the same time the wind music on the stage is interpenetrated by the orchestra in the pit to create a dramatic counterpoint of growing intensity. The process culminates in the climax of the scene. This climax gives the clue to the true nature of the drama of *Gloriana*. When the 'Victor of Cadiz' theme rises like a dark tide in the orchestra and gradually overwhelms the stage band's coranto, what we are hearing is not merely a powerfully ironic comment on Essex at the height of his pride and ambition and a prophecy of his fall: it is the sound of history itself, the roar of the 'dangerous flood'.* It is history being enacted that we hear in the scurrying yet momentous pizzicato motif in the first scene of Act 3, as Essex's return hot-foot from Ireland sets the Queen's servants in a flurry; history in the implacable tread of authority which sounds through the dark sonority of the trial scene; and history that finally takes possession of the opera as far-off voices, recalling the reconciliation music of Act 1, sing of the 'crownèd rose among the leaves so green', before the curtain falls. *Gloriana* is a drama of history even before it is a psychological drama—or rather it is both, but the one within and interfused with the other.

Failure to understand this may account for the accusations of dramaturgical diffuseness that are still heard from time to time. Superficially considered, the opera is divided into 'public' and 'private' scenes; but the two concepts colour each other from the first: the libretto's systematic concern with their interaction is matched by the music at

---

* Its significance is beautifully realized by Colin Graham in the Sadler's Wells production, in which the lighting slowly fades with the onrush of the orchestral crescendo, until the still-whirling dancers before our eyes take on the air of ghosts, once sentient creatures now fading further and further into the past.

every turn. This conflict is the master principle of Britten's
score, and it is carried out with a thoroughness and imaginative skill that would require pages of analysis. But consider only—to take one example—the composition of the
second scene of the opera, set in a private apartment at
Nonesuch, in which Essex attempts to woo the Queen from
statecraft to the business of the heart. Note the contrast of
textures—sustained strings and harp replacing busy, burrowing woodwind and being themselves replaced—which
dramatizes the opposition, and the subtle harmonic tensions
and resolutions that plot the transition from one mood to
the other. The motif which appears when the Queen dis-
cusses with Cecil the endless cares of state is a fine example
of Britten's genius for summing up an idea or attitude in a
single musical shape:*

the stealthy flourish up to the top of the phrase, like an
anxious thought, almost a stab of pain, that will not leave
one, and the slow even descent, diminuendo—its consequences, spreading silently, pervasively, like widening
ripples. The motif momentarily dissolves into a radiant high
string chord at the entry of Essex ('Queen of my life'), but
continues to dog and question his ardent appeals, preventing
the melodic line from taking wing. It is silenced at last by
the second lute song ('Happy were he'), only to come back
at the end of their Duet when Elizabeth conquers her
longing and dismisses him on the plea that 'the business of
the kingdom waits'—the motif, in its insinuating persistence, expressing the patient, ever-watchful spirit of govern-
ment which Essex cannot endure. It returns once more, with

* Reproduced by permission of Boosey & Hawkes Music Publishers Ltd.

a sense of never having been wholly absent, and with 'Queen of my life', now subdued and clouded, at the great moment of decision in the third act when the Queen, having yielded for an instant to his pleading 'Happy were *we*', for the last time commands Essex to leave her presence.

The two great scenes between Essex and the Queen are only the most obvious instance of a continuous confrontation of interests. But it is a confrontation in which the public overcomes the private and the issue, however agonizing, is never seriously in doubt. Ultimately, indeed, the public becomes the private. The scenes of pageantry and cere- monial are thus integral to the dramatic argument, not more or less splendid distractions from it; the matter of *Gloriana* is the merging of the Queen's private life into her public life. Once we grasp this, the other main objection that has been raised to the dramaturgical structure of *Gloriana* dwindles and disappears. It was no miscalculation on the part of Britten and Plomer not to develop Essex into a full- length portrait, but a deliberate and correct artistic decision. To have done otherwise would have been to deflect the work from its chosen and constantly adhered-to course. The sub- ject of the opera is not 'Elizabeth and Essex' (for all that it is indebted to Lytton Strachey's book for many details and ideas), but the ageing Queen and the deep and painful dilemma which besets her, between her royal and her 'other' self, and which finally can be resolved in only one way. Of course her relationship with Essex is of fundamental and riveting importance. It is the symbol of her dilemma, enticing her saddened heart with a vision of recaptured youth and gallantry, and its ambiguities are a rich source of irony and tension which Britten has drawn on to masterly effect; but in the end it is secondary, and it is precisely this fact that is the motivator of the dramatic resolution. The Queen over- shadows all and is protagonist, visible or not, of every scene. Everything that happens is designed to add a further detail to her portrait. To remove Essex progressively from the stage, so that there is no action shown between his departure for Ireland in high glory and his desperate return, and so that we never see him again after his dismissal in the second Nonesuch Scene, neither during the rebellion nor at his trial, is a bold stroke; but it is a stroke entirely consistent with that purpose. Essex is developed just so far as to contribute what is necessary and no further; the balance is exactly held. As Plomer and Britten have drawn him, he is a character alive in his own right: impetuous, charming, quick to anger but also to love, overbearing, sudden in sympathy yet helplessly egocentric, grand, and nervous to the verge of madness. But structurally he exists as a foil to the Queen and the central theme of her union with the realm.

That is why his rebellion is represented only indirectly, in stylized form. We see a group of his followers attempting to drum up support in a London street, and the reactions of the local inhabitants. At the same time, the course of his ill-judged bid for power is recounted, in metaphorical terms, by a blind ballad-singer whose verses punctuate the brief action. The oblique, epigrammatic character of the scene is so different from what the richly wrought high drama of the two preceding scenes has led us to expect that it comes as a shock when we first encounter the work; we may even be inclined to conclude that, at the crucial moment, the librettist has let his grip slacken and the composer succumbed to his weakness for the folky and the whimsical. In fact they have solved their problems in a most original way and achieved a change of dramatic mood and texture that enriches the opera. By giving the scene something of the character of an interlude, by stepping back from the dramatic argument and, in doing so, lending it a new emphasis, they contrive at once to serve their main purpose and to widen the angle of vision without loss of focus. The setting of a public street where anonymous citizens gather or pass, the excited, windblown orchestral music alternating with the ballad-singer's blunt, characteristically elliptical utterances and simple guitar accompaniment, and the very fragmentation of the action, combine to convey the sense of a cause already lost, a short-lived challenge from an outmoded feudalism to the acquired solidity of Elizabethan authority. At the same time the contrast between the alarm of the prosperous middle class and the indifference of the poor creates a sudden shift of perspective: history as the struggle for power gives way momentarily to history as the people to whom it happens. And fiery Essex declines more swiftly from his zenith.

The static ceremonial scenes are conceived in equal harmony with the governing idea of the work. That their role is far more than one of mere decoration should not need stating. The notion, put forward by more than one critic, that the picture of the Queen 'on Progress' at Norwich is extraneous to the main action can perhaps be explained by reference to the independent existence which the Choral Dances led for ten years while the work from which they were extracted languished in obscurity. In writing them Britten was certainly inspired to some of his most brilliantly 'Elizabethan' music, and at Sadler's Wells, as choreographed by Peter Darrell and danced by the Western Theatre Ballet in Alix Stone's delicate yet earthy costumes, they made an irresistible and archetypally English effect (an effect intensified by the sly, sweet, elusive face, innocently lascivious, mysteriously passive, of the girl who danced Concord). But quite apart from the obvious function of such an island of repose in a drama of turbulent power-politics, the Norwich Scene is vital to the scheme of the work—as, in a smaller way, is the reconciliation ensemble in Act 1. It is essential, for that scheme, to insist on the Queen's relationship with her people, for which she gives up so much and in the consciousness of which she dies at something like peace with herself; and the opera does so insist, with a niceness of judgment which we should be in no danger of mistaking.

There remains the question of the ending and its resort to the spoken word. The ending is typical of the freedom with which Britten and Plomer conceived their opera. It is also consistent with the idea that guided them throughout. But, like the ballad-monger scene, like any change of genre, it naturally encounters resistance even among those who do not object to speech in opera, and is found puzzling while its style is still unfamiliar and its purpose not yet clear. We may well think, at first, that it is dangerously abrupt. Without any change of scene the action is discovered to have moved forward two years. The Queen is dying. We see her at last, the least and most solitary of beings, truly alone. Time and place have grown dim for her. We look into her mind as it carries her back over her long reign. Speech, used for her remembered public utterances and for her regal but down-to-earth rebukes to the courtiers who urge prudence upon her, alternates with brief orchestral reminiscences of Essex; and speech, until the final offstage chorus, has the last word.*

To say, as has been said, that such a dénouement retrospectively reduces the importance of everything that has gone before is at least to acknowledge the power of that dénouement, but it is also to misjudge its significance and indeed the whole character of the work; for if *Gloriana* is a drama of history before it is a psychological drama, it is a psychological drama before it is a drama of events. Once we have grasped that, we can see that it is consistent to the end. The epilogue is the culmination of everything that has gone before. It brings to fruition the drama's main theme, adumbrated in the opening scene, but it does not deny the tragic reality of the lesser theme. At the end the sadness of the Queen's relationship with Essex is not evaded; it is absorbed in her wry acceptance of the only love open to her, a kingdom's. All the threads of this complex, wide-ranging work are finally drawn together in the person of the woman who represents her age. The portrait of Gloriana is complete.

The effect of this epilogue and its disjointed, stream-of-

---

* As performed by Sadler's Wells the scene is a little shorter than in the version printed in the published libretto and vocal score and seen at Covent Garden in 1953. The cuts, which reflect the authors' second thoughts, affect only the length of the scene; the principle remains unchanged.

consciousness technique is to jolt the spectator into a new state of awareness. Once again, and in a way that is wholly appropriate, Britten has chosen to end an opera by placing the drama at a distance from us. The mood is at once personal and heraldic; it closes the action on a melancholy cadence, and it fixes Elizabeth ritually in history, 'a crownèd rose among the leaves so green'. The spoken word is integral to it; it is part of the process by which she too is made to recede. When the curtain falls she has already melted into myth; the Elizabethan age is no more. The myth is not a falsification; it was forming during her lifetime. It corresponds to a greater reality, ultimately the highest reality of her life. The vision of private felicity held out and for an instant nearly reached for ('Happy were she') was an impossible dream. The spoken word is symbolic of the mortification of the Queen's personal life, the price she had to pay; music is heard only in connection with Essex, her Robin, whom she killed. *Gloriana* is an allegory of the burdens of kingship, of Shakespeare's 'hard condition, twin-born with greatness, subject to the breath of every fool'. 'Upon the king! . . . We must bear all.' What a Coronation opera it should have made!

Public memory is short; and, though certain misunderstandings persist, *Gloriana* may now be said to have lived down its gloomy start in life. Yet one cannot help wondering about the possible consequences of so discouraging an experience to Britten's career as an opera-composer. It is of course impossible to measure the effect of external pressures in an artist's development. Nevertheless, if *Gloriana* had not been so churlishly received, would seventeen years have elapsed before Britten wrote another large-scale opera (and that for television, not for the theatre)? Would his gift for big theatrical gesture have lain so long unused? Would the sense of the past which is to him so potent a source of suggestion have found outlet only in the attenuated medievalism of the church parables? The scope and brilliance of *Gloriana* make such speculations unavoidable.

Les Troyens and the Aeneid

Tristram Shandy's father, who knew the power of names, would have approved the notion—put forward by I forget which French critic—that, by calling him Hector, Dr Berlioz determined his son's fate: from the first the name marked him out for glory and tragedy, heroic deeds and the bitterness of failure and mutilation. The more one considers Berlioz's life, the more it seems almost mystically inevitable that his crowning work should be an epic on the Trojan war and its aftermath, the wanderings of Aeneas and the myth of the founding of Rome, and the more one comes to see his discovery of Virgil during boyhood and his precocious response to the passion and tenderness of the *Aeneid* as the most important single event of his imaginative existence. No less inevitably, such a work was bound to bring defeat and misery on its creator in the cultural climate of Second Empire Paris. As Gounod justly remarked, Berlioz, like his great namesake, died beneath the walls of Troy; for the final blow in a lifetime's struggles against a hostile musical environment was the rejection of the work that he knew to be his culminating achievement and artistic justification.

The conviction of its supreme significance in his life pervades the letters that he wrote during the two years of the work's composition. In their mood of exhilaration and their sense of destiny fulfilled, they recall the passage at the end of *The Gathering Storm* where Churchill describes his emotions on taking power in May 1940: 'I felt . . . that all my past life had been but a preparation for this hour and for this trial.' *Les Troyens* is a summing up of everything that Berlioz stood for. It marks the furthest point in the development of his musical style; and in it the characteristics of most of his previous works—the electric energy of the Fantastic Symphony, the ceremonial splendours and terrors of the Requiem, the exaltation and sensuous beauty of *Romeo and Juliet*, the massive grandeur of the Te Deum, the sweetness and archaic simplicity of *L'enfance du Christ*, the refinement of *Nuits d'été*—are united.

The determination to write a grand opera on the *Aeneid* crystallized in the early 1850s. In 1854 Berlioz confessed that the idea had been 'tormenting' him for the last three years. His writings around this time are full of allusions, comic and serious, to Virgil. In *Evenings in the Orchestra* (published in 1852) the narrator, asked by his friends to tell them about the Paris Opéra, answers in the ominous words with which Aeneas begins his account of the catastrophe of Troy: *Si tantus amor casus cognoscere nostros.** Later in the same book, modern music torn by conflicting ideologies is likened to Cassandra, 'prophetic virgin fought over by Greeks and Trojans, whose inspired words go unheeded, who lifts her burning eyes to heaven—her eyes alone, for chains bind her hands' (*Aeneid* II, 405–6). In a letter to Hans von Bülow written in 1854, Berlioz humorously attributes the bad luck suffered by *Benvenuto Cellini* to the workings of the 'Destiny of the ancients', and compares the opera's successive resurrections and collapses to the wounded Dido 'thrice raising herself upon her elbow, thrice falling back'; then, as if unable to contain his admiration, he bursts out, 'What a great composer Virgil is! What a melodist, what a harmonist! *He* could have made the deathbed remark *Qualis artifex pereo*, and not that humbug Nero, who was gifted with only one bright idea in his life, the night he had all Rome set on fire . . .' By this time, although he was still fighting against it, the ambition to write a Virgilian opera was fully acknowledged.

* 'If you are so eager to hear our misfortunes.'

It is hard to believe he had not dreamed of it much earlier. *Les Troyens*, planted in boyhood, casts its giant shadow over the years between. The conscious decision to compose it was like the emergence of an underground river to the surface. With hindsight we can see the work pursuing a secret subterranean course during the years when its composer is taken up with other, quite different preoccupations. Even in a jocular context it pops up, reminding us of its future existence—as when, describing his hurried departure from the island of Nisida under threat of a storm, Berlioz likens the Neapolitan fisherman in charge of their coracle to Aeneas cutting his vessel's cables and putting out from the port of Carthage on his destined journey to Italy (*Voyage musical*, 1844, later incorporated in the *Memoirs*). Earlier, in 1836, he looks back, with a quizzical eye, on his bouts of musical improvisation in the countryside near Rome, when under the stimulus of the landscape's Virgilian associations, guitar in hand and chanting 'a strange recitative to still stranger harmonies', he would hymn the great figures of the later books of the *Aeneid*, Pallas, Evander, Turnus, Aeneas, and yearn for 'those poetic days when the heroes, sons of the gods, walked the earth'.

In 1848 he began his *Memoirs* and wrote the chapters dealing with childhood and youth, including the famous second chapter which describes his discovery of poetry under the influence of Virgil and his profound distress at the death of Dido. The action of reliving such an experience must have helped to develop and define the still-shadowy, half-formed idea of a great Virgilian work that would bring his career full circle. 1848 was a watershed in Berlioz's life— the year of the Revolution (which threatened to make his daily existence even more precarious, and disenchanted him still further with Parisian musical life), the year of his father's death and of his return to the scenes of his adolescent awakening, of the first step in the bizarre pilgrimage that led him back to his boyhood infatuation with Estelle Dubœuf: the year when the nostalgia that is such an important aspect

of his nature took decisive hold. But the period that immediately followed, though it produced the Te Deum and
La fuite en Egypte, the second part of what was to become
L'enfance du Christ—music steeped in a sense of the past—
was not propitious for a major dramatic work. The lessons
of the calamitous failure of *The Damnation of Faust* were too
painfully recent; he was still resolved 'not to stake twenty francs
on the popularity of [his] music with the Parisian public'.
It was at about this time that in the same mood of defeatism
he deliberately suppressed the inspiration for a new symphony
that had come to him. *Les Troyens* continued to grow and take
shape in his mind. But it needed help from without.

The impulse to commit himself unreservedly to a project of this
kind and on this scale came from the changed circumstances
of his external life, combined perhaps with an inward and
reckless sense that the moment had come and that, whatever
the likely consequences (the taste of Second Empire Paris
being what it was), he must seize it before it was too late.
If he finally—as he put it—succumbed to the temptation to
write *Les Troyens*, one reason was simply that he could
afford to. Since the death of his wife Harriet in 1854, he
had no longer had the burden of two separate households to
support. By the end of the same year *L'enfance du Christ* had
been completed, and performed with a success that seemed
to confound his earlier pessimism. The following year, 1855,
apparently confirmed the new trend in his fortunes. His
activities during that year kept him busy. Tours of Germany,
publication of several major works, the Paris Exhibition
and the first performance of the Te Deum, left no time
for sustained composition. But the project was certainly
discussed at Weimar with Liszt's mistress the Princess
Wittgenstein, who urged him to undertake it. By this time
he must have known that he would have to: he had no
choice. His Virgilian passion must be satisfied; the great
business of his life was upon him. And in 1856, after further
encouragement from the Princess, he began. The first line of

the libretto was written on 5 May, the anniversary of Napoleon's death ('an epic date, if there ever was one,' Berlioz remarks in a letter to his uncle Félix Marmion, a veteran of the Grande Armée). Slightly less than two years later, despite illness and the distractions of journalism, the huge richly wrought work was complete.

Such rapidity of creation was the fruit of a lifelong germination. Berlioz himself acknowledged it in a letter to the Princess which is the prime text for our understanding of the subject:

> As for the principal object of the work, the musical rendering of the characters and the expression of their feelings and passions, it was always the easiest part of my task. I have spent my life with this race of demi-gods; I know them so well that I feel as if they must have known me. And this recalls to me a boyhood experience which will show you how fascinated I was from the first by those splendid creatures of the ancient world. It was during the period in my classical education when I was construing, under my father's direction, the marvellous twelfth book of the *Aeneid*. My mind was possessed by the glory of its characters— Lavinia, Turnus, Aeneas, Mezentius, Lausus, Pallas, Evander, Amata, Latinus, Camilla and the rest. I was like a sleepwalker 'lost in my starry meditations' (to borrow Victor Hugo's phrase). One Sunday I was taken to Vespers. The sad persistent chant of the psalm *In exitu Israel* had the magnetic effect on me that it still has today, and plunged me deep in the most real and vivid daydreams of the past. I was with my Virgilian heroes again: I could hear the clash of their arms, I could see Camilla the Amazon in all her beauty and swiftness; I watched the maiden Lavinia, flushed with weeping, and the ill-fated Turnus, his father Daunus, his sister Juturna, I heard the palaces of Laurentium ring with lamentation—and I was seized by an overwhelming sadness. I left the church, sobbing uncontrollably, and cried for the rest of the day, powerless to contain my epic grief. No one could ever get me to tell the reason, my parents never knew nor had any inkling what sorrows had taken possession of my childish heart that day. Is that not a strange and marvellous manifestation of the power of genius? A poet dead thousands of years shakes a guileless, ignorant boy to the depths of his soul with a tale handed down across the centuries, and scenes whose radiance devouring time has been powerless to dim.

Forty years later, his 'Virgilian passion satisfied', Berlioz dedicated *Les Troyens* 'to the divine Virgil', *Divo Virgilio*. It was a repayment of his debt to 'the poet who first found the way to my heart and opened my budding imagination'. A special sense of affinity bound him to Virgil, an affinity only strengthened by the supreme artistic experience of transmuting his poem into music. Near the end of his life he wrote: 'I must be reconciled . . . to not having known Virgil —I should have loved him.' Earlier, standing on the site of Maecenas' villa at Tivoli, he could imagine he heard 'Virgil's melancholy voice reciting . . . some splendid fragment of the *Georgics*'. (It was a passage from the *Georgics*, invoked to fill out the bloodless rhymes of the official versifier, that had inspired one of his finest student pieces, the epilogue to the competition cantata *La mort d'Orphée*.) Not even Shakespeare occupied a more personal place in his Pantheon. Shakespeare, to Berlioz, was a kind of humanistic God the Father; artistically, he was the most farreaching influence of all (an influence vitally felt in *Les Troyens* itself, which in Berlioz's words is 'Virgil Shakespeareanized', the libretto articulating the poem by methods learned from the history plays: open form and bold juxtaposition of genres, lofty soliloquy and vernacular conversation, private emotion expressed in a framework of public action). But with Virgil it was something more intimate, a companionship, a sense of identification. While composing *Les Troyens*, he felt that Virgil was alive again in him:

The countryside [at Saint-Germain] seems to make my Virgilian passion more intense than ever. I feel as if I knew Virgil, as if he knew how much I love him . . . Yesterday I finished an aria for Dido which is simply a paraphrase of the famous line: *Haud ignara mali miseris succurrere disco* [My own troubles teach me to help the unfortunate].* When I had sung it through once I was naïve enough to say, out loud: 'That's it, isn't it, dear Master? *Sunt lacrymae rerum!*' just as though Virgil himself had been there.

* A misquotation for *Non ignara*, etc.

He was justified in feeling it. Studying the opera and the poem together, we cannot but become increasingly aware of deep correspondences between the two artists. If this high theme was (in every sense) Berlioz's fated goal, it is equally true that one of the poem's many destinies, 'across the centuries', was to be its musical incarnation in a work that is among the last great manifestations of the unique hold of Troy and its legends on the mind of Western man.

Les Troyens is Virgilian in many ways. There is the blend of romantic rhetoric and classical restraint, of monumentality and pictorial vividness; the fondness for mixing genres and in particular for using the lyrical to diversify the tragic and at the same time to bring it into sharper focus; the combination of an aristocratic aloofness with an awareness of the sufferings of ordinary humanity; the sense of fatality, of obscure inimical powers that lie in wait for man, and of the madness that can strike a people and drive it blindly to its own destruction. (The two men have also in common their fear of the collapse of civilization as they knew it, and the doubts that assailed them at the end about the value of their work.) As with the *Aeneid* in Virgil's life, *Les Troyens* grew from seeds planted in youth. As Virgil went back to Homer in order fully to realize himself, so Berlioz turned to Virgil. The opera's outward structure, too, shows Berlioz's fidelity to his model (he has shared the criticism sometimes levelled at Virgil that the character and fate of Dido are treated with such power that they dominate the epic and deflect it from its course). *Les Troyens* follows the *Aeneid* in making the tragic death of an individual the last action that the audience sees enacted on the stage. And just as the *Aeneid* is an epic constructed of two personal tragedies (Dido's and Turnus'), so is *Les Troyens*. Even in consisting of two distinct though interlocking halves the opera reflects the shape of the poem, which is divided into the wanderings of Aeneas, including his narrative of the sack of Troy, and the struggle to found a new Troy in Italy. And though the action of the opera does not take the Trojans as far as Italy, the poem's central idea of the founding of Rome runs through it; Italy is the leitmotiv of the drama.

A study of the libretto in relation to the poem reveals Virgil as its constant guiding spirit. It is not only that a great deal of it is direct translation or paraphrase of the Latin of the books from which the main action is taken—Books I, II and IV. The whole poem is pressed into use. Even the stage direction at the beginning of the opera, 'three shepherds playing the double flute'—represented in the orchestra by oboes—is derived from the *Aeneid*, echoing a passage in Book IX where the Rutulian warrior Normanus taunts Ascanius with 'Go and dance to the double-mouthed pipe on Mount Dindyma, that's all you're good for.' Where Berlioz adds to the poem for dramatic purposes, he nearly always goes to Virgil for his material or his inspiration, working in ideas taken from anywhere and everywhere in the poem. Thus the scene in Act 1 where Hector's widow Andromache and her son Astyanax, dressed in the ritual white of mourning, lay flowers at the altar and receive Priam's blessing, springs from two different sources, one in Book II, where Aeneas, getting out onto the palace roof through a postern gate during the sack of the city, remembers that through this gate Andromache used to bring her child to see his grandfather Priam, the other in Book III where Aeneas meets Andromache in the Epiran city of Buthrotum, performing the rites of the dead at an altar dedicated to the ashes of Hector. Virgil, in fact, has inspired both the visual content and the tragic irony of the scene.

The episode in Book V where the disgruntled Trojan women gaze out to sea, and groan at the thought of the endless voyaging that lies before them, is transmuted into the scene in Act 5 for the two sentries who march up and down by the Trojan ships, grumbling at the prospect of leaving Carthage, where they are comfortably billeted, and entrusting themselves to the sea's tedium and the rough mercies of the storm (a scene whose Shakespearean ethos is so contrary to orthodox dramatic ideas in France that it is usually cut out when the work is performed there). Cassandra, urging Corebus to fly from the wrath to come, is answered with sentiments similar to those of Aeneas' reply to Anchises in the burning house: *Mene efferre pedem, genitor, te posse relicto/Sperasti?** Aeneas' words to his son, spoken before he goes off to fight the Numidians, paraphrases the hero's words in Book XII on the eve of the final battle against Turnus and the Rutulians. The invasion by Iarbas and his Numidian hordes, an interpolation made in order to provide a climax for the third act and give dramatic emphasis to Aeneas' arrival in Carthage, is a development of an idea put forward by Dido's sister Anna when she argues that Dido ought to marry Aeneas and share her kingdom with him: Carthage is surrounded by wild tribesmen, among them the Numidians and their chief Iarbas, who is all the more dangerous since Dido humiliatingly rejected his offer of a dynastic marriage.†

The process by which Berlioz fashioned his libretto is most clearly illustrated in Acts 1 and 2. The opera follows the main events of the sack of Troy.‡ But new material is added by the development of hints in the poem, and a good deal else has necessarily been subjected to compression or expansion. Thus the one-and-a-half lines in which Virgil tells of the cold fear that creeps over the Trojans at the news of Laocoon's death are built into a full-scale ensemble which shows the city poised at the fatal moment of decision. In

---

* 'Father, did you really expect me to run away and leave you behind?'

† A possible influence here is Piccini's *Didon*, which Berlioz had got to know during his student days (though written in 1783, it remained in the repertoire at the Opéra until 1826). Much of the action of Marmontel's libretto is concerned with Iarbas and his unsuccessful wooing. There are also verbal similarities between the two librettos in the later scenes, where Marmontel stays closest to Virgil.

‡ Originally Act 1 included the episode of the Greek spy Sinon. It was later removed by Berlioz, though not until several years after the completion of the score. The scene, 235 bars long, has survived (mostly in short score) and is published, for the first time, in the New Berlioz Edition, vol. 2c, pp. 875–86.

Act 2 Aeneas is made to succeed in his desperate attempt to relieve the citadel (in the poem he merely conceives the wild idea of doing so*); and he escapes with the royal insignia of Troy. The motive for this change may partly have been tidiness and coherence: Ascanius later presents a rich selection of Trojan relics to Queen Dido (a scene which is a conflation of two separate passages in Book 1). But the main reason, as with the finale of Act 3, is one of dramatic emphasis, to clinch the act with a decisive forward-looking event. In this case the action is not shown. We hear of it, from Cassandra, in the course of a scene which does not figure in the *Aeneid* except by implication, in the cries of the wailing women in Priam's palace (*plangoribus aedes femineis ululant*), in the glimpse of Helen cowering by the entrance to the temple of Vesta, and in the brief description of Cassandra being dragged from Minerva's sanctuary.

The development of Cassandra into the protagonist of Acts 1 and 2 is the biggest single change that Berlioz made. But here too he went to Virgil, deriving the character from a few lines in the *Aeneid*, just as Virgil derived Aeneas from the merest hint in the *Iliad*. Cassandra fills the role taken in Book II by Aeneas, who in the poem recalls Troy's downfall several years after the event. In the opera the tale comes to us through the eyes of the prophetess cursed with second sight. We see the catastrophe twice over: as it gradually forms in her mind (from the vague fears of 'Malheureux roi' to the fierce clarity of her vision in the following scene), and when it comes. This double process has the dramatic effect of heightening the sense of tragedy and doom. The vehemence and certainty of her unheeded prophecies throws the blindness of her fellow-countrymen into more merciless relief—that of Corebus in particular; the young warrior is mentioned briefly by Virgil as being 'on fire with desperate love for Cassandra' and as refusing to listen to her warnings, but in the opera he is betrothed to her: a lyrical addition

---

* If indeed we are to read *arcem* as 'citadel' and not simply 'strong point'.

which, by holding out the possibility of a happiness that will never be fulfilled, sharpens the cruel irony of Cassandra's personal tragedy. The text of Cassandra's scenes inevitably contains few direct Virgilian echoes; the prophecy to the Trojan women about the founding of a new Troy in Italy, based on Anchises' words in Book III, is a rare exception. Yet the whole character and her heroic, despairing utterances are in a sense simply a personification of Aeneas' tragic cry at the moment when he describes the entry of the Wooden Horse into Troy while Cassandra vainly prophesies:

> *O patria o divum domus Ilium et incluta bello*
> *Moenia Dardanidum!**

Cassandra is the first of the two tragic pillars which support the edifice of *Les Troyens*; across her fate, and Dido's, the epic of Roman destiny marches to its fulfilment. Berlioz had no choice but to kill her off in heroic circumstances at the end of his Act 2. The scene is not in Virgil; but its conception does not dishonour him.

In adapting the *Aeneid* to the totally different medium of opera, Berlioz also made some changes in the order of events as recounted by Virgil. The conversation (already referred to) between Anna and her sister Dido, with its tender urgings on one side and its barely suppressed emotion on the other, prompted the very similar duet in Act 3, 'Reine d'une jeune empire'. But whereas in the *Aeneid* the conversation occurs after the Trojans' arrival in Carthage and is very much concerned with them, Berlioz places it just before, as a means of projecting the state of Dido's heart at the moment of Aeneas' intervention in her life—her restlessness, her half-conscious yearning for love, her ripeness to yield. His dramatic judgment is correct. By doing so he is able partly to compensate for the fact that he has had to unfold the

---

* 'Oh my country! Oh Ilium, home of gods, oh walls of Troy renowned in war!'

events of the plot in straightforward chronological sequence and therefore to start the Carthaginian part of his story cold, where Virgil, by recounting the sack of Troy and its aftermath in flashback, through the mouth of Aeneas, with the fascinated Dido devouring his words, can accumulate tension over two or three thousand lines of verse and so prepare gradually for the explosion of passion which comes at the beginning of Book IV. (Yet such is music's power of suggestion, and so vibrant the impression of a woman of peculiar radiance and energy that Dido makes on us in those early scenes of Act 3, that the disadvantage is partly overcome.) The opera also redistributes and telescopes the sequence of events between Aeneas' decision to leave Dido and her death—a sequence which in the poem occupies four or five hundred lines, or well over half Book IV. A chart of the various sources, line by line, of Dido's soliloquies in Act 5—'Dieux immortels, il part', 'Je vais mourir', 'Adieu, fière cité' and the final invocation from the pyre—would show the text as woven of threads freely drawn from many different points in the last 250 lines of the book. The result is clear, logical and compelling, and does no violence to Virgil's psychology.

The third and final category of change concerns the new emphasis that Berlioz gives to certain events or ideas in the poem, his intention normally being to make explicit and theatrically telling what in the poem can afford to take its time and grow by degrees in the reader's mind. To take one of the most obvious instances: the theme of *fatum*, destiny, which is fundamental to the *Aeneid*, has had necessarily to be much more simply and directly set forth (a process in which the traditional importance of the chorus in French opera plays a vital part). This need applies also to the specifically Italian direction of the destiny of the Trojan survivors; not being native and instantly intelligible to Berlioz's audience as it was to Virgil's, it had to be made plain. In the *Aeneid* there is some doubt about the true identity of the mysterious object of Aeneas' wanderings. The ghost of his wife Creusa tells him, on Troy's last night, that his goal is Latium; but after that, uncertainty descends and it is only subsequently, several false scents later, that Italy is defined as the destined site of Troy reborn. An opera composer cannot afford such inconsistency (if indeed it is not deliberate and subtle poetic realism on Virgil's part) and, as we see, Berlioz is at pains to state the theme clearly and re-emphasize it at regular intervals, so that we shall be in no serious danger of not recognizing it as the majestic impulse of the epic, before which everything must ultimately give way. Contrary to Virgil, he makes Hector's ghost specify the object of Aeneas' wanderings. Later, he ends his picture of the sack of Troy with the Trojan women's defiant repeated cry of 'Italie'. Similarly, when the Trojans land at Carthage, their spokesman Panthus is more emphatic about the god-fated and only temporarily frustrated aim of their voyage than is Ilioneus in the equivalent passage in the *Aeneid*. In the opera, at the peak of the lovers' ecstasy, Mercury appears in the moonlit garden and, striking Aeneas' shield, intones three times 'Italie'. Mercury's larger role in the *Aeneid*, as explicit messenger of the gods, is not sacrificed but is filled, with the greater directness appropriate to drama, by the spirits of the illustrious Trojan dead, who rise up in turn to whet Aeneas' almost blunted purpose. Again, Berlioz sees to it that Aeneas is fully awake and conscious when Hector's ghost delivers his message; in the *Aeneid* the apparition comes to Aeneas in a dream, through the veil of sleep. All this makes for a necessary gain in clarity and conciseness, inevitably at a slight cost in poetic suggestiveness and truth to life.

In the same way, Aeneas' heroic role and his conscious-ness of his destiny as a hero have to be spelled out; the point must be established quickly—it cannot be left to the cumulative effect of epic verse. In *Les Troyens* the last words uttered by Hector's ghost before the vision fades tell of the death that Aeneas will meet in Italy; the final line, 'Où la mort des héros t'attend', is not in Virgil. Later Panthus, in his speech to Dido in Act 3, refers to it as an accepted fact. Aeneas himself, in his monologue in Act 5, says that he could not sway the outraged Dido even by reminding her of 'la triomphale mort par les destins promise'—the end awaiting him on Ausonian fields that is to crown his glory; and almost his last words to her, when she confronts him by the ships, speak of the death to which he is going.

It is sometimes objected that Virgil, concerned with the overriding theme of the epic of Rome, failed to make Aeneas sufficiently sympathetic. This is usually said by people who have fallen in love with his glorious Dido and who consequently regard any man capable of abandoning her as an unspeakable cad. Such indignant charges do more credit to the critics' chivalry than to their careful reading of the poem. Berlioz might appear to belong to their number, from the references in his *Memoirs* to the 'hypocrite', the 'perfidious' Aeneas. But the composer of *Les Troyens* understood the depth of passion hinted at in Virgil's resonant understatements and justly praised silences; and he was quite right, on Virgilian as well as on operatic terms, to make Aeneas' love for Dido whole-hearted and avowed and to dramatize the resultant conflict in the hero's mind. The famous duet in Dido's garden is not only obligatory for the composer of grand opera but also artistically essential to the drama as a whole. The words, adapted from the scene between Lorenzo and Jessica in the moonlit garden at Belmont in the fifth act of *The Merchant of Venice*, represent the one major textual innovation that is not Virgilian in origin. Its setting gave Berlioz the opportunity to lavish all his lyrical and orchestral art on a poignant evocation of the warmth and vast splendours of the starlit Mediterranean night. The *Aeneid* is not abolutely precise about the season of the Trojans' sojourn in Carthage. In *Les Troyens* it is, unequivocally, summertime; the great feasts with their bards and heroic tales and jewel-encrusted goblets take place out of doors under the open sky. Berlioz has also transferred the setting of the hunt and storm from open mountainous country to virgin forest, and has peopled his scene with the woodland satyrs, bathing naiads and glinting streams and waterfalls which help to make it the neo-classical masterpiece it is, a movement that has been compared to some great Claude or Poussin, and that combines attributes of both painters, Poussin's grandeur and universality and dynamic form, Claude's numinous clarity and sense of the golden moment.

An example of all three types of change—the interpolating of new material derived from Virgil himself, the re-ordering of the sequence of Virgil's narrative, and the making explicit what in the poem is implied—is the Quintet in Act 4, 'Tout conspire à vaincre mes remords'. Here we see Berlioz's dramatic imagination at work on the *Aeneid*, distilling from it a scene which, as such, is not found in the poem, but which is necessary to the scheme of a dramatic work based on it—in this case, the moment of Dido's change of heart, from lingering attachment to the memory of her dead husband Sychaeus to unreserved commitment to her new love. In the first place, the picture of Dido feasting Aeneas and begging him to repeat the tale of Troy's woes is moved on in time so as to follow the acknowledgment and consummation of their mutual passion; in Virgil it belongs to the preceding stage of their relationship (a part of the poem not included in the opera, except by implication). Then, Virgil's divine intervention (Venus and Juno in league) is discarded. In the *Aeneid* Cupid, in the likeness of Ascanius, fans the flame and 'gradually dispels from Dido's mind all thought of Sychaeus', while she, unaware of his true identity, 'fondles him and holds him close'. Berlioz retains the visual setting but replaces the supernatural with a dramatic idea developed from a reference, in Book III, to Hector's widow Andromache having married Pyrrhus. In the opera it is the discovery that Andromache is now the wife of the man whose father slew Hector that acts as a catalyst on Dido, severing the threads that bound her to her old life (and at the same time setting up in the spectator's mind a sudden resonance with the almost forgotten moment, three acts ago, when the desolate figure in white walked silently through rejoicing crowds by the walls of Troy). Finally, an echo of Cupid substituted for Ascanius survives in the stage direction which shows the boy 'leaning on his bow, like a statue of Eros', and in the smiling comment of the royal entourage that he resembles Cupid, as he slips Sychaeus' ring from the heedless Dido's finger. This last action is one of the very rare non-Virgilian ideas in the libretto; Berlioz took it from Guérin's painting, *Enée racontant à Didon les malheurs de Troie*.

Most of this examination has shown only the skill with which Berlioz reshaped the *Aeneid* into a fresh mould—a mould for the music that was waiting to pour out of him. It is the music that makes him a true descendant of the poet he loved. 'As for the principal object of the work, the musical rendering of the characters and the expression of their feelings and passions, it was always the easiest part of my task.' But not only the characters' passions, one wants to exclaim, but the Virgilian ambience itself, the whole environment of the epic, has been absorbed by the composer into his inmost being and given back reborn in his own language. A re-reading of the *Aeneid* with the music of *Les Troyens* in one's mind is a startling revelation of artistic correspondence. Feature after feature of the poem reappears in the score. Certain elements may be isolated. On the level of individual images, we find details such as the violin harmonics which in Act 5 suggest the electric effect of the apparitions on Aeneas, matching Virgil's graphic description of the hero rigid with fear, his hair standing on end (*arrectaeque horrore comae*). At the beginning of the opera the combination of shrill, rapidly pulsing woodwind chords, a texture devoid of bass, the absence of strings, and the curiously jaunty melodic material, at once trivial and possessed, conveying a sense of ritual madness, help to establish from the outset the idea of *fatum*, of a people rushing to ruin. An ominous rhythmic figure,*

first heard as part of the
orchestral texture in the opening scenes and stated explicitly
in the Octet 'Châtiment effroyable' which follows the death
of Laocoon, recurs as a kind of reminder of fatality at
moments where the action of destiny is most manifest or
the tragic irony most intense—the apparition of Hector's
ghost in Act 2 and of the spirits in Act 5, the tumultuous
exit of Aeneas as king-elect at the head of combined Trojan
and Carthaginian forces at the end of Act 3, the climax of
the Royal Hunt, Dido's farewell—'ma carrière est finie'—
and the solemnities which precede her immolation. But for
the most part the corespondence needs no analysing. It
leaps out at us. The Octet, for instance, once heard seems
the inevitable setting of the dread words *Tum vero treme-
facta novus per pectora cunctis/Insinuat pavor*—a whole
people's blood running cold, panic spreading as an inkling
of their doom 'works its way' into the back of their minds.
How much of Cassandra's music directly echoes, in its
piercing sadness, Aeneas' cry of anguish over the horror,
the pity of it—*O patria o divum domus Ilium!*

Or what could be more Virgilian than the scene in Act 2
where Hector, 'recalled to life by the will of the gods',
appears before Aeneas and lays upon him his sacred mission,
then sinks back to nothingness, his task accomplished—
the apparition materializing to the sound of stopped horns
groping from note to note, accompanied by pizzicato
strings, then uttering its message on the successive notes of a
falling chromatic scale above a dim fabric of divided cellos
and basses, with occasional interventions from the trombones,
at once nightmarish and majestic; Aeneas staring and
motionless, except for a sudden lurch in the orchestra, like
a missed heartbeat, at the words—the most terrible in the

---

* Borrowed, perhaps, from Max's scena in *Der Freischütz*, via Herod's
aria in *L'enfance du Christ*.

Aeneid—*hostis habet muros*: 'the enemy's within our walls'. In the orchestral prelude to the same act the very sound and feel of Virgil's lines are reproduced in the rhythm, texture, colour and harmonic movement of the music—*clarescunt sonitus armorumque ingruit horror*:* war and rumours of war, the hideous confusion of battle. Again, how true to Virgil are the music's insights into the effect of war and the great national enterprises born of war on the ordinary human being—poignant in the case of the Palinurus-like figure of the young sailor Hylas, eaten with nostalgia for the homeland he will never see again; humorous in the case of the two grumbling sentries who would like to stay in Carthage and have done with the whole senseless idea of Italy; tragic in the case of Andromache, whose grief, though it pales before the cataclysm to come, remains the ultimate comment on the misery of war. How deeply Berlioz has absorbed the example of the humanity of the *Aeneid*—those little touches that mark Virgil out among ancient writers, like the picture of the women and children waiting in a long line beside the piled-up loot in the courtyard of Priam's blazing palace. Such sudden shifts of viewpoint give a new dimension to the epic, in Berlioz's music as in Virgil's verse.

Dramatic effects of sharply contrasted colours, textures and rhythms are a common feature of the two works. The moment in Book I when the magic cloak shrouding Aeneas is stripped away to reveal him in all his glory is paralleled by the sudden change that occurs in the music when Aeneas throws off his sailor's cloak and steps forward in shining armour. Acts 1 and 2 of *Les Troyens* mirror Book II of the *Aeneid* in their alternation of light and dark, their evocation of flaring light amid surrounding blackness—the doomed splendour of the great processional entry of the Horse through the torchlit darkness, the smoky glare of the Temple Scene shot through with gleams of martial trumpets. The feeling we experience in the opera when the harsh, possessed

* 'The noise grew clearer and the roar of battle swelled.'

sound of Berlioz's Troy gives way to the lyrical and sensuous sound of his Carthage (flute and clarinet in octaves, piccolo trills, softer string sonorities), is just such as we experience in Book I of the poem when Virgil cuts abruptly from the clangorous description of the frescoes depicting the Trojan War in the temple of Juno to the delicate and luminous vision of Dido making her way through the throng, attended by young courtiers.

The criticism sometimes heard of Act 3, that the lengthy ceremonies in which Carthage celebrates its first seven years are a distraction from the main business of the drama and a concession to Meyerbeerian grand opera, is in effect a criticism of a too close fidelity to Virgil, for the plan of the opening scenes of the act is inspired by the intensely vital and brilliant first impression of Carthage that we receive in Book I. Berlioz's purpose in following Virgil, however, is a dramatic one, being both to provide an interval of repose after the concentrated fury of Act 2 and to emphasize the rising star of the new city so that the tragedy of its fall may be fully felt. To this end, and perhaps also borrowing an idea from Book VII (the picture of Latium as a kingdom of Saturn, still enjoying the blessings of the golden age), he has made his Carthage something of a matriarchal Garden of Eden, absorbed in the beneficent work of building and cultivation, fearful of the enemies surrounding it, yet defence- less until saved by the hero who is destined to be its des- troyer (the limping, melancholy strains of the Trojan March in the minor mode telling not only of Trojan sufferings endured but of Carthaginian disasters to come). But in his development of this gentle pastoral state the composer is, as always, the disciple of the poet—especially the poet of the *Georgics*, who is heard through the mouth of the bard Iopas. In the *Aeneid* Iopas sings of the elements and the movement of the stars, but in *Les Troyens* of the shepherd and the farmworker and the fruits of the well-tilled earth.

In this fourth act, set in Dido's gardens at night within sound of the sleeping sea, Berlioz matches Virgil's mastery of verbal magic in music beneath whose beauties lies the same sense of the pathos of life and the brevity of human happiness. Yet the fifth and final act is in some ways the most profoundly Virgilian of all, both in its heroic sweep and in its classicism: on the one hand the great arches of extended melody in Aeneas' scena—the huge stride of the vocal line above the surge and stress of the orchestra, the powerful swing of the rhythmic movement between agitation and serene exaltation; on the other hand the simplicity of Dido's grief. In response to the tragic dénouement of Book IV Berlioz strips his art to an extraordinary economy of gesture. One thinks of the gentle swell of the sea cradling Hylas to a death-like sleep; the two-note semitone figure which suggests Aeneas rocking to and fro in the anguish of his indecision; the brief shudder in the strings, like a premonition of a life escaping into air (*in ventos vita recessit*), that abruptly breaks the trancelike calm of Dido's first words from the pyre; the bareness of the vocal line a moment earlier as Dido, speaking as if in a dream, gives the order for the last rites to begin—a passage whose broken phrases and slow chromatic descent through an octave recall the music of Hector's prophecy which was to be the cause of her grief. (Virgil would have recognized here a poetic device of his own, whereby resonances are set up between pairs of similar or ironically contrasted incidents located in different parts of the epic.) While at work on Dido's recitative 'Je vais mourir', Berlioz wrote of his conviction that the music he was composing had a 'heartrending truthfulness'. What is even more remarkable is the sense of a calm beyond suffering that he achieves in the aria, 'Adieu, fière cité' (*urbem prae-claram statui*),* which succeeds the torment of the recitative. Nothing in music is more expressive of utter finality than the aria's concluding bars—the voice dying away, a last flicker of agony (the cor anglais' flattened sixth), then a mysterious peace, with a rustle of pianissimo strings and, on trombones, the quiet beat of the rhythmic motif of

* 'I founded a noble city.'

destiny, stilled in a cadence of such purity and simplicity that the silence which follows is almost palpable: there is nothing more to be said. Dido accepts her fate.

In the tragic climate of the ancients, redemption is neither demanded nor expected. Alone among Romantic dramatists, Berlioz was able to re-create it because it was his own imaginative world. It had become his natural element. The memory of the emotional shock that Dido's death had been to him, forty years before, and of all that had followed in his adolescent imaginative life, remained with him, fresh and undiminished. To it was added long experience as a composer of dramatic music and a capacity for feeling, for pain, for regret, that life had sharpened to a fine point. He had been waiting for this. His musical style, with its long flexible melodic line and its use of timbre and rhythm as subtly varied means of poetic expression, was ideally suited to the task. So was his temperament. The call of Virgil's heroic world was irresistible. A concept of human existence as it might once have been in some possible dream of a golden age took root in boyhood and grew till it possessed his mind. The Virgilian vision—a vision of grandeur without illusions, of destruction lying in wait outside and within man, and life lived subject to the will of implacable fate but, while it lasts, lived fully and ungrudgingly even in the shadow of doom—answered his deepest longings. It is the heroic temper expressed in Hecuba's proud prophecy in the last scene of *The Trojan Women*:

> We sacrificed in vain. Yet if the god had not seized this city and trampled it beneath the earth, we should have disappeared without trace: we would not have given a theme for music and the songs of men to come . . .

the mood that is expressed in the ardent, exalted music to which Aeneas, drunk with his mission, already part of history, apostrophizes Dido in sublime farewell, then turns and embraces his fate and the knowledge of his death.

As with Aeneas, there could be for Berlioz no turning back
once he had begun. But like Aeneas he knew the outcome.
'What agonies I am storing up for myself by becoming so
passionate about this work!' Its likely fate had been one of
his strongest reasons against being drawn into composing it.
The indifference of the French musical establishment was
nontheless a crippling blow. He had schooled himself in a
proud stoicism, but his resolve broke down. 'I know that I
promised you I would resign myself to whatever might
happen,' he wrote to the Princess, 'and here I am, failing
completely to keep my promise. I feel a terrible bitterness of
spirit.' The bitterness was not relieved, even by the momentary pleasure of seeing the second part of the work staged and
rewarded with a *succès d'estime* despite poor performances and
numerous cuts. It is the sense of defeat that *Les Troyens*
engendered which, more than anything else, even his son's
death and his own painful and incurable disease, accounts
for the gloom of Berlioz's last years. At least he was spared
the tragi-comedy of the work's subsequent fortunes in
France: non-publication, non-performance, performance in
versions mutilated almost beyond recognition, critical dismissal, lawsuits, and the rest of the scene he knew so well.
To quote the late Claude Rostand, in an act of public
recantation of dramatic completeness:*

Relying purely on received opinions, with a wilful blindness
that has persisted, to be precise, for one hundred and seven
years, France has always refused to accept that *Les Troyens* is a
great masterpiece, the high point of its composer's genius . . .
According to the official view that we used to be taught, *Les
Troyens* was an operatic 'monster', fruit of the old age of an
artist in decline, its occasional beauties set in an ocean of feeble-
ness, and in any case humanly impossible to perform or to listen
to in one evening. These judgments, these summary convic-
tions, repeated ad nauseam—till recently even by the most
enthusiastic Berliozians—were in fact based not simply on
incomprehension but first and foremost on a liberal measure

* Reviewing the Philips recording of *Les Troyens* in *Le Figaro Littéraire*,
21–27 September 1970.

of pure ignorance. What a confession! . . . We have here one of the most astonishing musical scandals of all time . . .

In the seventh book of the *Aeneid* an indignant Juno looks down on Italy and exclaims in wonder that the Trojans have endured so many cruel vicissitudes: half-drowned, blasted with fire, their might scattered; yet they are still unbowed, and life lies ahead of them. She might have been prophesying the destiny of Berlioz's opera. Despite all that has and has not happened to it, it has survived. Its worth is at last coming to be recognized. In a real sense life lies ahead of it for, with the publication of the full score (in 1969, a hundred years after the composer's death), the work may be said for the first time fully to exist. It can at last be recognized for what it is, the vindication of its creator's faith in his lifelong vision, and proof of the magic power of a great poet working, two thousand years later, on the mind of a kindred genius.

Part II

Performers—1

Klemperer

In the seventeen years since he began appearing regularly in London, Otto Klemperer has become an object of such veneration that it is hard to discuss him rationally: the musician is entangled in the myth. To some extent that is normal. The conductor is a natural cult-object; the impact of his interpretations can never be wholly dissociated from the image that people have of him. But special factors have been at work. Any foreign conductor over the age of 70 is eligible for that mysterious process whereby, in English lore, a Kapellmeister is transformed into an old master. When the conductor has overcome by sheer strength of will an illness that would have killed most men and which leaves him permanently crippled yet carrying on with a magnificent disregard of his disabilities, and when on top of that he is known for his caustic wit, disconcerting bluntness, and utter indifference to appearances, he qualifies as an institution; and once we institutionalize an artist, it hardly matters what he does: his spell is sufficient.

Occasionally, when Klemperer's gaunt frame, having been helped onto the platform by attendants, sits there almost immobile throughout a long movement, I have caught myself wondering whether it would make any difference if he were not actually alive: like the lifeless body of El Cid leading the armies of Christ to victory, the aura of the man would bring the evening to its triumphant conclusion just the same. But that would merely show the validity of the Klemperer myth. The spell creates the performance not only in the minds of the audience but also in the minds of the orchestra giving it; but it is founded on fact. There is more than sentimentality in the equation of extreme physical suffering endured and conquered with an understanding of Beethoven's music (especially the heroic Beethoven of the Third and Ninth symphonies and *Fidelio*), just as there is more than mythology in the Kapellmeister-to-old-master alchemy, age itself conferring an extra allowance of the wisdom, authority and detachment that help to make a great conductor. What Klemperer does, or what he causes his orchestra to do, is demonstrably remarkable. Its worth is seen in all that his performances, of Mozart, Schubert, Wagner and Bruckner as well as Beethoven, have meant not merely in ritual satisfaction but in enlightenment, joy and consolation to countless thousands. Such experiences are the material of myth.

Nevertheless the Klemperer cult has fostered one serious delusion: that the admirable clarity and sobriety of his interpretations constitutes the 'truth' of the music, in contrast to the more or less subjective approximations of most other conductors. If he now lets things appear simply to happen, where a younger musician would more obviously direct and impose, the result is no less uniquely and subjectively Klemperer's. Even the textual fidelity we hear so much about, the insistence on what is written, can in practice be surprisingly qualified, and by nothing more exalted than the old German performing traditions that he was brought up in. It is true that he scorns the additions made by Wagner and others to Beethoven's wind parts (how much more evocative of chaos and mental strife is the opening of the finale of the Ninth Symphony as Beethoven left it, and as Klemperer performs it, with the trumpet line gap-toothed, without the F naturals, a note not playable by the natural D trumpet of the time!). But that merely shows that he is an inconsistent human being and not a saint. The man who can quicken the tempo for Tamino's entry after the Armed Men's chorale in *The Magic Flute* (thus destroying the mood of fortitude and resolution inherent in a constant tempo), or who can remove the greater part of the second half of the finale of Bruckner's Eighth Symphony in one swingeing cut, is a conductor, like any other. Klemperer's illuminations, like anyone else's, are personal. They are not achieved by the abnegation of the egoistic interpretative artist's sovereign right to interpret.

And they do not invariably come. In him there is, if you like, a prophet with the sacred fire, but there is also a touch of the old Kapellmeister of his previous incarnation. Sometimes what he does seems inevitable in its calm, unfaltering grandeur, filling you with the conviction that Klemperer, like God, is working his purpose out and that everything has its place in a divinely ordained scheme which will justify all in the end. Sometimes, as with God, you do not feel prepared to take the higher providence on trust, while so many good and deserving points are being thrown away. The Kapellmeister is still active when Klemperer conducts the Missa Solemnis. Noble though his interpretation is, the work's sublime intoxication escapes him. The phrases do not surge, the rhythms refuse to 'leap as an hart'; the contrasts of colour, texture, weight, dynamics—generally a striking feature of Klemperer's conducting of Beethoven, and fundamental to the work—are curiously muted. There may be a partly technical reason for the sense of caution that keeps much of Klemperer's interpretation of the Mass on solid earth: the physical difficulty, for a half-paralysed man, of controlling and animating such large forces.

But it is not only in big choral works but also when he conducts his orchestra, which has learnt to read his mind and decipher the swiftest glance and the vaguest flutter of his hands, that the sense of larger movement can be lost in the concern with clarity and balancing of parts, so that the music ceases to flow and exists from bar-line to bar-line. A certain ponderousness of rhythm is the negative side of his bass line's granite strength. His fondness for very deliberate tempos and his refusal to be stampeded into external excitement can make the more fiery scherzos of Beethoven and

Schubert sound over-articulated and wanting in exuberance and animal spirits, their rhythmic reiterations a source of monotony rather than of energy. On an off-day even the pulse can falter and become wayward (so that the listener has a strange sensation akin to that of riding on a bicycle with a flat back tyre). Nor is his grand severity at home in the purely lyrical or the humorous. His conducting of *Lohengrin* at Covent Garden in 1963 lacked sensuous beauty in the love music, while a quintessential Haydn joke like the one in the finale of No. 98, where a raging fortissimo unison is promptly deflated by the reappearance of the tune, cocky as ever, a semitone higher, passes him by apparently un-noticed. He can rise to the heights of Mozart's more regal symphonic utterances and conduct performances of the Prague or the Jupiter that are unsurpassed in loftiness of temper and singleness of dramatic purpose; but it would be idle to look to him for the instinctive Mozartian sense of movement of a Beecham. In some ways Klemperer is the least *natural* of the great conductors. It is his weakness as well as his uncommon strength.

All this is only to repeat that the hero-figure is human. To harp on his limitations is to be provoked by the Klemperer cult into labouring the obvious. That an old man should conduct an exceedingly slow-paced *Figaro* because that is how, at 85, he feels it, is less odd than that people nearly half his age should fall about and hail it as a sign. He should be allowed to nod. He was 70 by the time he became a regular visitor to London in 1955. It would be inhuman to expect him to be able, or even to wish, to live up to his exalted image and produce unfailing revelations as a matter of course in a repertoire that, for all his continued keenness of mind, is restricted to works in which his intentions can be conveyed to his players by the simplest of gestures (thus the music of composers such as Stravinsky, Schoenberg and Janáček, with which he was very much associated in the 1920s in Germany, is necessarily excluded). It would be equally absurd to ask of him the nervous intensity and the dynamic performances of a younger man. If Klemperer was ever that sort of conductor, which I doubt, the truths he now reveals are of a different kind. They are such as a man of austere and penetrating mind, who has lived longer and been through more than most men, and who still searches but has long ceased to want to prove anything, would see when he stood back and looked at the music from a slight distance. To call such truths objective is pure moonshine. The angle of vision is peculiar to him. But the light it casts on familiar works is so individual and at the same time so strong and clear that, as always with a great artist, it gives us the illusion that we are hearing them for the first time 'as they are'.

The exceptional lucidity of Klemperer's performances is, however, a verifiable fact; it is achieved by cunning balancing, which means giving less of one thing rather than more of another, but the impression we receive is not of prudence and economy. The different layers are boldly defined, the pianos and the fortes. It is dynamic in both senses—horizontal as well as vertical. Sometimes, as I have said, the musical mobility can become encumbered in the preoccupation with detail. But in such cases it is the execution that is at fault, not the intention. Klemperer has a profound feeling for architectural unity and, at his best, the ability to present a work or a movement in one embracing gesture, so that each detail, however vivid, seems subordinate to a governing principle. When he is in the vein, the first 120-odd bars of Bruckner's Seventh Symphony come to us (as they should) shaped as one wide arc of melody; the whole movement sweeps forward with the majesty of a great river. In Klemperer's interpretation of the Fantastic Symphony the two final movements belong to the same design and idea as the other three; they are not genre pieces, spectacular but separate, but nightmarish intensifications of the mood of isolation and mingled fever and melancholy embodied in the earlier part of the work. And though the interpretation may leave out something of the music's mercurial vivacity and nervous élan—what one might call its specifically Gallic attributes—we hardly notice the omission, in the beauty and conviction of what it includes: the impassive, relentless power of the finale, emphasizing the quality of obscene ritual which is missed in conventionally lurid performances; the mixture of grandeur and intimacy in the opening Largo, which, while losing nothing of its sadness, is laid out on the largest scale; the phrasing of the *idée fixe* in such a way as to bring out its proud, exalted character, the shaping of the allegro as one constantly developing symphonic entity, the marvellously disciplined welter of sound at the final tutti statement of the *idée fixe*, achieved by scrupulous instrumental balance; and in the adagio the sense of Beethovenian spaciousness and immense distances that he evokes by a combination of broad tempo, generous phrasing, careful observance of dynamics, just proportion of weight and flow, and precise ear for colour, and which pervades the whole movement from the opening dialogue of cor anglais and oboe to the last soft horn note—rightly sustained a whole beat beyond the final string chord, with magical but predictable effect.

Most of the qualities that distinguish Klemperer at his best are there. Many of them are different functions of the same thing: the music unfolds at a pace which allows so much to happen, resonances to be set up, sonority to establish itself, colours to be placed exactly, climaxes to be unhurriedly prepared for, horizons to open. The deliberate tempos which can weary us by their plodding insistence are also part of the secret of his greatness. Only at such a pace can one feel the exhilarating clash of rhythms in the first movement of the Great C major Symphony. Only at such a pace can one truly register the grandeur of Bruckner's Miltonic images—for example, in the passage in the first movement of the Eighth, where, after a radiant paean from the whole orchestra, a fragment of the main theme sounding darkly on cellos and basses, as though from deep chasms, is answered by an oboe high above, playing the same figure inverted, while a barely audible shimmer of violins hovers in the middle air between. (Who, after experiencing such a passage, as Klemperer conducts it, could wish to cavil at Bruckner's naïveties again!)

Choosing almost at random from my memories of Klemperer's performances, I recall the indescribable excitement of the long crescendo which heralds the arrival of Lohengrin in the first act of the opera, when Klemperer conducted it at Covent Garden; the superb control of the diminuendo at the beginning of Leonora No. 3, the darkening of colour spreading over the music as the descending C major scale settles onto the pianissimo F sharp, and the still deeper hush of the modulation into A flat; the wonderful blossoming of phrase, near the end of the adagio of the Ninth Symphony, when the theme returns after the first of the fanfares, and the huge expansion of perspective at the turn into D flat major; the combined gravity and serene absence of effort in the March of the Priests in *The Magic Flute*; in the same work, the ability to place and accent the most apparently ordinary things, like the simple octaves and tonic chords which intersperse the voices in the D major priests' chorus, so that they are charged with unutterable mystery; the epic scale of his grandest conceptions, whether of Beethoven or Schubert or of Richard Strauss, and the emphasis on firm, ringing horn tone which is a vital part of it; the command of ample, unforced orchestral sonority, which perhaps comes to a conductor only when he no longer strives for it, and which enables Klemperer, in the finale of the Pastoral Symphony, to produce out of an already full fortissimo a sudden blaze of sound for the four final bars of the climactic tutti (an effect that is not indicated in the score but that is justified harmonically, Klemperer's *fff* coinciding with the great culminating chord of the ninth); the feeling for the clinching detail of dynamics and colour: the overwhelming effect of the trumpets' entry in the Prelude to *Tristan*, or the magnificently decisive underlining of the forte that follows the four fortepiano chords at the end of the development section of the overture to *Don Giovanni*.

I remember the performance of this overture at a New Philharmonia concert in 1964 as among the finest demonstrations of Klemperer's power to conceive and project an interpretation as a single comprehensive experience. So strong was its imaginative force and conviction that even the concert ending—normally an outrage against nature—seemed inevitable. Belief in what he is doing has become a hallmark of Klemperer's musicianship which, to the willing listener, communicates itself as a moral quality transforming a concert into a public rite.

In the 1960s, in London, one piece of music came to symbolize the great doctor, his steadfastness and his far-sighted breadth of vision—the Ninth Symphony. In Klemperer's reading we lived the work as a journey of the soul, beginning in groaning and travailing, a darkness of tribulation lit only by the unconquerable will and ending in a triumph which, for all its transcendent splendour, was a triumph of humanity, won amid the howling tempests of an inhospitable universe. No wonder such a man has been made a cult. Its votaries may be blind to his limitations, but they are acknowledging the presence of a great original in our musical life, which is brighter for the light of his heroic sanity.

(1970)

Beecham

'The greatest conductor' is an idea void of meaning and altogether preposterous, and to apply it to Sir Thomas would be to invite from that genial spirit an explosion of ridicule ('you idiot, you fustilerian, I'll tickle your catastrophe!'). But to me, as to thousands of music-lovers, Beecham was incomparable. This is something that went far beyond our appreciation of his personality and physical presence on concert platforms. He gave us not only more enjoyment than any other musician has done, but more enlightenment, a deeper understanding of music, a more acute sharpening of our musical instincts, a closer communion with the flesh and blood of the art. That, it seems to me, was for a very simple reason: he was the most instinctively musical conductor of his time. Beecham is being celebrated as the great hedonist, the arch musical *bon vivant*, the prince of connoisseurs. It is pointed out, as evidence of a certain unsoundness in the man, that he started many enterprises but built none; his restless genius spent itself prodigally but left no monument behind. In this way the 'character' is made to overshadow the artist. Such assessments miss the truth. It was not pleasure he communicated but love. He made us for the moment as musical as he was, as passionately in love with the art.

Time and again this essential musicality took him to the heart of things. There were great composers in whose music he was undeniably surpassed by other conductors. Bach he described as having done 'some very pleasant things in the smaller forms' (there was an element of pure provocativeness

in such judgments, for, music being a social activity, he saw
it as among his functions to shock English taste out of its
puritan provincialism and narrow Teutonic rut; but his
infrequent and unfruitful encounters with Bach's music made
it clear that that was how he reacted to it). In Beethoven he
chose what was real to him. It was, he seemed to be saying,
the music that interested him and not the moral preoccupations. These sometimes stirred up the demon of icono-
clasm in him. He never measured, nor perhaps presumed
to measure, the sublimity of the Ninth Symphony. But on
occasion he gave beautiful and satisfying performances of
the Second, Third, Fourth and Sixth, and his interpretation
of the Seventh, until latterly he wearied of its hammering
insistence and would drive through it like a Jehu, was
titanic in the force of primal energy generated from tremendous rhythmic tension. It is not true that he was
congenitally unsympathetic to grandeur. The National
Anthem alone blew that myth to annihilation. Handel's
choruses conducted by him were more truly majestic for
being reduced of superfluous fat and made light on their
feet. His interpretation of Schubert's Great C major Symphony was the best I ever heard—finer than Toscanini's
because the tempo of the second movement was better
judged—and it is a curiosity of his career that this work
which he admired above all others he adamantly refused to
record.

Like any conductor he had his blind spots. But over an
astonishing range of composers the freshness and vitality of
his musical taste, which was unconditioned by theories of
any kind, led him straight to a style characteristic of the
music, so that it seemed more truly alive than when anyone
else conducted it. I use the word style deliberately. The
Pharisees beat their breasts over Sir Thomas. To purists his
versions of 18th-century music were a blasphemy. Such
people could not see how ardently the Handelian spirit—
the largeness of scale, sensuousness of line and delicacy of
colour—burned on in Beecham's performances. In an

imperfect world his *Messiah* and *Solomon*, big brass and all, were paradoxically more faithful to Handel than many far more authentic performances. Even in Haydn his occasional emendations would, one swears, have delighted the composer because they were loyal to a characteristic humour in the music which Beecham was almost alone in recognizing. To change the strings' off-beat chords at the end of the Trio of Symphony No. 93 in D to pizzicato was of course wrong, but for a splendidly right reason; it was such a quintessentially Haydnish touch that Haydn must have kicked himself for not thinking of it.

One cannot overemphasize this question of style in the sense of an atmosphere native to each work. It was not a conjuring trick, performed with or without the aid of the composer; it was an essence which he drew out of the very core of the music. He divined what the composer had put into it, and made it speak as the composer meant it to speak; so that—for example—one felt the sense of the brevity of human relationships expressed in phrase after phrase of *La Bohème*, one had the almost physical sensation of thunderstorm and cloudburst at the climax of the *Royal Hunt*, one experienced the exotic, deranged world of *Coq d'or*, glimpsed the vision of an enchanted existence behind the horn flourishes and swirling harps and strings of the *Valse des fleurs*, and saw Don Quixote plain in the leisurely but incisive opening paragraphs of Strauss' masterpiece, with unprecedented vividness. There was something different about such things, beyond analysis but impossible to mistake. Nor was it only in romantic music that he possessed this gift of poetic penetration. Think of the many moments when Haydn stood before us. In the slow movement of the Surprise Symphony, after the strings' imposing C minor octaves, there was a wonderful pomposity-pricking impertinence in the violins' answer in A flat such as I have heard from no other conductor. Again, at the end of the slow movement of No. 93, who else, after the bassoon has laid his great egg on a monstrous bottom C, could make the orchestra settle back and crow and cluck with such audible satisfaction—and then, having done so, make the quiet final bars an image of such deep rustic contentment? He did not impose—he simply characterized the music correctly, allowed it to be most richly itself.

Beecham had few equals in Haydn or Schubert, or in Richard Strauss; few if any in Mendelssohn, Puccini, Sibelius and much of 19th-century French music; and none in 19th-century Russian and Bohemian—Tchaikovsky, Borodin, Rimsky-Korsakov, Smetana. He was a great Wagner conductor. The faults of his Handel were those of his day, the virtues are timeless. His Mozart style, formed in reaction to the almost unbelievably flat and inexpressive playing common in English orchestras when he was young, had a tendency to over-refinement; but the origin was in an excess of insight—he had found so much that had formerly been overlooked. His understanding went much deeper than his mannerisms. He could give marvellously intense, vivacious performances of the E flat Symphony, the Prague, the Haffner and the little C major, K.338. The rare examples of Verdi's music included in his available recordings fully bear out, in their fire and trenchant energy, his reputation as a superb Verdi conductor. Even in music by composers with whom he professed to be not in sympathy (Elgar, for instance), instinct often led him to the truth.

The elements of his own personal style were several. First was his unique rhythm, on which everything else rested: a rhythm, perfectly sprung, flexible but undeviating, which was the explanation of his orchestra's extraordinary unanimity in tuttis, and which enabled him to shape a phrase unhurriedly, yet at the same time gave such an impression of inevitable momentum that the music seemed to spin along by its own motor power; this, when it happened, was exciting as nothing else was. Then, a feeling for correct accentuation; an acute sensitivity to the shape of a phrase and an unwearying ear for contrasts and blends of instrumental colour; a care for beauty of tone, a sense of sonority, that prevented the sound from losing quality in whatever extreme of fortissimo or pianissimo; right up to the end, an enormous vitality that could blaze through a whole work like a forest fire. Finally, an innate grandeur of manner, a nobility—in both senses of the word—for which nothing was common or mean, and by which the most battered melody, like the andante theme in the first movement of Tchaikovsky's Sixth, regained the dignity that belonged to it in the first place.

Beecham's humanity—a humanity which lay behind the seigneurial mien and below the streak of destructive malice —was touched on by Malcolm Arnold when he spoke the other day of the reason why Beecham was supreme from the orchestral musician's point of view: 'Unlike so many of the big names, he had the ability to make a player feel that what he was doing was worth while . . . His musical standards were of the highest, but he never made the players feel that they were beyond them.' Knowing his men as individuals, he 'never attempted to inflict a style on a player which was foreign to his nature'. To his own orchestra his dying must seem an irreparable loss, something inconceivable and even absurd, as Jack Brymer has said. But to the concert-goer or opera-goer who loved him, he is not dead. He lives on not only in his recordings (which catch most, though not all, of his greatness), not only in countless memories of inspired performances, but above all in the fact that we are nationally and individually a more musically aware people because of him and what he gave us. That is his monument.

(*1961*)

Furtwängler

The present-day cult of Furtwängler among musicians, critics and music-lovers in Britain is both an act of retrospective justice and a sign of our belated maturity as a musical nation. This may seem an unwarranted conclusion to draw from what can after all be represented as a perfectly normal phenomenon: the reissue of old gramophone records, at cheap prices, coinciding with the emergence of a great musician's reputation from the trough which naturally followed his death. But Furtwängler's genius, far from being generally accepted here in his lifetime, was frequently derided, and derided in the name of a delusion. He had his fervent admirers; but to many others he became a byword for the wilful and arbitrary imposition of the conductor's extravagant fancies on the pure long-suffering truth of the music. This ill-repute had little to do with his equivocal actions under Nazism (which only became a serious point of dispute after the war), but a great deal to do with the doctrine of objectivity in interpretation. Rejection of Furtwängler was inspired and justified by the concept of 'the score', 'the notes', the 'correct way' of playing a piece of music—the conceit that it is all there, written down, only waiting for the truly great interpreter who, like Toscanini, is content to observe what the composer says. Furtwängler's greatest antagonist, Ernest Newman, the critic who put his shirt on objectivity, was fond of declaring that when he wanted an ideal performance he went to his study and read the score. In other words, there was nothing left for him to learn about it from anyone. From such a point of view Furtwängler could not have seemed more wrong-headed.

The notion that there is one ascertainably right way to perform a work is curiously persistent, perhaps because it is part of the process of first discovering music. At its lowest, it means that the work is assumed to exist in the one definitive form, i.e. the performance through which one got to know it. In the case of the critic, who has probably forgotten long ago what that was, it is symptomatic of a hardening of the sensitive arteries and a contraction of horizons and sympathies under the pressure of his trade. It is more a listener's notion than a practical musician's, though in practice it can also go with the egoism to which all successful performers are liable. But wherever it is to be found, it is a force for impoverishment. It not only limits response to the music, it negates its very existence. This is as true of the performer as of the listener. The performer must be free in order that he may be faithful. The listener must be free in order that he may experience the music as it comes to him. Furtwängler has, I am sure, contributed to our liberation from the tyranny of this notion. He, who in his lifetime was always being pitted against Toscanini (who despised him), has helped to bring about the abolition of rigidly opposed schools of interpretation and the recognition that the notes tell you only so much; a score is not a blueprint but an encouragement to re-creation, and a variety of conclusions may be drawn from it.

Such tolerance does not mean an end of critical discrimination; interpretations are still valid or unacceptable according to the criteria of experience and personal taste. It certainly does not mean swallowing Furtwängler whole. Everyone can point to performances in which, in his search for the music's inner life, Furtwängler risked breaking its outer shell, if he did not indeed split it into fragments. He could set slow tempos in *Don Giovanni* which must have seemed to many, as they did to me, fundamentally at variance with the manifest spirit and intentions of the music (though slow tempos are by no means generally characteristic of his interpretations, of Mozart or of anyone else).

But such idiosyncrasies, if that is what they are, now command respect at least, because of—in a double sense—what he has shown us: the existence of no 'correct way', and the profound discoveries that come when his search is successful. Furtwängler's undependability is implicit in his greatness. His habit of going faster when a crescendo is marked can be disconcerting or worse (I say 'can be' where ten years ago I would have said 'is'): but it is not the action of a musician of diminished responsibility. We may still dislike it in a given instance; but we can hear it without scorn, realizing that it is an aspect—a negative aspect, maybe—of the loftiest attitude of mind: an attitude for which nothing is taken for granted, nothing is irrevocably set, nothing ever exactly the same; for which truth is approached through study, of course, but study inspired and led by instinct, a work or movement is an organism and an interpretation of it a living thing which, being alive, is unpredictable at every moment, and the element of creative accident is present in every performance worthy of the name. Such an attitude could be unfortunate in a conductor of lesser gifts and weaker understanding. With Furtwängler himself it can lead to some very strange results.

Yet it would be wrong to picture Furtwängler the musician as a child of nature, magnificent when the spirit blew but stumbling when it deserted him. He probably *thought* more about interpretation than most musicians. His sense of form was built up from an accumulation of carefully weighed and pondered details. He was aware of what he was doing and worked patiently and tirelessly to put it into effect. To hear him rehearsing the first dozen bars of the Unfinished Symphony with the Vienna Philharmonic and going over and over them until the players phrase the music as he thinks it should be phrased is to be left in no doubt of that. He knew what he felt and why. For that matter, Furtwängler was quite ready to carry a movement like the opening molto allegro of Mozart's G minor Symphony right through in a single unswerving tempo when this seemed to him the right way to perform it. But his achievements in the last resort depend on what for want of a less vague word one must call intuition. The organic unity he tries to find is an inner, not an outer, unity, which has to be sought beyond the notes, and if necessary round them. Sometimes, in this quest, the outer unity is neglected to an unacceptable degree; or perhaps, to put it another way, the inner unity which would make all things clear on a higher plane of reality is not fully attained. When that is so you can be left puzzled as to why he should have thought it necessary to do as he does. One would have said—for example— that the first movement of the Eroica must move at one comprehensive tempo, and indeed has no need to do otherwise, or that in the first movement of Schubert's Great C major Symphony the second subject must have the same basic tempo as the first. I would still say they should. We are at liberty to feel maddened by what Furtwängler is apt to do in these movements. But he has taught us that there is never any 'must', even in what we like to think of as the most clearcut cases (though I admit that I would make a pretty strong plea for the Schubert as one exception to the rule).

The most obvious qualities of Furtwängler's musicianship concern things that are not written down and yet belong to the blood and sinew of musical performance: sense of line, of the weight and density of chords, of the length and sound of notes. Such things, which by their nature cannot be laid down, expose the fallacy of 'the notes'. They are not in the score but they are in the music. The literal truth rarely stares at us from the page. Are the conductors, like Klemperer, who make a point of clearly articulating each group of sextuplet semiquavers in the opening bars of the Ninth Symphony truer to Beethoven's intention than Furtwängler, who interpreted them as a kind of multitudinous murmur, and in doing so seemed to take you to the threshold of a new universe? No conductor filled the short notes so full of tone. Listen to Haydn's Symphony No. 88 played by the Berlin

Philharmonic under him: the meanest semiquaver sings. Yet—evidence again of the most scrupulous and systematic rehearsal—the orchestral texture remains clear and uncongested; there is nothing in the least sluggish about it. The music breathes. And it 'goes', at a tempo unhurried but irresistible. The whole thing has a kind of solemn jubilation that delights the heart. Even at the most rapid tempo—as in the molto allegro of the G minor, which few conductors have taken so fast—the music has time to sing.

Furtwängler's characteristic sonority is built from the bass. He is just as concerned with weight as with tone; they are aspects of the same thing. The music always has roots; the forte chords in a Furtwängler performance are planted like trees. When he conducted Brahms' Third, the tonic chord in the third bar seemed to release the whole work in a rush of energy; the rest of the symphony was the inevitable consequence of it. This was no isolated stroke or act of sorcery but a calculated process in which the colour, accentuation, dynamics, timing and precise degree of crescendo of the two previous bars played their part. But it had a miraculous, spontaneous character as of natural growth. Similarly, his recording of Smetana's *Vltava* unfolds the work's various stages in one great complex sweep; the performance moves with the naturalness of the river whose progress from source to mouth the music evokes. This is no hypnotism but the art of conducting at its most masterly and true. One cannot imagine the music more faithfully realized.

Yet there remains a visionary quality in Furtwängler's conducting, a sense of the lifting of veils, that is above analysis. That is why he has become something of a god, warts and all. We do not have to respond in every instance, but by rejecting him we deprive ourselves. He sees things that others do not see. In Furtwängler's recording of Leonora No. 2, the horns' answer to the second trumpet call comes as though from the deepest darkness of the prison, almost from another life, while the orchestra listens in

motionless wonderment. It is a moment of revelation, uncanny in its illusion of distance and its power of poetic
suggestion. The effect is doubtless achieved by the most
careful placing and colouring of the notes; but the source
of the insight lies beyond thought, and dungeon depths
below objectivity. But there was never any pretence of that
in Furtwängler's music-making. He was a German to whom
German mysticism, with its profundities and its tendency
towards vaporizing, was native. To him the conductor
could never be a mere reflector or transcriber; he was a seer,
a vessel, and at the same time a constantly enquiring intelligence. This was not a particularly acceptable concept between the wars, in critical ideology at least. And, great
artistic personality that he was, the spell of his presence was
an obvious factor in the impression his performances made,
and helped to impose his conception of the music on those
who succumbed to him. There were also those who disliked
what he did and were impervious to the spell. They ration-
alized their dislike, finding no lack of fuel for it in Furtwängler's eccentricities, and thought of him as an arbitrary
distorter of manifest truths, an unholy magician. But Furtwängler was not the only conductor to exert an appeal that
that has nothing to do with music. Personal magnetism, to a
greater or lesser extent, is a factor in our response to all
great artistic figures, no matter how lucid and impersonal a
character we like to read into their art, and we delude ourselves if we believe otherwise. We find what they make us
think we find. I exaggerate, but there is a truth in it that
is not confined to Furtwängler. It depends whether you
respond, and whether you let yourself respond. His pianissimos were accused by indignant critics of going beyond the
point of audibility. They may have done. But if you were in
tune with him, you heard them.

On gramophone records, where personal magnetism is not
directly active, Furtwängler's most unconventional readings
carry less conviction than they might have done in the flesh

and in the shared heat of the moment. But at their best his recorded performances need no living presence to persuade us of his greatness. His virtues shine out in the recording of *Die Walküre* (which, though made nearly twenty years ago, does not disgrace the splendour of the performance). In the first act, for example, how superbly Furtwängler rises to the height of Wagner's conception, encompassing it in a single arch of understanding. The opening bars at once announce the interpretation's epic scale and character: the giant tread of the bass, massive, rugged, but carrying us powerfully forward, the surge of violins and violas, the gloriously full sonority of the Vienna Philharmonic. The music's lyricism is not neglected or overlaid; the playing is full of tenderness. But it is a momentous, superhuman tenderness. In the full statement of the love theme on solo cellos the effect is of an incandescent beauty, appropriate to the children of Wotan at their destined reunion. The treatment of this passage is characteristic of Furtwängler: the individual lines are drawn with a strong and generous hand; every note glows, yet the phrases are perfectly poised, the relation of the details to the whole gauged exactly. There is no false husbandry in Furtwängler's conducting of Wagner. The climaxes are achieved by raising the temperature even higher, not by keeping it down at other times. Each smaller moment has its own life and intensity, its lesser climax within the larger. Listen to Siegmund's great cry 'Drum muss ich Wehwalt nennen': every drop of anguish is wrung from the notes. But Furtwängler's mastery of conducting enables him to do so without lingering over them. While the notes sing, the tempo moves. The music is always going somewhere; the place which each moment, however expressive, occupies in the total design is never forgotten. Furtwängler moulds the phrases into sentences, the sentences into paragraphs, the paragraphs into scenes, the scenes into one indivisible act. His grasp, conscious and instinctive, of the music's formal processes, his feeling for transition, and his control of tempo, rhythm, accentuation, dynamics and phrasing are such that when the grand climactic moment comes—the drawing of the sword from the tree—it comes with absolute punctuality and overwhelming force. Everything that has been happening during the last hour seems concentrated and fulfilled in that heaven-shattering eruption of sound. Furtwängler is also, incidentally, one of the few conductors (Toscanini is another) who observe that the final chord of the act falls on an off-beat.

But it would be a betrayal of all that we have learnt from him to exalt him as the greatest of all conductors, the man who alone possessed the inmost secret of organic unity. Furtwängler no more invalidates Toscanini than Toscanini invalidated Furtwängler. Klemperer's conception of the opening of the Ninth Symphony has its own truth. It is enough that Furtwängler is appreciated for what he is, one of the supreme interpretative musicians of the 20th century, and enjoyed for what he gives us. He is a great broadener of understanding. He opens doors into worlds we had hardly guessed at, or only in dreams.

Geraint Evans

To call Geraint Evans one of the great singing actors of the age is by no means to exaggerate his greatness. Neither is it to slight his singing. He acts with the voice: the Figaro he sings on the Klemperer recording of Mozart's opera is proof of that. His conception of the character—an uncommonly fiery, rebellious conception—imposes itself no less forcefully than in the theatre. But the voice itself is not especially remarkable: not ugly but certainly not beautiful, somewhat dry in tone, slightly constricted in production, rather narrow in compass. One accepts it for what he has made it, the servant of his comic inspirations. Its limits help to dictate what parts he can and cannot play. Its relative lack of warmth and expansiveness put even the lighter romantic Verdi baritone roles beyond his reach. Falstaff is its furthest point—a character part, despite the lyrical beauty that keeps springing up in the cracks of the old man's ruined life. His occasional attempts to widen the range and type of his repertoire have not usually been successful; his Rigoletto was overtaxed by the vocal demands of the role, and even his Posa was not convincing.

It may be that such attempts were doomed to failure in any case: the very brilliance of his comic persona rose up before us and prevented us from taking them seriously. If so, our instinct was surely correct. Dramatically as well as vocally, that persona is anti-romantic; it is fundamentally resistant to large-scale gestures unaware of their own absurdity, and subversive of all rhetoric that does not laugh at itself. It includes the grotesque and the malevolent but not the grandiose. (Evans's Balstrode, the one unequivocal achievement outside his normal range, is successful because *Peter Grimes* is not a romantic but a realistic opera, and because the part does not demand vocal splendour and is well served by the craggy vehemence he brings to it.) His Scarpia glowers and struts and declaims without persuading us, or itself, that this is the man before whom all Rome trembled. Even his cleverly conceived and well-executed Wozzeck seems the product of effort undertaken against the grain; the grim picture of the Victim is qualified by a slight but obstinate touch of the comic.

If this is an unjust criticism, it is a measure of how powerfully the comedian has impressed himself on our imaginations. His loss is, in the long run, our gain. The field of his talents may be limited, but within it he is supreme. And it is not confined to the merely 'comic'; it is comedy in the fullest sense. The theatrical genius of Geraint Evans goes much deeper than the superficial business of the stage, master of it though he is. His comic characterizations are no doubt meticulously studied; but they strike us as spontaneous creations, born in a flash of sympathy yet illuminating the whole character. Like all great comedians he touches the roots of human life and reveals the universal in the particular. And like all great comedians he is continuously inventive, rarely content to repeat himself from one performance to another. I remember a marvellously effervescent moment at the dress rehearsal of Britten's *A Midsummer Night's Dream*, the first time it was put on at Covent Garden, when, returning from the wings at the head of his troupe after the play scene, he broke into a grotesque high-stepping gallop and wildly brandished his fist in the air. The action perfectly summed up the mood of heady triumph; but although I went to several performances I never saw him do it again.

At the same time, with all his natural, intuitive brilliance he is a performer of scrupulous tact; his instinct for the stage includes an acute sense of the drama as a whole and of his exact place in it at any point. He can play to the gallery without once stepping outside the charmed circle of dramatic illusion. He magnetizes the attention, but he never steals the scene. No one who saw him in *La Bohème* can forget his sudden tensing, and the swift involuntary movement of curved fingertips to lower lip, when Schaunard realizes that Mimi is dead: it was a gesture of inspired simplicity, which caught the full horror of that realization yet remained securely within the non-tragic, pathetic context of the opera.

A typical Evans performance is alive with this sort of effect, touched in with the nicest judgment. Yet it is done without a hint of calculation. Rather, his sense of the character is so profound that, when allied to a thorough technique, it leads naturally to the right execution. He can appear to fix a character like Ned Keene, the raffish but debonair apothecary in *Peter Grimes*, in a few decisive strokes; but it is rather that he has felt himself under the character's skin to the point where everything about his performance is Ned Keene. Geraint Evans is an uninhibited artist. He is a master of slapstick. When he was one of the Bohemians at Covent Garden the student pranks in Act 1 took on an almost alarming abandon. His Bartolo in *The Barber of Seville* is a stumping, fuming anthology of crusty humours and low comic tricks that, old as Aristophanes though they are, seem freshly improvised that instant and are all the funnier for being timed to perfection. His exit from Sachs' room in the third act of *Die Meistersinger* is sometimes so irresistibly comic that the entire house, devout Wagnerites and all, is compelled to drown the orchestra for a few bars in spontaneous tribute to the sheer genius of the man and the completeness with which his whole body expresses the dazed Beckmesser's unholy joy.

Such intense visual impressions are a vital element in his art. His sense of character, his Celtic instinct for the dramatic and his command of facial expression and gesture combine to create images which, once seen, are stamped on one's memory. I shall always treasure the sight of his Tonio, in Zeffirelli's production of *Pagliacci*, hobbling away from the meeting-place of Nedda and Silvio with a struggling gipsy child clamped under one arm and, later, the kind of dogged frenzy with which he played the scene of Tonio's attempted rape of Nedda. Such details are unforgettable because, far from being isolated strokes, they spring from a total conception whose effect is to enlarge the scope and widen the resonance of the role in question. His Tonio seized and held the imagination from the first *coup de théâtre* of the blanched clown-mask thrust through the curtains at the opening of the Prologue; he lived the part, to the least twitch of the awkward limbs or black glint of the darting, sad lost eyes. And his interpretation of Tonio as a peasant Iago was characteristically matched to the volcanic jealousies of Jon Vickers's Canio. As Leporello in the 1962 *Don Giovanni* at Covent Garden, and many times since, he presented an unusually sharp, sidelong view of a part whose music suggests a certain rotundity of vocal style (it was a view perhaps conditioned by the lack of this quality in his voice); yet he made one aware, as few have done, of its universality: he was at once uniquely himself and the eternal servant, mean, furtive, indestructible.

In *A Midsummer Night's Dream* he found his way unerringly to the truths embodied in Bottom's character. The solemn chewing-over of experience which follows Bottom's awakening inspired him to one of his subtlest and profoundest performances. He grasped as though by instinct the significance of Britten's motivic transformations: the metamorphosis of Flute's last cue, a vacant, tripping little figure, into a ruminative phrase for clarinets over a pedal A, then the brief reminiscence of the four magic chords that presided over the previous night's activities, before the bass settles back onto the A and the clarinets softly repeat their phrase. The way Geraint Evans performed this scene and then, at the end, wandered off still talking, puzzled by the dream, absorbing it into his shrewd mind, was a marvellous

picture of *sancta rusticitas*—the shrug of the sensible country-
man, the acknowledgment of a mystery which he accepts as
unfathomable yet keeps returning to with a sense of ever-
widening wonder.

Geraint Evans's most famous role is Falstaff, a role in
which he has no serious rival today. But splendid though it is,
and constantly though he enriches it, I would not myself
choose it to represent him at his greatest. Within its limits
it is a masterpiece of full round humour exquisitely touched
with shades of the mortality that Falstaff so superbly scorns.
But I remain conscious of those limits. I miss the air of
cultivation which should linger round the old reprobate, for
all the low company he keeps, and a little of which has
rubbed off on it (even Bardolph makes classical allusions).
Geraint Evans encompasses Falstaff, the archetypal English
old boy, standing imperiously on his dignity yet incurably
juvenile, fertile in resource, inexhaustible in cunning, brazen
in effrontery, making defeat look like victory, talking his
way out of anything; but the cloud-capping fantasist, the
great creative liar whose inventions are truer than other
people's reality, still eludes him. The part which, to my mind,
epitomizes his genius is Papageno. In it his finest qualities
are united—his mercurial humour, his flair for the stage, his
tact, his sudden dazzling insights that spring from a deep
half-intuitive comprehension of the whole character, his
humanity, his musicianship and sense of Mozartian style.
There is never any shortage of good Papagenos; the part is
so simply and immediately appealing that it is hard not to
be a success in it. But Geraint Evans's Papageno is much
more than that. It is an education as well as an unending
delight, complete as no other Papagenos have been, in my
experience at least, and perfectly judged—pantomime and
allegory, the particular and the general, held in exact balance.

The unpredictable comic artist has, of course, full play (if
the business with the magic bells is not made up afresh
each time, it always seems so—and often is). Evans the card
is in his native element, rejuvenating the hoariest gag or

double take with the refreshment of his personality, button-holing the audience while remaining impeccably within the drama and the character—the little man gibbering with fright yet alert to snatch the slightest chance that may help him to come through with a whole skin. And Evans the natural mime, tirelessly inventive, riveting a situation or mood in a single gesture with the skill of a cartoonist, helps himself with both hands and feet. Since Schikaneder played Papageno and Mozart sent him up from the wings, the music-hall humour of the part can never have been more gleefully and comprehensively milked. But the humour stirs deeper laughter for being rooted in common humanity. Nothing in his performance is more moving or more typical than the silent sympathy for Pamina that radiates from him during the first of her ordeals, while he munches his food and thanks his stars it isn't him. Geraint Evans's Papageno is Everyman in his baser but no less necessary aspect, stubbornly unheroic, bent on survival, thinking of the next meal and the lack of women, not at all sure that it wouldn't be better to have done with the human race and become a bird, yet moved by an inextinguishable fellow-feeling for every creature he meets along his pilgrimage, and in his simplicity demonstrating a wisdom as central and perennial as that which is achieved through the long labours of the spirit.

Gré Brouwenstijn

The name of Gré Brouwenstijn, the Dutch opera singer who finally retired from the stage in 1970, will possibly be forgotten when others who had a fraction of her greatness are still remembered. Gramophone records have artificially extended the natural brevity of the performing artist's span; but Brouwenstijn made very few recordings, and such as there are do not show her true genius. Hers was an art of the theatre, and in the theatre her vocal imperfections were lost in the glow of her presence and the vibrant sincerity she brought to roles which suited her. Her Elisabetta in *Don Carlo*, when seen and heard in the flesh, seemed the very embodiment of the 'soul, not *solfeggi*' which Verdi wanted from his interpreters. But her recording of 'Tu che le vanità' from the fifth act of the opera suffers from technical deficiencies that one hardly noticed when she performed the role: a comparatively weak lower register, a slight unsteadiness of tone exposed by the music's wide intervals and largeness of phrase, and declamation that does not always make the most of the words (though in the opera house she could give the poignant exclamation 'Francia!' a thrilling intensity of regret). Nor, in itself, does the quality of the voice—a warm, appealing, G-majorish quality—seem particularly striking. She sings touchingly, even nobly; it is a good account of a difficult piece. But you could hear it without having the impression that here was one of the great operatic artists of our day.

Brouwenstijn excelled in roles whose moral grandeur or heroic austerity are out of reach of most singers. Her

Elisabetta set a standard; it showed one what the part was capable of, what it must be. She was suffering nobility incarnate. She made the self-denial, the sheer goodness of the reluctant Queen of Spain wholly credible and intensely human. At the same time she conveyed the reality of the Queen's plight, not by any sudden violent inflexion or vehemence of gesture, there was nothing flamboyant about her, but, I suppose—for one did not stop to examine, one simply experienced it—by small significant movements of head, hand and eye and by her whole quiet, agonized demeanour. You felt the pain of a spirit bound to the wheel of political necessity, the grief of a heart imprisoned in the stiff brocaded ceremonial of empire but still beating wildly. Yet—and this was part of its truthfulness—she never broke out from the formality of the queen; she kept rigorously within the unflinching restraint of her interpretation. Even in the final scene, that saddest of all partings—where Verdi, after an Andante in C sharp minor which is the apotheosis of his *lamentoso* style, turns to an infinitely compassionate B major and depicts the lovers' frozen grief by an inspired use of repeated notes over a bass that moves below the voices in wordless sympathy—she seemed to be holding herself unyieldingly in check; she harrowed us with the sense of emotions whose full magnitude would never be revealed, even to herself.

This characteristic sense of heroic fortitude animated Brouwenstijn's greatest and most admired interpretation, her Leonore. Where, in *Don Carlo*, it was a small, subdued point of light, in *Fidelio* it blazed with a flaming fire. The impact in the small theatre at Glyndebourne in 1959, the first year she was seen there in the part, was devastating. You believed in her the moment she appeared. Her tall, loose-limbed athletic grace was a natural advantage that not many Leonores possess. But it was her inner conviction that gave the performance its terrible intensity. She might pass for a youth, but to the spectator her face was a map scored with sorrow, fear, empathy, resolution and greatness of heart. We knew the outcome, but she did not, and every step and look was laden with a fearful consciousness. She made you aware from the first of the danger of her quest—danger not so much from without, though that was ever-present, as from within. You could feel what it cost her. She was a human being near the end of her tether, her nerve stretched so tight that it might snap at any moment. This, you felt, *was* Beethoven's *holdes Weib*, interpreted as he meant it by a compatriot of Rembrandt's: a Leonore who had truly dared everything for Florestan and suffered for him and with him, but with a love so selfless that her 'Nichts' was a simple statement of fact. I cannot now re-member how she sang, but I shall never forget the desperate exaltation her singing communicated. The tension was so tremendous that when the trumpet call had broken it, and the sublimities of 'O namenlose Freude' came to their quiet, radiantly simple end, the normally sluggish audience cheered for ten minutes.

Another work in which Brouwenstijn showed her gift for rising to the drama's tragic heights was *Die Walküre*. I can still see the slim figure of her Sieglinde, taut, touchingly vulnerable, standing before the tree in Wieland Wagner's first production of *The Ring* at Bayreuth. She conveyed un-forgettably the loneliness and the youth of the character, the eagerness and the capacity for joy, the sufferings past and to come. But it was not only such romantic or emotional roles that called forth her genius. She was the greatest Gluckian heroine I have seen, indeed the only great one. Her Iphigénie in the 1960 Holland Festival production of Gluck's German adaptation of *Iphigénie en Tauride* was a vindication, an explanation of Gluck's style and dramatic method. Like the character she interpreted, she was the priestess and sacred mentor of the performance, inspiring everyone involved in it with her fervour and high serious-ness. For once, the fire that Gluck's noble plainness pre-supposes, and without which he can seem so stiff and limited, descended and made all things clear. The drama was a seamless unity and the music, not a note too short or too long, moved with it at every turn. For such artists great composers write their masterpieces, and for such revelations Brouwenstijn will be remembered so long as there are people alive who saw her.

Jon Vickers

Like all singers for whom truth and vividness of expression is the guiding principle of what they do, Jon Vickers has his detractors. Great dramatic singing is, almost by definition, singing that is disliked by as many people as passionately admire it; the quality that strikes one man to the soul grates on another man's nerves. I can well imagine Vickers not being a favourite of that type of opera-goer who treats singing as a higher form of interior decoration and opera as the glorification of bel canto. But without doubt there are others too, confirmed believers in the gospel of opera as drama, who simply do not take to the very individual timbre and manner through which he expresses the outsize emotions that are his natural element. It is no use reminding them that singing of such rugged force is not compatible with smoothness and refinement, that ruggedness is part of its character, and that the feeling it communicates is all-important. Singing is not a subject for argument. The response to any singer is a matter of personal chemistry, but never more so than when the singer is cast in the heroic mould of Jon Vickers.

This is not to say that he is all vehemence and little if any subtlety. On the contrary, he has developed into a highly conscious artist, husbanding and nurturing his voice (which has confounded all the prophecies of doom once confidently pronounced upon it), and constantly restudying and deepening his interpretations. He is that rare phenomenon, a tenor who thinks, and who feels with something more sentient and sophisticated than his entrails. Yet, with all his artistic seriousness, he remains what he was when, lately arrived from Canada, he first startled London fifteen years ago with the untamed zest and energy of his Riccardo in *Un Ballo in maschera* at Covent Garden—a force of nature. And it is to this primordial emotional quality that people react. The almost evangelical fervour with which he strives to project his dramatic conceptions only intensifies the reaction, whichever it is. You can discuss his vocal characteristics, and point to this or that fault or mannerism of style or method, just as you can criticize or warm to his stage personality and the air of transatlantic geniality that still clings to his playing of certain roles; but that is not really what the issue is about —or rather it only externalizes a disagreement of instinct. In expressive passages he has a habit of scooping up to the longer notes, as though lifting them from his boots. He can lapse from high sentiment into sentimentality. He has never fully mastered the technique of even voice production within the whole range of dynamics; his full-voice and his mezza-voce singing tend to be more like two different voices than two aspects of the same voice, and the mezza voce is sometimes so quiet that the musical line is broken. To his detractors such things provide rationalization for their antipathy. To his admirers they are the reverse side of his strength; without them he would be another and less extraordinary kind of singer.

Thus an admirer can concede that Vickers would be a still more effective Peter Grimes if he were to sing a passage such as 'Now the Great Bear and Pleiades' with the firmness of line it demands. But were he to do so, his Grimes would not be what it is, and he would not be Jon Vickers: the pressure of emotion which impels him to disrupt the musical phrase in the instance quoted also gives the interpretation as a whole its ferocious conviction. Certainly there are times when he allows emotion to obliterate singing. But that is the price one pays for his prodigious power. He is that kind of singer; it is because of what he has to say. Even at his magnificent best, he suggests emotion only just contained,

Titanic impulses wrestled with and barely overcome. A great performance by Vickers is like giant sculpture on which the hammer-blows are still visible. Struggle is native to it; a more polished style would be incongruous. His is a voice predestined, like Aeneas and his men, to toil. The scoops themselves are an essential expression of it; they suggest immemorial yearnings, ancient griefs and triumphs dug from the collective unconscious by the sweat of his brow. His world is the world of epic passions

> such as rais'd
> To height of noblest temper heroes old
> Arming to battle.

Restraint is as much a part of their expression as is struggle. He is the least ranting and posturing of tenors, the most formidable in dignity and inner strength. You feel that what comes out is only a fraction of what stirs and seethes within. This sense of turbulent energy held under stubborn control can generate a tension unequalled in opera today. When Vickers plays an introverted character goaded to violence—Canio, Don José, Otello—the whole house sits as though on the edge of a volcano. In the final scene of *Pagliacci* in Zeffirelli's production at Covent Garden, his explosions of fury were the more terrible for the stillness that preceded them; sheer intensity of suffering forced a breach in the grim façade, through which you glimpsed a hell of jealousy. The anguish of Vickers's Canio lifted the work temporarily onto the plane of tragedy. His Don José is overwhelming in its truthfulness to the tragic vision of *Carmen*—the brutalization of a once proud, reserved nature, the subterranean pressure of conflicting passions slowly increasing to the point where they burst out and destroy their object and themselves.

His performance in the last act of *Carmen* is comparable as an all-absorbing operatic experience, to Callas' in the last act of *Traviata* or Jurinac's in the Prologue of *Ariadne*.

Vickers belongs to that élite of opera-singers whose grandeur and veracity of utterance justify the pretensions of the genre. This is what it is about, and for this one waits and keeps the flame of one's faith alight. The higher opera aspires the more vulnerable it is in practice. It incarnates pure concepts—nobility, innocence, evil, the heroic, the good—with a completeness and instantaneousness which no other art that exists in time can equal. (This is one of the difficulties of writing about it: words are necessarily vague, general and diffused where music is precise, particular and concentrated; how can 'purity', 'holiness', 'serenity' begin to suggest the reality that Mozart creates in a few bars of *The Magic Flute*?) But the loftiness of opera presupposes performers who are at home in it and who breathe its eager air without gasping. *Otello* with a tenor bent on vocal self-aggrandizement is still an exciting score; but it is not the music-drama that Verdi wrote. Opera of that degree of heightened reality demands, ideally, a breed of demi-gods, and at the least singers of the intelligence, imagination and vocal authority to make you experience what the music tells you is there. Vickers is one of these. When he throws off his disguise in the third act of *Les Troyens* and sings 'Reine, je suis Enée', the audience, like the orchestra, catches its breath: at that moment he *is* Aeneas. In the second act, where Aeneas questions the shade of Hector, Vickers' voice is charged with the pity and wonder of the words: 'De quels bords inconnus reviens-tu? . . . quelles douleurs ont flétri ton visage?' The idea of the hero, in all its austerity and intoxication, its mixture of stoicism and obsession, comes alive when he sings the last act of the opera. Whatever his vocal shortcomings may be (in a role that asks for at least two different types of voice), you realize that nothing less than this will do.

But the role that brings out and unites his greatest qualities is Otello. His Italian diction is more convincing than his French; and in Italian music he shows a feeling for the shape of the phrases that does not seem to come naturally to him in German music (memorable though he can be in *Fidelio*, *Tristan* and *Parsifal*). Vickers is the only modern Otello who commands both the notes and the moral grandeur of the part. He has the vocal range and the true tenor ring, as Vinay never had. He is a credible leader of men, the chosen general of the State, where del Monaco is merely an Italian tenor and McCracken, for all his exertions, cannot avoid the suggestion of a saloon-bar tycoon. And he has the aura of greatness—greatness of heart, of bearing, of musical and dramatic conception—without which the work remains mere grand opera: the grandest, but no more than that.

The characteristic control of Vickers's interpretation is not what we associate with the conventional operatic Otello who, like a dictator distracting attention from inadequacy at home, throws everything into outward strife and show, and plays the part throughout in Ercles' vein. Vickers gives us something altogether different, deeper, more inward, more gradual, and finally far more catastrophic. In the light of it, the eyeball-rolling, jaw-dropping and air-clutching that are normal almost from the beginning of Act 2 (as though the first drop of Iago's poison produced an instant and total chemical change) seem cruder and less germane than ever. The restraint which makes Vickers interpret the repeated A flats in 'Dio mi potevi' literally and sing them quite simply, without the usual declamatory distortions, is not a negative virtue but part of his whole idea of the role. Perhaps he has reacted a little too much against the melodramatic. The self-regarding, hyperbolic side of Otello's nature—Otello the histrionic artist—is played down (it is in any case a less marked feature of Verdi's characterization of the Moor than it is of Shakespeare's). Vickers' idea is simple; but it has the measure of the tragedy. The natural authority and innate nobility of this Otello bear out the clear intent of the music in phrase after phrase, from 'Esultate' and 'Già nella notte densa' to 'Niun mi tema'. Mastery of himself is his foundation, and its overthrow is in the strict sense tragic. His rage, never merely external, grows within and is the more appalling when it finally masters him. He plays Act 2 mindful that the disintegration of Act 3 lies in the future, still only hinted at. His dismissal of Iago after the Quartet is dignified, abstracted. Even in Act 3 it is only his overhearing the conversation between Iago and Cassio that drives him to frenzy. The preceding Duet leaves us above all with a sense of the pity of it; when Desdemona protests her innocence, he turns away weeping, shaken by deep sobs. Even the repeated 'Indietro!' is delivered without obvious fury, with a quiet, desperate intensity: she must get out of his sight, because he cannot bear to look a moment longer on the image of what she once was to him. The numb horror of 'Dio mi potevi' is in keeping with this mood, as it is with the unequivocal meaning of the music. All this, while making manifest psychological and musical sense, and rather deepening than diminishing the effect of these scenes, reserves to the fulfilment of the tragedy its true character of climax and resolution. The collapse in the castle hall, the murder, and the finality of the end, owe part of their impact, in Vickers's performance, to the long slow build-up of which they are the inexorable culmination.

He rises to them superbly. Indeed, when the great moments come, they do not find him wanting. His strength, when at last it is unleashed, is truly Herculean. At the end of the third act of *Aida* he fills the house with the agony of Radames' despair. He alone makes Grimes's final madness awesome as well as pitiful. The tragic is his native habitat. It pervades his style. We feel it in the casual remark as well as in the resounding statement. When he sings Grimes' first words in the opening scene of the opera—'I swear by almighty God'—one's heart misses a beat: an alien force breathes through the theatre, lifting you suddenly from the bustle of the courtroom into the mind of the proud man apart; the dramatic conflict at the heart of the work is re-vealed in that instant. So indeed the music plainly tells us, in the contrast between the woodwind's spiky semiquavers and the quiet, searching chords on the strings, sustained then abruptly cut short. But such simple strokes are the stuff of great singing, which is the art of communicating the obvious with an urgency that takes possession of us. Great singing is singing that involves us to the soul in the drama's fundamental being.

Vickers does this. And he does it by his singing. There are singers who impose themselves and their interpretations mainly by other than vocal means. But with Vickers the sound of his voice is an inseparable part of the effect his performances have on us and of the way we remember them afterwards. (Although it was thirteen years ago, I can still hear his opening phrase in *Don Carlo*, 'Fontainebleau, foresta immensa e solitaria', and the mixture of grandeur and melancholy with which he infused it.) He is a singer of large virtues as well as of shortcomings. His sense of rhythm is a gift uncommon among tenors of his type. So is his vivid declamation. And despite the fact that his zeal for expressive intensity sometimes tempts him into breaking the musical line, he has an acute sense of the dynamic of a phrase, which he makes you feel with him and follow through from beginning to end so that, though its shape may not be perfectly clear, its meaning is. As with all the great dramatic artists, his singing is not to everyone's taste. You must be able to respond to it in order to receive what it has to communicate. But to those who can, there is no one quite like him. It is as though he were the embodiment of some ancient prophetic cry, with a power to move feelings touched by few in this or any age.

Part III

Performers—2

Sir Thomas in Paris

The tiny gnomelike figure in a rumpled tailcoat, still awesome in its shuffling progress to the rostrum; the body sprung easily but perfectly on bent knees; the bapgipe lift of the elbow, the wristy right hand thrusting haughtily in aristocratic swordplay, the left, wreathed in two inches of white cuff, signing rococo phrases on the astonished air or clinching with clenched fist a crashing fortissimo; the suggestion of a sultan disposing courteous favours on distant provinces of brass and woodwind—these are sights that the English musical scene has been too long without.

But Sir Thomas Beecham, though in exile, is not in retirement. He is taking his orchestra on a tour of Europe and on Thursday and Friday could be heard in Paris. It is, for an Englishman, extraordinarily pleasant, after dining somewhere off the Champs-Elysées, to stroll round the corner and see the familar faces of the Royal Philharmonic Orchestra on the platform of the Salle Pleyel, and find that their great chief looks exactly as he did when one last saw him (except for a haircut of almost Prussian severity) and is, in his 79th year, to all appearances in rosy health and unimpaired vigour, his concentration unflagging, his joie de vivre unquenched, the famous rhythm still one of the prodigies of our time, the vast, dedicated appetite for music unappeased.

Paris has responded with an equal zest. *Le Figaro* writes of 'sa barbiche royale, son air conquérant, sa bonhomie majestueuse, son allure débonaire'. Superficially, it is his 'éton nante personnalité' that has made the greatest impression—

that and his playing of the French national anthem. 'Mais la Marseillaise!', in accents almost of ecstasy, was an exclamation frequently heard during the interval, and *Le Monde* remarks that many French conductors could profitably take it as their model.

What of the performances? It is not Beecham's fault if the sheer force and panache of his personality blind one to his essentially musical virtues, the ungrudging absorption of his whole nature in the work in hand, the search for the creative life at the heart of it, in which, rather than in any 'wizardry', lies the simple secret of his genius. Tchaikovsky's Fourth Symphony at the first concert, which I did not hear, was described by one critic as fulfilling the composer's intention more exactly than any performance he had ever heard, and I can believe it.

Beethoven's Pastoral, the first work on Friday evening, sounded slightly weary. I have heard him give it with more fire and feeling. The Storm was no less academic than Klemperer's at the Festival Hall last Tuesday, the playing of the first horn as unpolished as his instrument. During the interval Sir Thomas must have told the orchestra what to do with the performance and then himself shed twenty years. The second half was a feast. Schubert's Sixth Symphony was a miracle of wit and beauty. Two pieces by Delius, passionately played, sounded almost bearable. At 11.20 p.m. Sir Thomas was settling into his stride. The Festivo from Sibelius' *Scènes héroiques* glowed like an old brandy, a Second Symphony in miniature. Then, with a hoarse cry of 'Come on brass, give 'em hell,' he launched into a performance of the Trojan March which must have reached Berlioz in Elysium and caused him to think more charitably of his ungrateful capital.

(*1957*)

Hotter's Farewell

It was not altogether the fault of Herbert Fliether, the substitute Wotan hastily summoned from Hamburg on Tuesday morning to replace the indisposed Hans Hotter in *Die Walküre* at Covent Garden, that his competent, routine performance was overshadowed by the spirit of the absent god. We had come to witness Hotter's last appearance in the work, and the memory of his tormented grandeur—the deep-set eyes dark with foreknowledge of doom, the huge, baffled gestures, the moist lips pronouncing scorn or benediction—was, unfairly, active throughout the evening. It was no compensation to see instead a Wotan whose exit after the scene with Brünnhilde in Act 2 suggested a grizzled pikeman going off sentry duty, who delivered the terrible prophesy 'das Ende, das Ende' like a barber agreeing that things were not what they had been, and who stood contemplating the sleeping Brünnhilde with the air—no doubt understandable in the circumstances—of a man trying to remember what he is supposed to do next.

The whole evening suffered. Without Hotter's presence or the expectation of it, the old irritations were more obtrusive: the hut door flying open to reveal not the beauty of the forest under the spring moon but an interior view of the far side of the Schneider-Siemssen 'Ring'; the hopeless mismanagement of the fight; the neglect of many of Wagner's stage directions for no discernible artistic reason; the excessively bright lighting in Hunding's hut, which makes Siegmund's failure to identify the object sticking out of the tree as the handle of a sword incredible even when that unhappy character is played by the monumentally obtuse Ernst Kozub; Kozub's fatal impassivity of voice, gesture and expression, all the more exasperating because of the stentorian power with which he sings; the general drabness of the stage pictures, their inadequacy as visual equivalents of the force and colour and poetry of Wagner's music.

The conductor, Edward Downes, was new to the work, and since he was taking over a performance prepared by someone else (Solti, who directed the first cycle), he cannot be altogether blamed for the sluggish rhythmic pulse of the first act and much of the second, and should be praised for his sensitive and generous response to the warmth and tenderness of the third. But even the good things of last year's performance seemed partly eclipsed. Deprived of her natural antagonist, Josephine Veasey's admirable Fricka, her tea-gown scarfed about her, was not quite the radiant termagant I remember. Dvorakova's appealingly youthful, almost girlish Brünnhilde was only spasmodically effective; the concentration, vocal and dramatic, seemed lacking. One could sense the flame waiting for the breath of the god to blow on it.

So Hotter dominated by his absence, and Wotan's farewell was in the end no more than a memory. He was the supreme Wagnerian artist of the mid-20th century. He had his detractors; but he embodied as no one else did the grandeur of Wagner's conception. As Wotan commanding the elements or looking down on the shattered body of his son, as Kurwenal scanning from the ramparts of Kareol the empty sea, as (once and unforgettably at Covent Garden) an inbred, corrupted Gunther, he evoked the heroic simplicity of the sagas, reinterpreted and enriched by Wagner's psychology. Stature, physique and physiognomy were only part of his authority. He put them to superb use. No one else wielded a spear so easily and majestically. No one, not even Otakar Kraus, could stand so still. No one had his power to sustain a large slow gesture like a musical phrase. Finally, he was a great singer. This is not to deny his im-

perfections. But how many Wagnerian singers of the fifties
and sixties have sung better? How many can be considered
other than imperfect? How many, that is, have united
smoothness of line and purity and steadiness of tone to
dramatic insight and expressive intensity? Who, except
perhaps Ludwig Weber, has sung Wagner's music as Lotte
Lehmann, Schorr and Schumann-Heink show us, through
their recordings, that it should be sung? Opera is the art of
the possible. Hotter's voice was far from being an absolutely secure or perfectly focused instrument, nor was it in
itself strikingly beautiful. But it was enormous, and he used
it with such artistry that it could on occasion seem beautiful.
He was a master of subtle, varied and powerful declamation,
without which no amount of splendour of tone will take you
very far. Wotan's long narration in the second act of *Die
Walküre*, a traditional operatic bore, became one of the
most enthralling passages in *The Ring* as he sat, hands on
knees, massive head bowed, eyes staring, delivering it in that
cavernous, incisive whisper. Even at his most 'woofy' he
conveyed the music. He was seen at his greatest at Bayreuth,
where Wieland Wagner's designs and lighting enhanced his
genius. But what we saw at Covent Garden is enough to be
grateful for. He taught us what *The Ring* is about, and all
other attempts at it will be judged by his example.

(1967)

Caro Johnny

Giovanni Martinelli ('Caro Johnny', as the immortal Geraldine Farrar addressed him in one of the many messages of salutation that have been pouring in) was on stage at Covent Garden on Tuesday, between the second and third acts of *Aida*, to receive a gold medallion the size of a plate from Eva Turner in commemoration of his first performance here, in *Tosca*, fifty years ago. It was a stirring occasion, not even marred by the revelation when Miss Turner read out the inscription—after Sir David Webster had been moving us with talk of 'fifty years ago tonight'—that the historic debut occurred not on 22 May, the anniversary date, but a month earlier. The great man enlivened the house with tales of his last appearance here, in the Coronation season of 1937, when the curtains parted to reveal Radames, the returning victor, brandishing an immense Union Jack. The conductor on that particular occasion was Sir Thomas Beecham.

Signor Martinelli, in the fluctuating way that is common with singers' ages, is now said to be nearer 80 than the 76 with which *Grove* credits him, but he looked superb, with his leonine head and serene countenance, and seemed full of vigour. He can apparently sing strongly up to A (his doctor has only forbidden him B flat), and I could not help wishing, during the succeeding Nile Scene, that he and Miss Turner, who was in magnificently vibrant throat and made the 'British Institute of Recorded Sound' roll round the theatre like Brünnhilde's *Todesverkündigung*, would take over for a moment and give us a sample of the heroic style. Charles Craig presents an impersonation of the fiery Egyptian

warrior torn by the great Verdian conflicts of love and duty
that is as phlegmatic as a pork butcher, though it must be
recorded that his voice has grown in power and quality and
fills the house comfortably. Vishnevskaya is a singer of
unusual intelligence and sensitivity to phrasing and colour, a
bit harsh in forte but clear and melodious below it, and she
has the attributes of an actress, with her lithe figure and
catlike presence. But she is not yet an Aida, either in
feeling for the part or in deportment (an air-clutching, white-
of-the-eye-exposing anthology of silent-film gestures with
occasional sideslips into Nineteenth Dynasty, Bow Street
style), or in grandeur of melodic utterance. I am not suggesting that it is Madame Vishnevskaya who is chiefly to
blame for the charade, but only that we have not yet seen or
heard anything like her best in opera. In some ways the
most interesting performance is Louis Quillico's sonorous,
dignified Amonasro, which does something to rescue the
part from the blustering style of recent years. But the current
production's image of the Ethiopian king, bald as a coot and
shiny brown like a milk chocolate Easter egg, remains
unacceptable.

(*1962*)

Sutherland's Sleepwalker

La Sonnambula, which opened at Covent Garden on Saturday with the announcement, to an aghast house, that Joan Sutherland would be singing under the handicap of a heavy cold, ought to have been insufferable deprived of its sole raison d'être, a nightmare of mummified triviality; and I must admit that the alacrity with which we all sat up and took notice at the entry of a quartet of basset hounds in the final scene was a just measure of the dramatic interest to be found in the opera at the very highest point of the plot. Mummified it is, even with a prima donna at full strength to throw a veil of glorious irrelevance over its inanities. The story, set, like *L'elisir d'amore,* in an Alpine village square and concerned with the jealousies and misunderstandings that delay a wedding, has almost none of the wit and local colour and credibility of character which help to pass the evening in Donizetti's work, and the sleepwalking which afflicts the heroine, though a praiseworthy variant of the usual lunacy, never becomes more than a transparent device to keep things going for three acts.

Yet even last Saturday *La Sonnambula* justified itself, by that priceless gift of Bellini's besides which all Donizetti's theatricality and Rossini's high spirits are as sounding brass and tinkling cymbal—his sad, serious, gentle, unfailing musicality. Music is only the beginning of opera, but an opera is nothing if it does not begin with music. Bellini always does that. There is heart in his most routine roulades and a vein of sincerity running through the silliest string of thirds and sixths, not to mention his famous power of self-perpetuating melody. *La Sonnambula* may be the least impressive of his well-known works, in a large theatre at least, but it is still vastly more rewarding than *Lucia*.

At Covent Garden it does not get the full *Lucia* treatment, though Serafin is again there to preside guilefully over the musical side of the proceedings. There were one or two somnambulistic passages in his conducting on Saturday when the ensemble went astray, but these were unimportant compared with his grasp of style and spacing and his wonderfully tactful accompanying of the singers. Filippo Sanjust has designed conventional but quite agreeable sets, and some of his costumes are excellent, but he is no Zeffirelli, while the producer Enrico Medioli does not even seem to have heard of that great man, being content to handle his chorus in the incorrigible old pantomime style which Zeffirelli and Visconti have thoroughly discredited, and to track his principals about with that ancient abomination, the cupola spotlight. On the other hand the resident company comes well out of the evening. Jeannette Sinclair, as the vixenish *ostessa* who fails to get her man, gives a clever study of meanness and envy. Joseph Rouleau, sonorous of voice and twinkling of eye, makes splendid strides both as singer and as actor in the role of the genial *deus ex machina* Count Rodolfo. And the chorus, under Serafin's loving hand, sing with real sensitivity. Agostino Lazzari, as the tenor, is a pleasant-voiced specimen of his tribe, above the general level of Covent Garden importation—though I wish he would not prance onto the village square with quite such a blatantly spurious air of one who a moment before was clearing his tubes in the wings.

But it remained Miss Sutherland's evening. Her triumph —and the gallery was still in full cry when I left the theatre after her umpteenth recall—was partly a triumph of sheer technique. But the part of her voice which was affected most, her middle and lower registers, is in any case the least remarkable. Her supreme achievement—the power to produce from the mezza voce of a large voice apparently effortless

high notes of perfect evenness, radiant purity and, in that
register, unique beauty—was substantially unimpaired; and
in 'Ah non giunge', with the end in sight, she suddenly
cast aside caution and burst out in an ecstasy of jubilation
and relief. Dramatically, we have been here before: the
piteous smile, the pale, lost moon-face, the air of one who
has just been struck by a sandbag. Even her routine enquiry
about the tenor, who is a few minutes late for the celebrations
in the first scene, has to become a faltering, near-to-tears
suggestion of imminent abandonment, more appropriate
to Miss Havisham on her wedding eve. Miss Sutherland's
sleepwalker, as might have been expected, is first cousin
to Lucy of Lammermuir and Elvira in *I Puritani*. We
have not yet heard the last of that *Lucia*.

(1960)

Anna Russell

Anna Russell, a beefy comedienne with a receding wit, had a huge audience in stitches at the Festival Hall on Tuesday. Miss Russell, according to the *Chicago Tribune*, is 'one of the world's greatest entertainers'. The *Melbourne Sun* considers her 'the funniest woman in the world'.

To question this supremacy is to proclaim oneself a prig, a square, a humourless bastard, a beastly spoilsport, like poor old Wotan (from whom she extracts a lot of jolly fun) 'a crashing bore', and—whisper it not in the streets of Kensington—a highbrow. But question it I do. One cannot stand by impassive and unmoved at the spectacle of a minor talent strenuously pumping itself into a major genius, and being hailed as a kind of prophet in the process. Lampooning the pomposities of the music world is her business, a job worth doing but one that requires the sharpness and soft precision of the satirist, who can prise open a rib and extract the mickey before the self-satisfied smile has faded from the patient's lips. Miss Russell thumps her subjects with Indian clubs, pelts them with custard pies, pins rude notices on their backs, sets traps for them with buckets of water which sometimes fall on herself. Occasionally, in all the romp, a genuine victim is laid low, but the wastage of ammunition is appalling. If the technique of art is to conceal art, Miss Russell's lies buried feet deep in sawdust.

But art is not what she is about. On the contrary she is the High Priestess of Anti-Art. This is the reason for her meteoric rise and what makes her the phenomenon she is, if not in the sense intended. There are other reasons too. LP records assure her in advance a prefabricated audience

with built-in responses; her fans have had a ripping evening
before it has begun. She can raise howls of mirth with the
oldest joke in the world, the Joke about the Haggis, which
Archie Rice in his most abject moments would hardly stoop
to. While pretending to ridicule snobbery, she shamelessly
exploits it. No audience keeps up more eagerly with the
Joneses than an Anna Russell audience. She flatters their
knowledge, giving them the scent, leading them on with
craftily dropped morsels (spiced with a pinch of sex)—the
familiar quotations from Schubert, 'l'après-midi d'un quel-
que chose'—so that they feel they are very knowing to be
able to keep up.

But her deepest appeal is at teddy-boy level. She is a
cultural demagogue, a philistine rabble-rouser. The line,
however crudely put over, can't fail. That is why people
do not see that as an artist she stands for amateurism rampant
and the spirit of the charade. All the bewildered antagonism
they have ever experienced at the obscurities of modern composers ('for the tone-deaf singer I would suggest contemporary music'), all the uneasiness at being forced to strike
musical attitudes for social reasons ('it isn't only on this side
of the footlights that the acting goes on'), the sneaking, half-
repressed suspicion that opera is absurd, find in her their
outlet. Here is a woman who is clever, who knows and who
feels just as they do! It is a victory of brawn over brain, and
the British sporting public, who traditionally believe that
art is bunk but have been too much awed by snobbery to say
so, cheer with almost hysterical relief. There was, I swear, a
note of bloodthirsty resentment in the applause which
greeted her jubilant dismemberment of *The Ring*—as if the
ranks of the culturally patronized and downtrodden were at
last wreaking their revenge on the upper classes. If she had
only said the word, we would all have blindly followed her
across Waterloo Bridge, invaded Covent Garden, and broken
up the performance of *Die Walküre* just at the point where, as
she inimitably put it, Wotan was 'nagging Brünnhilde to sleep'.

(1958)

Karajan the Conqueror

Karajan, master of half Europe, has conquered London. At the Berlin Philharmonic concerts last week he drove his glittering war chariot over the outstretched necks of the multitude and they loved it. After the Brahms C minor Symphony at the second concert such a deep-throated roar went up as can rarely have been heard in a concert hall. You felt that anyone daring to dissent would be thrown to the horns. Through the tumult the heavy brass and percussion moved up and the conqueror, who smiled with his lips while his level gaze took us in dispassionately, celebrated his triumph with a performance of the *Tannhäuser* overture so ruthlessly insensitive that, as I stared at those spidery arms feeling at the controls and the faceless trombones, their yelling bells raised to the roof, images of Attila and Frankenstein went feverishly through my brain. It was superb, irresistible, and terrifying. I was glad to get out into the air.

Yet to say just what was wrong with the performances is not easy. With Karajan, just because there is so much beauty on the surface and so little music below it, one is forced back on vague statements about 'lack of feeling' and, still less helpfully, on descriptions of how he seems on the rostrum, the strangely machine-like movement of his arms. There are details of tempo you can criticize, but that never gets one very far. The first movement of the Pastoral Symphony was nowhere near allegro ma non troppo (this was Nature seen from the Autobahn), but did Toscanini never take Beethoven too fast? Karajan's fluctuations of tempo in the finale of the Brahms were disconcerting, but Furtwängler's

could be no less so. Yet Toscanini's structures had a singleness of vision and form besides which Karajan's seem prefabricated; Furtwängler was searching for a truth that
Karajan's performances do not admit the existence of.

Karajan is formidable precisely because what may be
politely called his limitations as an interpreter are indissolubly linked with an exceptional sensitivity in training an
orchestra to perfection. Everything is in place. And it is all,
in a superficial way, intensely alive and musical. You could
not ask for more exquisitely spun lines of violin melody than
in the Scene by the Brook as he conducted it last week, more
ravishingly tender string texture than in the opening bars
of the Brahms slow movement. Karajan, though pre-
eminently a synthesizer of orchestral tone, is no mere flash
boy; his skill is subtler than that. In Beethoven, he does not
crudely flaunt his ego and crack the music into submission
with a showman's whip. He plays what is written, and plays
it beautifully.

Too beautifully, for, once you have got used to the sheer
sound—and with the Berlin Philharmonic that takes a long
time—you suddenly see how essentially undramatic his
interpretations are. Smoothness of line and tonal blend are
the be-all and end-all. Even in the Eroica he ironed out the
accents: there was not a true sforzato to be heard. Except in
his codas, Karajan's range of dynamics is surprisingly
narrow. But all that is forgotten in the crafty blaze of sound
which he rarely fails to summon at the end. Here, I think, is
where this supreme technocrat gives himself away. It is
significant that he, normally the most scrupulous of conductors, should have added cymbals to the last two chords
of the *Meistersinger* prelude. Save everything up till the end,
then let them have it—the formula is fundamental to
Karajan's approach. They are on their feet before the final
bar. What matter if it has little to do with the music?

To dignify this bread and circuses technique by talking of
classical restraint and mastery of form, as some have done,
ignores the fact that classical form is a matter of organic

growth, unity of opposites, resolution of tension; that a symphony is a drama, and truth arrived at by argument. Karajan, the Supermac of the musical establishment, does not like argument and sees to it that awkward facts (explosive sforzatos, unpredicted modulations, extreme disparity of dynamics) are safely smoothed over. There is usually very little inner tension about a Karajan performance. Take away the vote-catching codas and the most striking thing is the lack of incident. Until the end, the scherzo of the Eroica was simply dull; nothing happened—the music did not grow, did not even live. For all the trace there was of the high spirits, the excited suspense, the energy which on any reckoning Beethoven poured into this revolutionary movement, the composer might as well have torn up the whole score and not merely the title page. And this is only one example. Whatever outward adjustments may be taking place, the underlying mood remains the same. Tannhäuser's song to Venus (an exalted, springing melody, but played last week with impersonal brilliance), Falstaff's delight in the Brook from which such rich liquor flowed—it makes no difference: the music purrs superbly and indifferently on. Beauty without form, sound without meaning, power without reason, reason without soul—it is the deadly logic of hi-fi. Machines, we are told, will one day compose symphonies. At present they merely perform them.

(1958)

Rostropovich

The London Symphony Orchestra, in occupation of Carnegie Hall for a couple of weeks, has been treating New York to one of those extraordinary cello circuses in which Rostropovich combines the roles of ringmaster, lion-tamer, high-wire artist and performing seal.

A cycle of 32 cello concertos is not the surest criterion of the best an orchestra is capable of. It is a test of nerve, adroitness, quick thinking, even of survival, but not primarily of artistic excellence. Of the concerts I heard, it was a purely orchestral programme under Kertesz that stimulated the LSO to playing of the spontaneity and fire, the lithe rhythm and eager phrasing, that give them their own distinctive quality and entitle them, at their finest, to be ranked among the leading orchestras of the world. Strauss' *Don Juan*, in particular, was done with a mixture of control and abandon that was ideal. On the other hand *Don Quixote*, in the Rostropovich cycle, was a pretty rough-and-ready affair. It is not a work that fits comfortably into such a syllabus. Its contrapuntal complexity and range and subtlety of characterization can be mastered only with thorough rehearsal, even by the most alert and resourceful players, and only if the conductor, not the cellist, is in command. Rozhdestvensky's tactful, self-effacing efficiency is an important ingredient in the success of these cavalcades; but *Don Quixote* is not a concerto, and much though one may admire the strength and speaking eloquence of the great cellist's playing and splendid though it is to hear and see him as he attempts to gather the whole work in his bear-like embrace, the composer is inevitably the loser.

Rostropovich, if not yet the demigod we have made him in England, has conquered New York by his outsize musical gifts and personality, his stupendous dynamism. The audiences, scanty at first, grew steadily larger and more appreciative. What can one say that has not already been said about this amazing man? I am struck once again by the same contradictions, which are perhaps different facets of the same thing: the combination of mastery and untamed power. He is at once an intensely professional artist and a force of nature which can destroy as well as re-create. In the sheer size of his tone and the wide-spanned grandeur of his line he stands alone. His range of dynamics and tone colours is almost that of a great singer. He has widened the technical and expressive possibilities of the instrument, as Casals did in his time. The voraciousness of his musical appetite, the indefatigable energy and high spirits, the ferocious concentration and unfailingly retentive mind, stagger the imagination. At rehearsals he reveals a conductor's knowledge of the orchestral score. As always, he played everything from memory, including a formidably difficult new work by Lukas Foss, commissioned by Rostropovich for the festival.

Then abruptly you are confronted with the other side. When he plays a concerto by Vivaldi the result is, artistically speaking, impossible. At large in the baroque or the rococo, he is like a peasant running amok in a St Petersburg drawing-room, a one-man revolution. He takes the allegros so fast that not even he can articulate the notes properly or play them all in tune; the music sounds rough-hewn and coarse. The mildly expressive adagios wilt in the fierce heat of a soulful, alien intensity. One cannot help smiling—there is something childlike and endearing in this naïvely rustic performance. But considered as a piece of interpretation, it is a monstrosity, the wonderful powers abused, applied without regard not only to the style but to the character of the music. In the Dvořák concerto his restless daemon, to my taste (brought up on Casals), subverts the structure by wayward rhythm and constant changes of colour, and turns delight to irritation. But then suddenly some phrase will awe criticism into silence by its beauty and rightness; a whole work will march with an inevitability that only a mature artist of genius can achieve. No doubt he will always be like this, as phenomenal for his splendours and insights as for his perversities.

(1967)

Fischer-Dieskau and Elisabeth Schumann

There will be many people for whom a new recording of *Die schöne Müllerin* by Fischer-Dieskau is such an obvious automatic winner that to suggest it has serious and even fundamental defects will be both useless and blasphemous. Yet that is what I must suggest after listening to this stimulating, sensitive and often beautiful performance.

The first defect is one over which the performers, once they decided to perform the work, had little or no control: Schubert's songs, in this cycle, do not suit the baritone timbre and register. Their whole character is that of tenor songs and, however much remains, an essential truth is lost when the brightness of the unreflecting tenor is replaced by something warmer, darker, more knowing. A song like the divinely fresh and artless 'Morgengruss' cannot, whatever the singer's art, make its effect if it is sung a tone lower by a baritone. In transposing them down, one also alters the character of the piano accompaniment. Fischer-Dieskau does not lower them as much as many baritones, and in a few of them he retains the original key; and thanks to the skill of Gerald Moore the heavier accompaniments are often cleverly lightened without becoming too discreet. Nevertheless, again and again the wrong character emerges. In the opening song of the cycle, 'Das Wandern', the piano already sounds too tubby; the footloose, carefree wayfarer has become a purposeful hiker with hobnail boots, rucksack and alpenstock. In the third song, 'Halt', the semiquaver figure in the bass which runs through the accompaniment like the noise of the turning mill-wheel growls and grumbles in the lower key, despite all Mr Moore's efforts.

The second defect, it seems to me, is that Fischer-Dieskau's deeply sensitive and thoughtful interpretation slightly but significantly distorts Schubert's intentions. It is simply too sophisticated. Of course lieder-singing is an art of extreme sophistication. But in such songs as these the singer must, so to speak, get the sophistication over beforehand. Fischer-Dieskau practises his art with such refinement and evident dedication that we become aware of it when we should be aware only of the young miller's emotions. It obtrudes on them and makes the miller himself seem intelligent, subtle, self-conscious. Characterization disrupts the song instead of being contained within it. The music's spontaneity is overlaid. In 'Feierabend', for instance, Fischer-Dieskau's sense of the ambiguities in the young miller's rather boastful, self-important exuberance leads him to 'put in' expression, with several dynamic changes in a single phrase, instead of letting it come out of the music. The singer, too responsive to the words (and that is after all possible even in lieder-singing), cannot resist the urge of his restless intelligence to colour the music according to their literal meaning. In the final song, 'Des Baches Wiegenlied', where the stream which set the young miller first wandering now laps his dead body to oblivion, Fischer-Dieskau has to 'register' the reference to the far-off hunting horn of the miller's successful rival. This seems to me an excessive subtlety. The point of the reference is surely that if the horn calls from the green wood the brook will only wrap the miller more closely in its all-obliterating arms: if anything, the allusion intensifies the mood of stillness and holy, mindless peace (so beautifully realized in the Pears-Britten recording) which is sustained throughout the song and which Fischer-Dieskau's word-colouring only succeeds in breaking. In the same song there is a self-consciousness in the phrase 'In dem blauen kristallenen Kämmerlein' which tarnishes the simple beauty of the image, making it slightly 'pi'.

There is no denying the popularity in this country of Fischer-Dieskau's high-powered, intensely decorative style of lieder-singing. But if so many English music-lovers prefer their lieder dressed up, it may be for the mundane reason that the words the singer sings belong to an alien language and therefore, not being immediately or fully apprehended, cannot properly play their part; the listener comes to depend for his experience on projection. It is a cult that could not flourish round a less than remarkable artist, and needless to say there are outstanding things in this performance, not only details which, however questionable, are in themselves superb—like the smile that Fischer-Dieskau gets into his voice in 'Tränenregen' at the words that describe the flowers nodding and blinking by the edge of the stream—but also some whole songs. 'Der Neugierige' is beyond reproach because, besides being sung with a most beautiful flow of tone, the feeling—the yearning and exaltation, the anxiety and eagerness of the lovesick miller—is conveyed vocally; the song is allowed to be a song and, for all the singer's subtlety, to seem to sing itself. But it is a rare example of Fischer-Dieskau restraining his inclination to smother Schubert with too much science.

With Elisabeth Schumann there was no such danger. And yet there was no lack of art of the finest delicacy in her lieder-singing, as the second volume of her collected Schubert recordings reminds us. These performances were made between her 49th and 62nd years but, frail though she sometimes sounds, they are hardly to be faulted. Schumann's mannerisms—the audible catch of breath like an up-beat, before certain words such as 'Lachen' or 'Liebe', the tendency to scoop up to a long note and attack it piano and then swell on it—can be maddening in the hands of her Viennese imitators. With her their effect is almost always natural and right. The silvery, birdlike voice, which she kept almost to the end, was admired by many in England for the wrong reasons—for its 'purity', 'unearthliness' and the rest. It was capable of expressing, or rather suggesting, the most intense and passionate emotion. But with her the spontaneity of song is paramount. She has the quality I miss in Fischer-Dieskau—a naturalness that comes from not forgetting that a song, before and after it is everything else, is a lyrical utterance. Schumann's singing is full of subtleties, but they are musical subtleties springing from a warm and vivid response to the song. Hearing it, one realizes that lieder-singing consists fundamentally in feeling—feeling allied to good diction, a strong and supple vocal line and an appealing voice. The words must be clear; the music does the rest. In 'Des Baches Wiegenlied' on this record, the hunting horns do not break the glassy surface; the words are allowed to make their point but remain subservient to the musical thought.

It is not only in lyrical songs that Schumann is superb—the exquisite 'Nachtviolen', or 'Der Einsame', where the well-being of the sitter by the hearth is unforgettably caught and summed up in the delicious lazy curve of the final phrases. 'Frühlingstraum' from *Winterreise* shows quite as impressively her power of dramatic characterization. The dead coldness of 'Da war es kalt und finster' strikes with a physical chill. The sadness of the dreamer who half-knows that his vision of spring flowers is an illusion is evoked with haunting poignancy, and from it follows inevitably the increase of tension in the tone and accent of her singing of the second verse, 'Ich traümte von Lieb um Liebe'. These and other truths are conveyed vocally, by variations in the musical intensity. Elisabeth Schumann, in fact, held the perfect balance between the old ideal of characterization within beauty of line and the modern ideal of subtlety and psychological realism. This is one reason why she sounds like a voice from another world and yet speaks to us directly, with such eager, unwearied freshness.

(1962)

The Leningrad Philharmonic

The supremacy of the Leningrad Philharmonic, demonstrated in four concerts at the Edinburgh Festival last week,
has a touch of the fabulous about it, even allowing for the
fact that orchestras commonly play better on tour than at
home. The orchestra struck Edinburgh like some force of
nature harnessed by science, a secret weapon of orchestral
technology. But its triumphs are based on the simplest of
musical formulas: the players all play together. This exotic
practice of an elementary principle always comes as a
revelation. How often do we hear anything approaching the
unanimity, the discipline and ravenous zest of the Leningrad
players? The RPO under Beecham can convey the sense
of an orchestra possessed by a single artistic purpose. The
LSO and the Philharmonia occasionally give glimpses of the
same thing. But we grow so used to the half-measures doled
out most of the time even by our best orchestras that
suddenly to be confronted with the singlemindedness of the
Boston or the Vienna Philharmonic or the Berlin Philharmonic is to experience with a shock, as if for the first
time, the startling sound of an entire orchestra, back desks
and all, playing what is written. The Leningrad players
belong in this rare class.

It is not primarily a matter of tone quality. The strings
(disposed by their conductor, Eugene Mravinsky, in the
old way, with first and second violins placed opposite each
other) do not achieve the effortless glow of Vienna or the
massive golden solidity of Berlin—it would not be in
character. They have a bright, fierce brilliance like perfectly

tempered steel. By Western standards the woodwind play with a vibrato that is sometimes uncomfortably wide and rapid. In solo passages the horns give forth a moan like displaced saxophones, the trombones move in slow waves of sound, the tremendous trumpets splay out their strident beat with quivering insistence.

These are questions of taste. What is beyond dispute is the sovereign mastery and accord of each section. The woodwind's precision and attack give unrivalled glitter to the orchestral tutti; the scale passages in the third movement of Tchaikovsky's Sixth Symphony can seldom have sounded so thrilling. The brass (with the horns placed directly in front of their noisier colleagues, not separated from them as they normally are) are welded into a single block of metal, superb in its strength and thrust; the trombones' low-lying triad at the end of the Tchaikovsky March stood out as I have not heard it before, with a wonderful refined ferocity, the horns' soft chording at many points was impeccable, while the playing of the whole section in the climax of the first movement was overwhelming in sheer weight and sense of catastrophe.

This perfection of ensemble is even more striking in the strings. Their tone is exactly gauged from top to bottom. The separation of first and second violins—an arrangement now rarely found in the West, though still favoured by a few conductors, notably Klemperer, Kempe and Boult—is no doubt a factor in the extraordinarily clear definition of the string texture (and has the incidental advantage of making sense of the opening of the last movement of the Sixth, where Tchaikovsky conveys the idea of a mind in turmoil by dividing the melody note by note between firsts and seconds —an effect that is frustrated when, as usually happens, the notes all come from the one direction). The double basses (bowing in Continental fashion) form a mighty foundation, leaner in tone than German or Austrian basses, but equal to the best of them. In the first allegro of the Tchaikovsky their fortissimo major third had the bite and sonority of only a very few orchestras in the world; the grinding minor seconds in the finale of Beethoven's Seventh Symphony would not have been disdained by the Vienna Philharmonic itself. The strings' attack is reckless in its enthusiasm, their concentration, seemingly to a man, unbroken in pianissimo and fortissimo. So disciplined are they that at any one moment the effect is of every first violinist, second violinist, violist, cellist or bass player applying the same force to the identical part of the bow. The rushing demi-semiquavers in the March were one whiplash of flashing sound, but they were not more remarkable than the deep hush of many pianissimo passages in the first movement, or the minute concentrated whisper of the opening bars of the *Figaro* overture. This same sense of total participation extends to the percussion, who play as if the enterprise hung on their lightest drum-tap. The warrior cymbal-player strikes his brazen plates with a downward movement unknown in the West, a slicing scimitar blow of Oriental ruthlessness and finality.

What is true of each section is true of the whole orchestra. They play as one man. The Leningrad concerts have given a new, a completer meaning to the conventional signs of orchestral dynamics. More than anything it is this passionate literalness, within a range which stretches at either end to the full *pppp* and *ffff* of Tchaikovsky's markings, that is the secret of the orchestra's power. When the music says crescendo, every player concerned does precisely that and does not let go the pressure until it tells him to. Equally, the diminuendos are graded with an evenness that would be notable in a single instrumentalist, let alone in a hundred; they sink down to a softness whose intensity comes from the fact that every player is contributing his atom of tone. The effect of this simple ability to increase or decrease the sound continuously right through a phrase or sustained note is revolutionary: the music grows and breathes with heightened life. Indeed I do not find anything machine-like and inhuman in their unanimity. They play together as they do because Mravinsky, a great orchestral trainer as well as a conductor of uncommon power, has wrought them to a fighting pitch of ensemble, but also, even more important, because they feel it so. Their phrasing has the vitality that can only come from individual musicianship freely expressed.

It is playing that likes to characterize the music. The woodwind in the scherzo of Shostakovich's Fifth Symphony were dramatized into figures in an ironic farce mimed by a team of grotesques. Mravinsky is a conductor who excels in dramatic music. His is not a relaxed art. The 5/4 movement in Tchaikovsky's Sixth was, I felt, slightly too unrelenting to catch the lilt and charm of the music. In Tchaikovsky's Fifth Symphony there were some exaggerated effects of crescendo and decrescendo which to my mind destroyed the natural shape of the phrases. But the main impression was formidable. In the finale of the Fifth the double bass crotchets beneath the long D major/C major melody stamped like the hoofbeats of medieval chargers. At the climax of the slow movement Mravinsky released the slowly accumulated tension with a quadruple forte of prodigious grandeur and intensity. The allegro vivo in the first movement of the Sixth, often a conventional 'outburst' of neurosis, was a cataclysm of stupefying dimensions (and as much by the tense pianissimos, faithfully observed, as by the engulfing fury of the whole orchestra in spate); one was staring down into the boiling vats of a human being's personal terror, face to face with the agony of mind that produced the notes. Such experiences do not often happen in a concert hall; but what else did the great composers mean when they wrote such music?

It is tempting to see signs of 'ideology' not only in the obvious dedication of the players to a collective idea but in the heroism of Mravinsky's interpretations. If the finale of Shostakovich's Fifth Symphony was made for once musically convincing by the fervour with which it was played, the finale of Tchaikovsky's Sixth was considered by many to have sounded unnaturally affirmative, skirting the pit of despair into which Tchaikovsky is plunged without reprieve. Mravinsky certainly did not linger over the movement; nor do Tchaikovsky's markings suggest one should. He did not wring the last drop of anguish from the suspensions, the separation between the horns' dissonances and resolutions being markedly emphasized. I thought that tragedy was present nonetheless, ennobled perhaps, but no less powerful for being treated with classical objectivity. But however one reacts to the Russian view of Tchaikovsky, it is impossible not to enjoy and be grateful for the stimulus, the excitement, the superb dash and vivacity of the performances of this great orchestra. It plays in London next week and should not be missed.

(1960)

The D'Oyly Carte

31 December 1961. Scene, the Savoy Theatre, at the conclusion of *Princess Ida*. It is the last day of the Gilbert and
Sullivan copyright, and the eve of war. Outside, the board
says House Full. Within, in the words of the *Guardian*,
'half the D'Oyly Carte company's administrative staff [are]
onstage with the singers to take a series of rapturously
insistent curtain calls'. All over the theatre Savoyards (one
of whom, a Cheshire schoolmaster, has popped his silver to
throw a party for past and present members of the company)
are joining hands, 'strangers and friends alike, laughing,
tearful and utterly loyal, [to raise] their hesitant British
voices in Auld lang syne'.

There is not, of course, the smallest danger that auld
acquaintance will be forgot. The mood of this season, of
which the demonstration on New Year's Eve was only the
most ardent expression, has all along been one of conquering
ease, happy comradeship, of going forward together in un-
troubled confidence into a new and more golden monopoly
with this great and characteristically British company of
whom we are so justly proud. There has been no sense of the
beleaguered defiance of a tradition declining into senility.
It is not even a closing of ranks, backs to the wall, against the
modern age. They believe they can afford to be tolerant
of their new competitors. When the general manager, Mr
Frederick Lloyd, says that 'as far as the D'Oyly Carte Opera
Company is concerned, 1961 is not the beginning of the
end but the end of the beginning', he means exactly what he
says.

What is there to be feared? For the audiences who throng
the Savoy, the modern age does not significantly exist. 1961
can be ignored because it is really still 1901. For them, to
attend a D'Oyly Carte performance is to have one's dearest
reflexes tenderly stimulated and to return, for an evening,
to an age in which the Empire is big and red on the map,
income tax is 1s in the £ and America has not yet been
invented. In *The Mikado*, at the words 'apologetic statesmen
of a compromising kind/Such as What d'ye call him,
Thing'em-bob and likewise Never-mind', while I was hesi-
tating between various members of the present Cabinet an
aged female voice nearby exclaimed 'Churchill!' The description hardly fits any of the last three bearers of that
name; but I swear she meant Lord Randolph.

But my impression is that it is the young as much as the
old who keep the torch burning. The sacrament of G and S,
preserved and administered by its chosen priests, nourishes
and draws strength from the national neurosis of not wanting
to know. It keeps our nostalgia green and always fresh. So
long as this mentality does not change, so long will the
tradition flourish. Indeed, of the few concessions to modern-
ity that the company has permitted itself to make in the
text, most strike a jarringly inconsistent note. 'That singular
anomaly, the televisionist', in Ko-Ko's list of people ripe
for execution, may be good for approving laughs, but it is,
like the policeman's lot, not a happy one. As for the replace-
ment of 'blacked like a nigger' by the feeble 'painted with
vigour', it carries no conviction and is only a reminder of
things better forgotten, an alien uncomfortable world
pressing beyond the walls of the theatre. Within those walls
all is still for the best in the best of all possible worlds.

This is the strength of the traditional productions. It is
not so much the particular lines themselves that tell—the
puns, the paradoxes, the tags, the topical allusions (Captain
Shaw, parliamentary trains, and the rest)—as the soothing,
splendid atmosphere they re-create of a past when Britain
really ruled the waves and Britain set the world ablaze. That

is why the jealous preservation of every move and gesture
hallowed by Gilbert's prompt-book, every semaphored sigh
and smile and tantantara, is axiomatic. Equally, no doubt,
the finer points of Sullivan's music and his parodies of opera
are lost on most of the audience, who never exercise their
brains (that is, assuming that they've got any) with questions
of musical standards and accuracy, and who take a skit on
sentimentality at its sentimental face value.

G and S D'Oyly Carte style, in fact, is a quasi-religious
institution: change must come imperceptibly, if at all. And
like most religious institutions, it embodies a denial of its
founders' intentions. By a final Gilbertian paradox its popularity is based on an exact inversion of the original spirit.
That terrible weapon of the English, the ability to laugh at
themselves just so far as is necessary to take the sting out of
satire, has once again been unfairly at work. The operas are
cherished for the very sacred cows they once mocked.

For this reason, if for no other, the challenge of competition is overdue. But there are, of course, other reasons. The
chief is the state of the music. It may be argued that Gilbert's
plots and period wit could not survive except in the stylized
productions that have been handed down. It can also be
argued that if the audience do not catch the echo of 'Why
do the nations' in the opening chorus of *The Mikado* or the
snatch of Bach's great G minor Fugue at the reference to
'classical Monday Pops', or even if it treats a bit of cod
pathos like Katisha's 'Alone and yet alive' as a serious and
very affecting piece of work, no matter. But it cannot be
argued, least of all by professed admirers of Sullivan, that the
D'Oyly Carte tradition has in living memory done more
than very rough justice to the music. In some respects, it is
true, standards have improved, particularly in the orchestra.
I remember performances of *The Mikado* in the not so
distant past in which the bassoon fluffed his solo in 'Three
Little Maids' with damnable precision. At the Savoy,
though the string tone is weak and uningratiating, there is
some good wind playing.

And, on certain nights, there is Sir Malcolm Sargent to restore a sense of musical values. I am tempted to regard this as his finest hour. It has not always been so. Sir Malcolm reorchestrating *L'enfance du Christ* for Anglicans, Sir Malcolm publicly asserting that Beethoven's Eighth Symphony could be an early work—these were, with respect, ridiculous figures. But Sir Malcolm taking the bandmaster's rigidity out of the rhythms, lightening the musical articulation, observing the spirit and letter of Sullivan's scoring, shaping the phrases with the affection of one who truly loves the music because he truly understands it—this is Saul among the prophets, and it does one good to hear it. The crime of the D'Oyly Carte has been that it has tended to reduce the English Offenbach to the level of a superior pier-end tune-smith. As it is, even with Sir Malcolm at the helm, the poor quality of the voices—bottled voices, breathy voices, pinched voices, wobbly voices, bleating voices, hairy voices and voices as bald as old tennis balls—is not to be disguised. There is hardly a singer at the Savoy who achieves a decent all-round standard of tone, rhythm and phrasing, and many who fall miserably below it. Yet how many Savoyards are not perfectly satisfied with the singing they get, and would not endorse Sir Arthur Bryant's words in the souvenir programme book about dedicated artists training to sing the operas as their author intended them to be sung? Whatever the debt we owe to the D'Oyly Carte for keeping the works in constant circulation (and I acknowledge it, along with millions), such complacency cannot go unpunished, nor the Guthrie and Sadler's Wells invasions arrive too soon. Even in the matter of stage personality—the strong suit of the D'Oyly Carte in the days of Darrell Fancourt and Sydney Granville—only John Reed, especially good as the Lord Chancellor, and Donald Adams, a splendidly overblown, disgusted Mikado, carry on the old tradition with the old authentic skill and panache.

Besides, it is the least compliment that ought to be paid to the vitality of G and S to put it to the test of new methods.

It may be found that Gilbert has no future outside the D'Oyly Carte straitjacket. Personally, I believe his wit should have no difficulty in proving its topicality in an age when What d'ye call him is Foreign Secretary, not to mention the perennially hot competition on both sides of the Commons for Ko-Ko's allusion to 'apologetic statesmen of a compromising kind'. I agree with the implication of Groucho Marx's dictum, delivered after he had appeared as the Lord High Executioner in New York: 'If this doesn't kill Gilbert and Sullivan, nothing will.' At the very least we may hope that the end of copyright will lead to performances which are imaginative, flexible and prettily designed within traditional lines, conducted as Sir Malcolm has shown how, and above all well sung.

(1962)

Part IV

Miscellaneous Essays and
Reviews

The Diabelli Variations

The Diabelli Variations is a classic instance, amongst other things, of the role of chance in the genesis of great art. The role is modest, being limited to giving the little push which sets the inner mechanism of the creative artist in motion; without a predisposition, the external prompting would be as fruitless and forgotten as the seed that falls on stony ground. It is clear, for instance, that Beethoven's predisposition to compose a work on the scale of the Variations must have been considerable, given that he was already involved in completing the Ninth Symphony and the Missa Solemnis. But when the soil is ready, a random hand—in Henry James' phrase, a 'dropped grain of suggestion'—may determine what grows there. Would *The Ambassadors* have come into existence if James had not heard of W. D. Howells' admonition to a mutual friend?—'Live all you can: it's a mistake not to. It doesn't so much matter what you do—but live . . . I haven't done so—now I'm old. It's too late . . . You have time. You are young. Live.' The whole glowing intricate masterpiece springs from that single germ.

The grain of mustard seed that grew into the Variations was a publicity stunt on the part of the publisher Anton Diabelli; and the work, with all its transcendent genius, retains a touch of the showmanship of its origin. It is the greatest work in the literature of the pianoforte, and it is the apotheosis of the Beethoven who, after improvising like a god, would startle his rapt audience with raucous laughter and the violent shutting of the piano lid. Diabelli's idea had been to get the leading Viennese and Imperial composers of

the day to write one variation each on a theme composed
by himself, as a contribution to a spectacular compendium
of modern piano music. He succeeded in assembling fifty
representative talents, including Carl Czerny, Vorsischek,
the Archduke Rudolph (disguised by initials), Mozart's son
Wolfgang Amadeus the younger, Moscheles, Hummel,
Liszt (then a boy of 12 or so), and Schubert, though not
Beethoven. But the fame that was to reward the enterprise
went beyond his wildest dreams for, like some unwary
merchant in the *Thousand and One Nights* who unwittingly
conjures up a mighty djinn, he stirred Beethoven into writing
not one variation but thirty-three. In the event Diabelli's
collection appeared (in 1824) as the hind quarters of a
fabulous monster whose head consisted of Beethoven's
personal compendium.

A contemporary critic observed that not the least remarkable thing about Beethoven's work was its being
based on a theme which 'no one else would have considered
capable of such treatment'. It is in fact the only example of
Beethoven writing a major work or movement in variation
form on a theme composed by someone else. Yet Diabelli's
sprightly, commonplace tune holds the key to the unique
character of the work. It was partly that the tune, with its
characteristic stepwise ascent and tonic-dominant-tonic progression, had the crucial virtue of a simple, clear-cut design
(one virtue it shares with the themes of the great variation
movements in the piano sonatas Op. 109 and Op. 111, composed in the same period) and thus lent itself to variation,
especially Beethovenian variation. But what must also have
appealed to Beethoven were the flaws in the theme, or rather
the stimulus they perversely offered. The harmonic awk-
wardness of its crude sequential repetitions challenged his
powers and aroused his instinct for the bizarre. It was
precisely its combination of primitive vigour and maladroit-
ness that marked it out as a basis of a work that is at once
a *summa* of his whole art and an intellectual *tour de force*
in which the sublime is constantly interfused with the

grotesque and the composer plays the dual role of quick-change artist and explorer of the universe, emperor and clown. Behind and within the Variations' paradoxical, even enigmatic character—mystical and histrionic, whimsical and exalted—stands Diabelli's unsuspecting but decisive waltz. Everything that happens during the work happens because of it.

Variation was the natural field for such an exploit. Till then, Beethoven's great achievements in variation form had taken place in a symphonic context. In the finales of Op. 111 and the Eroica Symphony, for instance, variation serves as an extension of sonata form, a resolution or sublimation of the conflicts proposed and carried on in the previous movements. Here, on the contrary, sonata is subsumed and absorbed; the drama of key relationships is largely set aside; variation is the alpha and omega; and, as the first principle of all music, it serves as a gigantic demonstration of pure creativity, with the most apparently trivial material chosen so as to show off the godlike art of transformation. The Diabelli is the highest expression of the great tradition of organic development which runs through German music from Bach to Mahler—the power of making a seemingly limitless variety of possibilities grow from the smallest germ, which we see at work in—for example—*Die Meistersinger*, Haydn's F major Quartet, Op. 77, and Bach's organ Fugue in B minor (the subject of which is hardly more than a five-finger exercise). In Beethoven's Variations even the little decorative turn which introduces Diabelli's theme is not too humble to bear the weight of the argument, and is forever appearing in radically different melodic and rhythmic characters. Earthy and cross-grained in the humorously protesting Variation 9, in No. 11 it is all tranquillity and light. In No. 16 it becomes an explosive trill with a dramatically delayed resolution, in No. 31 a florid baroque upbeat which blossoms into a wonderful profusion of ornament. In its last and most surprising metamorphosis, in the final variation, its childlike naïvety earns it an honoured place in paradise; here the turn merges with the complementary flourish from the third bar of Diabelli's theme to produce a beautifully serene figure, familiar from the Trio of the Ninth Symphony, where it contributes to a similar mood of unencumbered happiness.

With all their fantastical diversity, in fact, there is nothing capricious about the Variations. Even the burlesque reference to *Don Giovanni* (No. 22) is motivated. Each imaginative flight is a fresh exploration of the hidden potentialities of the theme. Beethoven's art both demands and makes possible a method of the utmost flexibility. He builds his melodic and contrapuntal designs with material evolved from whatever elements in the theme seem fruitful, however apparently insignificant; and for the foundations he uses its harmonic structure. The theme's total shape, remaining as a constant, provides at once a framework and a dynamic impulse for the free play of fancy. Invention, grounded in discipline, is released by it. Given the nature of Beethoven's genius, the scope is boundless; and the Diabelli Variations duly ranges across the Beethovenian universe. Every aspect of his artistic personality is distilled in it, from the heaven-challenging assertion of the power of the human mind to endow the raw clay of notes with infinite life, to the discovery of truth, at the end, in a simplicity beyond conflict. (Bach achieves a comparable effect at the end of the Goldberg Variations by returning to the unadorned quietness of the aria with which it all began; but, for a dramatic composer, something outwardly different was required, quite apart from the fact that to have returned to Diabelli's waltz would have been one surprise too much, even for Beethoven.) The sweet sublimities of the Op. 109 variations, the Eroica finale's delight in pure energy, even the visionary immobility of Op. 111, are present; but so are the tragic declamatory gestures of the Arioso of the Op. 110 Sonata, the lyricism of the F sharp major, Op. 78, the epigrammatic brevity of the Bagatelles and the intellectual breadth of the first Rasoumovsky Quartet, the rhythmic drive of the

Seventh Symphony, the horseplay of the finale of the Second, the manic exuberance and ferociously comic self-portraiture of the Eighth.

Comedy, indeed, is never far away. The whole work, in a sense, is a jest, a piece of Olympian sport at Diabelli's expense. The story of Beethoven marching into the astounded publisher's office and throwing thirty-three variations on his desk with a brusque 'take it or leave it' is no doubt apocryphal; but there is a symbolic truth in it. Similarly, though Schindler is the least dependable of witnesses, his account of Beethoven exclaiming ironically that Diabelli would 'have a variation or two on his cobbler's patch' corresponds to the reality of the matter. The obvious flaw in Diabelli's theme is the clumsy harmonization of the middle section of its two halves, in both of which a phrase in the subdominant (F) is repeated in identical form a tone higher —an example of the most primitive kind of sequence, the so-called *rosalia* or 'cobbler's patch', which all good composers are taught to avoid. Beethoven avoids it too (though here and there he disdains to—in Variation 19, for instance), but in doing so teaches not only Diabelli but also the succeeding generation of piano composers some instructive lessons in harmonic resourcefulness.

Diabelli's difficulties inspire a fascinating variety of solutions; his incautious venture into the subdominant is altogether momentous in its consequences. One or two of the variations look forward to Brahms in their rich chromaticism, as in their free handling of bar-lines (as others do, in their ornamentation and texture, to Chopin). The despised cobbler's patch is thus a precious source of colour, an element of contrast. And contrast is the immediate means of the work's progress through its protean changes of face. Extreme contrasts of mood and sonority such as Beethoven revels in in the Diabelli Variations are part of the act, the revelation of the almost unlimited number of possible transformations of the one banal theme, by which the composer exhibits the marvels of his art; they are expressions of the comic spirit which presides over and informs the work's prodigious display of contrapuntal invention.

The contrast between successive variations frequently comes with an effect of calculated shock, overturning the serious character just set up or, equally, awing irreverence into solemnity. Thus the dreamlike tenderness of the *dolce* No. 8, with its long, gleaming phrases arched over gently running quavers, is succeeded by the crusty humours of No. 9. The gravity and the deliberate, slowly piled-up climaxes of the massively canonic No. 14 are juxtaposed with the rapidity and lightness of the presto scherzando No. 15, which gives way to the laborious technical exercise of No. 16 (like inspired Czerny). No. 19's brilliant clamour is silenced by the magical atmosphere which, in No. 20, is created by the slow swing of soft chords in the lower register and the mysterious movement of the harmonies; yet the haunting mood of this beautiful and strange piece is itself unceremoniously dispelled by No. 21's flurry of trills, drumming semiquavers, and octave leaps up and down the whole extent of the keyboard.

Thanks partly to the cobbler's patch, many variations contain their own contrasting material, a darkening or lightening, an intensification or slackening of movement, according to the character of the piece. Such are the sinuous Brahmsian octaves in No. 18, the brief stillness that descends with the modulation into D flat in the second half of the cantankerous No. 9, the outbreaks of rhythmic violence in No. 5, the even more unexpected interruption in No. 3, when the airy contrapuntal discussion breaks off and we hear only a remote, sinister rumbling. No. 13 is made up of extravagant alternations of dynamics and registers, separated by pauses which underline the outlandish effect. No. 21's trills and octave leaps give way to a slower, more cantabile passage, and the variation ends quietly; but this contrasting impression is effaced by the macabrely humorous Variation 22, based on 'Notte e giorno faticar' in *Don Giovanni*. The allusion is not arbitrary: Leporello's grumpy soliloquy begins like Diabelli's bass line (even the orchestra's flourish in the second bar is matched by the quaver figure at the corresponding point in the theme); but Beethoven presumably intends an incidental dig at his 'master', for whom he is slaving night and day with (all publishers being robbers) little prospect of reward.

In the final variations internal contrast largely disappears; but the application of the principle of contrast between variations is taken still further and deeper. The marvellous fughetta, No. 24, which breathes a calm not previously heard, follows a particularly powerful display of virtuoso brilliance, and is itself followed by the jauntiest piece in the whole set, a dancing, jigging allegro in 3/8, which in turn yields to a gentle fluctuation of semiquavers, delicately ambiguous in their rhythmic grouping. In the next two variations invention attains its extreme point of eccentricity, with accented seconds clashing at breakneck speed at the top of the keyboard (No. 27) and frequent and regular sforzato chords which jerk the music along like a demented clockwork toy (No. 28). But just at this point the work moves into a dark world of suffering of which there has been scarcely a hint. Three variations are now heard, all in C minor, of increasingly searching beauty and sadness (each one corresponding to the successive minor-key variations in the Goldberg). The third re-creates the florid melodic style of baroque keyboard music to achieve within its brief, concentrated time-span an introspective intensity comparable to that of the last piano sonatas. As the intensity subsides, the variation (No. 31) comes to rest on the dominant of E flat, the relative major of the C minor which has been so carefully established. We are by now accustomed to Beethoven's shock tactics; but the double fugue into which the work now plunges seems a dramatic stroke to crown all. Only the key—which for the first time forsakes C and its minor for E flat—tells us that this tumultuous but rigorously controlled music, so formidable in sonority, so rich in harmony and relentless in rhythm, is not the grand finale of the work.

Beethoven has one more surprise for us, the strangest and, when we become familiar with it, the most inevitable. The triumphant fugue is suddenly checked in mid-career, on a diminished seventh over a pedal E flat. The chord disintegrates in a storm of arpeggios; and when the clouds have cleared, C major has been conjured out of the air, Diabelli has been canonized, and the theme has become a minuet of the most artless simplicity which proceeds on its course with the preordained momentum of the music of the spheres. We are back where we began, with the Dance. The variation flowers into a celestial coda, in which Beethoven, with a final gesture of mastery, seems to dissolve the work and return it to the pure elements from which, almost by chance, he created it.

Schubert: Promise and Fulfilment

Is there any composer loved as Schubert is, whom so many people have taken to their hearts? Is there any with his power to catch us by surprise and touch us to the quick in a single phrase? (We get a reminder of that power in John Schlesinger's film *Sunday Bloody Sunday*, when a fragment of the Octet is heard for a second or two on a car radio, with an emotional effect out of all proportion to its length.) But the above questions at once recall the other side. They prompt the reflection that to be so generally loved has its disadvantages: it may not be good for the serious reputation of a creative artist, particularly one who died young; he can easily become an artist who never grew up. Further questions suggest themselves. Is there, with any other composer, so wide a dichotomy, even now, between critical attitudes and the experience of musicians and music-lovers? (How often, after enjoying a work or movement of his, has one looked it up, full of zeal, in some authority or other, only to find that it is not nearly so satisfactory as one imagined!) Is there a comparable case of a great composer—one that many would unhesitatingly place among the half-dozen supreme creators, a junior member of the company of Mozart, Beethoven, Bach, Handel and Haydn—whom commentators feel so free to patronize: a master who is so often approached in the expectation of finding weaknesses, whether for censure or indulgent forgiveness? Was there ever a sadder example of the fallacy of judging an artist by preconceived criteria, or indeed by any criteria but his own?

Perhaps not, but it may be objected that this is no longer

so: the heyday of Schubert-belittling was in the now-distant past, the era of Parry, whose unimpeachable principles led him to the discovery that Schubert had 'no great talent for self-criticism, and the least possible feeling for abstract design and balance and order'. Since then Tovey, and more recently Maurice Brown, have put admiration for Schubert onto a respectable footing. His underestimation by 19th-century critical opinion was due to a combination of incomplete knowledge, his historical position, and the narrowness of contemporary academic ideas. Coming between two eras he was, even more than most geniuses, unclassifiable; but criticism relies on classification, to save it from the necessity of constant thought. The criteria by which Schubert's large-scale works were judged were those of Mendelssohn and Brahms, which were held to be themselves those that Beethoven had laid down for all time and every season. But we have long since rid ourselves of such barren and deluded notions.

It is true that the excesses of the Parry school are rarely if ever encountered today. Yet it seems to me that the prejudices that produced them still linger on in the collective mind. They can be seen reflected in the unthinking aside, the casual but revealing epithet, gently, often fondly reproving, that tends to come out when a Schubert sonata or quartet is being discussed, in conversation or in print. The legendary Schubert still floats across our consciousness. Maurice Brown's book was published fifteen years ago; but it needs more time than that to scrape off the deposits of a century's misunderstanding. Generalizations about artists are very hard to eradicate once they have taken root, however accidentally.* In short, there is still an effort required to see Schubert clearly and whole, and a case to be argued for his true greatness.

---

* Brown makes the intriguing suggestion that Schubert's reputation as a weak constructor may originally have had a lot to do with the accident of its being the E flat Trio, a work full of beauties but undeniably unsatisfactory as a whole, that the great song-writer was principally known by as a composer in large forms.

The reasons why this should be so are only partly con-
nected with scholastic disapproval. They are also inherent
in the problem itself. Paradoxically, the very immediacy of
Schubert's music is a barrier to understanding. Its marvellous freshness and directness, its sense of inexhaustible
fertility, its sensuousness, its melodic invention, its sheer
companionability, which can become a little too much of a
good thing when he is in his most garrulous and button-
holing mood—in short, everything that is meant by the
adjective Schubertian—combine to evoke a conventional
picture which, though it leaves out a good half of the truth,
seems neatly in accordance with the facts: the enormous
output, the incredible facility (whole songs dashed off on the
backs of menus, etc.); the uninhibited, direct response to
the world around him, seen in his general susceptibility to the
influence of Viennese popular music, as well as in his magpie
stealing of other people's tunes, which he took not because
he was short of his own but because he was incapable of
thinking beyond the first moment of rapturous discovery;
death at the age of 31, with its implication of promise yet to
be fulfilled—'a rich treasure but still fairer hopes'—so that
everything he wrote is an early work; the proximity of his
mighty predecessor Beethoven, composer of symphonic
masterpieces on an unprecedented scale, the pattern and
measure of all subsequent attempts at composition in large
forms. The picture is of a purely instinctive artist, a lyricist
who 'dwells with Beauty', and it has coloured critical
thinking and writing about Schubert from his day to
ours.

The ease and abundance that lies on the surface of
Schubert's music gives undeniable plausibility to such a
view. Does it matter exactly how he ranks? The treasure is so
rich as it is! We can help ourselves. The effortlessness of a
work like the Trio in B flat—perfectly formed though it may
be—gives the impression that the music has come into
existence by spontaneous generation, without requiring to be
composed. Even the great String Quintet can be included in

the picture, because it is so extraordinarily beautiful, and because of the intensely lyrical character of its utterance: the music is great by divine right of inspiration rather than by achievement of intellect; it is the songster *in excelsis*; beauty is Schubert's way to the highest truth. Yet at the end of his *œuvre* stands the towering form of the Great C major Symphony, a work of ferocious mastery on the grandest scale, handled with the conscious assurance of a mature and fulfilled artist. How does it fit into the picture? Not very easily; yet such is the persistence of the 'babbling brook' conception of Schubert that even the Great C major has been affected, and a whole school of mellow interpretation has grown up round it, associated in modern times with Bruno Walter and dedicated to the view that it is a lyrical, quint-essentially 'Viennese' work.

At its most extreme the critical classifying of Schubert manifested itself in doctrines of the following sort. He was a lyricist and, as such, not primarily concerned with the rigours of form, but content to sing of nature and the simple joys and sorrows of existence and capture the intensity of the moment. He was a melodist: ergo he was no contrapuntist (did he not himself recognize it when, right at the end of his tragically short life, he began going to a leading Viennese theorist, Simon Sechter, for lessons in counterpoint?). He composed as ordinary people write a letter, dashing his thoughts straight onto the paper, without troubling to work them out first.* As a fundamentally non-intellectual artist, his ability to sustain long movements was necessarily suspect; and when his attempts to do so were judged by the correct yardstick, that of Beethoven (whose forms he was quite capable of borrowing *in toto*, as though they were so many matrices to be filled with whatever one pleased), the suspicion proved only too well founded. As

* This rash deduction from negative evidence remained unrefuted until quite recently, when the survival of full sketches for a number of works began to become known.

often as not he fell victim to his melodic copiousness and harmonic over-exuberance. His very fecundity was his enemy, for his inability to resist its promptings deflected him from the true course of disciplined thought into lovely bypaths and winding mossy ways. In his innocence he did not realize that he was asking Beethovenian sonata form to do things that God, not to mention Beethoven, never meant it to do. He confused the functions of exposition and development and treated his second-subject material in a regrettably diffuse fashion. Mastery of small forms such as Schubert revealed at an early age in songs like *Erlkönig* and *Gretchen am Spinnrade* is plainly an instinctive gift (and a valuable one); it is not, alas, the same thing as knowing how to organize a large-scale symphonic movement—though the flowers he gathered on his vagrant journey are so charming that one almost forgives the lack of consistent purpose behind it.

Extreme though they may be, such opinions have had a pervasive effect on the general climate of Schubert criticism, colouring the assumptions and attitudes even of some of his staunchest admirers. Ernest Newman, while defending him against a charge of symphonic irresponsibility in the first movement of the Unfinished, could write of him that he 'seems to have racked his brains hardly at all over problems of structure, trusting to his inexhaustible invention to see him through anything'. J. A. Westrup regretfully concludes that the 'errors of taste' represented by such things as the café influences in the finale of the String Quintet are the price we pay for Schubert's miraculous spontaneity: 'if Schubert had been a more painstaking artist, given to revision and reflection, he would not have been the Schubert we know.' Tovey himself, devoted Schubertian as he is, cannot quite bring himself to let him alone. He adores him, but cannot quite reconcile his adoration with the self-evident truth that the great post-Beethoven master is Brahms (whose mastery is never in question). Tovey's tireless and superbly perceptive and knowledgeable eloquence in support of Schubert is qualified by niggling doubts. He cannot even accept the Grand Duo as it is but, following Joachim, must mystify himself into finding in it 'from beginning to end ... not a trace of pianoforte style'; nor can he resist characterizing the reminiscences of Beethoven's Second Symphony in the slow movement, with an affectionate wag of the pedagogic finger, as a 'naïve' surrender to impulse.

If Schubert's most eminent champions tend to think of him in this way, it is not surprising that a good deal of criticism should still reflect the prejudices that lie behind such thinking, and should still be too busy fussing over him, and repeating generalizations, to recognize the man that fancy's child grew into. To consider the question of his magpie instincts, the teenage Schubert was undoubtedly naïve in his borrowings; one would expect a boy to be. (Precocity need not include the sophistication of the young Mozart or Mendelssohn.) We can watch him, at the age of 17 or 18, encountering *Fidelio* for the first time and going straight home and adopting the First Prisoner's tune for the Credo of the Mass he is composing. But the mature Schubert's borrowings are quite another matter. The Beethovenian origin of the middle section of the Grand Duo's slow movement may be obvious but is of no significance except as further evidence of the extent to which Schubert was steeped in the classical period of Viennese music; the same can be said of the allusion to the Archduke Trio in the first movement at the point where the music touches the key of B flat. No one would seriously question the *echt*-Schubertian character of the C minor Piano Sonata; yet the immediate impulse behind the opening of the work is quite clearly the set of variations by Beethoven in the same key, and the sonata makes unmistakable reference to at least two other Beethoven works, the sonatas in E minor and A flat (Op. 26). Beethoven, again, prompted the opening of the finale of the B flat Sonata, which like the finale of the Op. 130 Quartet in the same key begins in C minor and reaches the tonic key in the tenth bar.

Mozart was an equally rich source of allusion. If the similarities between the D flat major episodes in the adagios of the Violin Sonata K.481 and the Octet are accidental (though it is hard to believe it, once you have noticed them), the first theme of Schubert's F minor Fantasy for piano duet clearly echoes Barbarina's F minor cavatina in *Figaro*. Halfway through the song 'Mein' in *Die schöne Müllerin* Schubert, having modulated to his favourite flat submediant, writes a melodic and harmonic pattern almost identical to that used by Mozart when expressing, in the dominant-key passage in 'Non sò più', Cherubino's similar pangs of adolescent ecstasy. The pitch of the notes in the two passages is again the same (the flat submediant of the one key being the dominant of the other). But in the light of the result the likeness is strictly superficial. As Brahms said when accused of plagiarism, 'any fool can see it'. It is the difference between almost and wholly that makes the music Schubertian and not Mozartian. The passage suits Schubert's particular purpose, so he annexes it. In such cases what we are witnessing is not blind impulse but an act of possession. As with the café influences, it is not the source that counts but the use which is made of it. Schubert makes these thefts as ruthlessly his own as does Stravinsky his similar depredations. His mind seethes with music heard and assimilated and ready for the chances of creative necessity to call it forth.

There is undeniably a strong element of nostalgia in Schubert's borrowings—an implied awareness that Mozart's music, and even Beethoven's, belongs to a world which has gone or is going, and that henceforth the artist is on his own and must create his own language and conventions. Schubert's exploitation of the past is one part of the sadness of his music. His use of classical forms in a non-classical way, though not invariably successful, is conscious and deliberate; it is not—as is sometimes suggested or hinted— like that of the savage misapplying the artefacts of civilization. And it has a right to be judged separately in each case, and not by the book but by the free response of each listener.

That is how Schubert, like any other composer, should always be judged. Try letting him alone, try coming to him on his own terms and going with him to the end before deciding whether he has succeeded—listen to his music without preconceptions—and the picture will change into something subtler, more complex and many-layered, grander, more purposeful, and more beautiful still.

The beauty of Schubert's music is frequently characterized in terms of a happy sensuousness darkened by no more than a wistful acknowledgment that one day it will have to come to an end. If it were merely that, it would not touch us so keenly. The reason for its peculiarly personal appeal lies deeper than felicity, below the sunlit surface; it is the combination of felicity with a passionate sense of its transience. Mozart moves us because we recognize in him both the perfection we long for and the sensation of our own longing. With Schubert the delights are all about us but man is mortal. Like Keats, Schubert

> dwells with Beauty—Beauty that must die
> And Joy, whose hand is ever at his lips
> Bidding adieu.

The beauty is so intense because it is passing and knows it. This is much more than a poetic convention, and it is independent of any thoughts aroused in us by Schubert's own premature death; it is in the flesh and blood and bone of his melody and harmony—the one seemingly spontaneous and unreflecting, the other shifting, ambiguous, betraying from within. Sometimes the consciousness of mortality becomes terrifyingly explicit, as at the end of the slow movement of the Octet (a movement shadowed with it from the first, though commonly described as music of serene loveliness by commentators who have not seen the skull beneath the skin). But it can lurk in the most innocent outpouring of happiness. It is a constant undercurrent of his music.

The Octet is an instructive work with which to consider

Schubert from an untraditional or Schubertian point of view. It is almost proverbial for its happy charm;* but that is not how it strikes us when we look at it more closely. It takes its legitimate place in the series of chamber works through which, in the mid-1820s, Schubert prepared himself for the 'big symphony' he intended to write; occasional though it may be in origin, it belongs in the evolution that leads to the Great C major. The commission which brought it into being was apparently for an old-style divertimento on the lines of Beethoven's Septet; Schubert obliged, and in doing so gave his patron, Archduke Rudolph's chief steward Count Troyer (an enthusiastic clarinettist) ample opportunity to shine. But what a divertimento! We hardly need be aware that it comes from a dark period of Schubert's life, or indeed do anything except open ourselves to it and learn to know it thoroughly, to recognize it as an affirmation of existence in the midst of despair.

At the time of its composition Schubert, then aged 27, was a sick man, convinced that his health would not recover. He told a friend that 'each night when I go to bed I hope I may not wake again, and each morning only recalls the miseries of the day before.' The contemporary string Quartets in A minor and D minor are the musical transfiguration of that mood. Between them, flanked by the dreamlike sadness of the one and the demonic restlessness of the other, comes the Octet, one of music's great celebrations. It is a celebration that does not delude itself about the sorrows of life; some of Schubert's most poignant music is in this work —in the Minuet, for instance, and in the A flat variation of the andante. And it has looked at death face to face. How else are we to interpret the adagio? The movement seems to carry within it the seeds of its own decay. From the first the tonic key of B flat is steadily undermined; harmonic flattenings attack the poised beauty of the main clarinet melody.

---

* Even Einstein finds 'no trace of dualism' in the work. Westrup notes the dark touches in the last movement but 'everything else in the Octet is serene and gay'.

Still more, when the clarinet's exquisite, floating counter-melody gives to the theme, now played by the first violin, a frailer, more attenuated quality, do we feel that this is music burdened with the knowledge of its end. Yet for all the progressive harmonic dissolution and increasingly hectic colour, and the intimation of the two eerie silences that break the music's flow in the second half of the movement, the blow, when it comes, falls with sickening suddenness. The main theme, returning for the coda, proceeds for four bars in a kind of exhausted tranquillity, a shadow of itself but apparently secure in the home key, then abruptly crumbles to dust: the melody, plunging down a diminished seventh, is cut short by the thud of a single low pizzicato note—a rattle of dry bones—then nothingness.

The character of this long but precisely controlled movement is the cause of and clue to its formal progress—form being not a set mould but the shape taken by the material, which is itself the expression of the poetic idea. A flatwards tendency is active throughout, burrowing from below. Tonality constantly threatens to dissolve. The tonic key of B flat is rarely safe, and in the second half or recapitulation (the movement is in the so-called abridged sonata form familiar from some of Mozart's slow movements) the music is in B flat less than half the time. In the coda, after the collapse, B flat is not regained for six more bars of groping uncertainty rising to a feverish climax in which the music seems to be reliving the nightmare.

Words only coarsen by attempting to spell out what notes suggest. But in Schubert the poetic idea, once grasped, explains the formal organization. In the light of it, what may have appeared, to the eye, and measured by other rules, the product of a rich but wayward fancy, assumes a purpose. Schubert has his own structural unities. At his best, the speed and diversity of his thought is matched by his ability to subject it to a unifying impulse; the music goes where it does in obedience to a plan. The impulse, the flow, may in origin be 'lyrical', but the word, so far as it tells us anything useful, tells us about the music's character, not about its formal construction. The plan does not invariably succeed. Given his large expansion of the harmonic vocabulary of music, it is not surprising that coherence should sometimes elude him. But in his mature works the footloose wanderer of legend rarely lets himself wander for the pleasure of it. The exploration of remote sharp keys at the beginning of the development section in the first movement of the B flat sonata is subtly pervaded with the deep nostalgia for home which eventually draws the music back to B flat and which we can feel as an undertow gently tugging on it from the beginning. When Schubert digresses he usually has a long-term reason. We should always try to seek out his intentions, and suspend judgment until we have heard what he does; otherwise we may miss the point. This is true of the details as well as of the structure. The passage half way through the finale of the String Quintet, where a canonic development of the opening theme twice breaks down after a bar or two, is not—*pace* certain commentators—an example of contrapuntal deficiency but a dramatic effect of frustrated energy in tune with the sense of striving with itself that increasingly comes over the movement as it progresses towards its exasperated conclusion. It will seem weak only if we come to it expecting it to be, our gaze fixed in the wrong direction. Schubert's counterpoint usually does what is required of it, which is the only relevant criterion; it is, as is proper, an extension of his melodic abundance and harmonic skill. To invent the countermelodies that he writes for his main themes in the slow movements of the Octet and the B flat Trio, or to provide the beautiful F major tune in the slow movement of the Great C major with a heavenly intertwining of inner parts, is the highest expression of contrapuntal genius. He had nothing essential to learn from Simon Sechter.

If harmony, not melody, is the main structural agent of Schubert's large-scale music, rhythm is its outward scaffolding. The Octet, mellifluous though it may be and is meant to be, is pervaded by rhythm, in particular by a rising phrase in dotted time, first heard in the introduction, which generates the unflagging forward thrust of the first movement, recurs in the second and briefly in the fourth, and again dominates the fifth. Rhythm, in Schubert's music generally, has a more than external, almost a symbolic significance. We can almost state, as a Schubertian principle, that Melody equals Beauty, Harmony equals Death that waits for it, and Rhythm equals the eternal Life-force that drives on even in the midst of dissolution. Rhythmic energy, in the Octet, is the means by which life asserts its indestructible vitality—springing up, in the tigerish scherzo, from the ruins of the adagio and, in the finale, banishing with the defiant verve of its relentless crotchet pulse plus irregularly phrased theme the spectre of annihilation which returns to cast its shadow over the introduction to the movement, and which beckons again with menacing gestures at the height of the revels.

In such ways a work commissioned to entertain (which it does, perennially), and written in the old-fashioned easygoing six-movement form, helped to prepare for the 'big symphony'. Even here, in fact, Schubert shows himself nearer to Beethoven than the traditional picture would have it—not in his formal methods, which are his own, and not so much in the scheme of the work (closely though it follows that of Beethoven's Septet) as in his seriousness of purpose, his approach to emotional content in music, the extra-musical meaning that a piece of music can embody while remaining wholly musical.

Schubert's preparations were not in vain. The Symphony is arguably the supreme masterpiece produced in the form since Beethoven's, if not the only one that can stand as an equal in that august company. Its rhythmic dynamism matches that of Beethoven's Seventh on a different plane, and gives it a physical power that makes live contact with it, in a good performance, one of the most exhilarating experiences in music; but the work is also Beethovenian in its intellectual discipline and its moral determination, its harnessing of lyrical invention to the drive of an all-suffering, all-daring will. Rhythm generates the momentum that carries the music, in the first movement, on its epic tonal journeys; that, in the andante, impels it on its march through the wilderness; that rises like a giant refreshed in the scherzo (where the andante's four repeated notes recur in a context of boisterous spirits, prefiguring the finale); and that erupts, in the finale, in a feat of sustained and tumultuous energy almost without parallel. But rhythm is only one means, if the most spectacular; rhythm is the agent of an unswerving purposefulness. Nothing that happens in the work is accidental or forgotten. The apparently playful, decorative trumpet counterpoint introduced half-way through the andante grows into a monstrous, obsessive figure that takes the music to the brink of destruction. The rising dotted phrase in the second bar of the symphony has consequences that continue to be felt right to the end and that are only most apparent in the allegro of the first movement: in the famous trombone passage and its derivatives (the work is a landmark in the treatment of trombones as an integral part of the symphony orchestra, going even further in this respect than the Unfinished) and in the momentous bars at the end of the development section, where the phrase flowers into a mysterious brooding melody played by clarinets, violas and basses, while horn-calls, in the ubiquitous dotted rhythm, softly summon the music back to C major. The repeated notes that lead to the climax of the andante—an awe-inspiring expression of spiritual anguish struggled with and barely overcome—are transformed into the triumphantly pounding minims of the finale; here the first movement's heroic images are brought together at an even higher pitch of intensity in a blaze of sound and spirit that for the moment obliterates the thought of all other music.

The Great C major Symphony, it may be objected, is not

typical of Schubert. No major work by a great artist is typical of anything but itself. But it can help us in various ways to look at him afresh; it can encourage us, by its mastery, not to come to him expecting diffuseness or uncertainty; to study his highly individual formal processes in the light of themselves; to realize, perhaps, that at their best they achieve by their own distinct methods a tension different from Beethoven's but comparable to it, and that a sense of purpose no less serious animates them; that the tension is harmonic even before it is rhythmic; that, contrary to the common assumption, tonality and harmony, not melody, are the chief preoccupation of Schubert's large-scale compositions. The exposition of the first movement of the Great C major, in which the *attainment* of the dominant constitutes the matter of the music, is a pointer to Schubert's highly personal adaptation of the tonal relationships of classical style to his needs—an adaptation which must be examined and listened to impartially before it is judged inferior. Musicology still has some investigation ahead of it before the full extent and character of what he did is appreciated.

What he might have done had he lived another ten years, let alone a full life span, is a speculation so deep as to 'tease us out of thought'. But, short though it was, his life was long enough for the naïve, instinctive genius to develop into an articulate and singleminded artist, and to achieve, in a dozen richly original masterpieces, a disciplining and organization of his miraculous talent, an assertion of creative self-reliance and pertinacity in a disintegrating world, that was perhaps the most miraculous thing of all.

Decorating Mozart's Piano Concertos

Ornamentation and the grammar of musical performance are, strictly speaking, separate questions. The one concerns how the individual performer understood and responded to the music he was performing, the other what all performers were expected to do as a matter of course. In modern terms, however, they are in practice aspects of the same problem. To take a topical case, the performance of Mozart's piano concertos, the issue is whether we can, and consequently should, revive the conventions of Mozart's day. Is it possible for the spirit and function of 18th-century ornamentation to be recaptured by audiences or—a necessary condition for that—by performers, nearly two hundred years after the event? Can we deliberately re-create a convention whose essence was improvisation? Can modern interpreters re-learn a forgotten art that was itself the faint echo of a much earlier, pre-interpretative tradition in which the performer and the composer were one? Can it again become a part of our experience, so that it ceases to confuse our awareness of the music and actually enhances it? If so, should we go so far as to restore to the solo pianist his long-superseded role of providing continuo support for the strings?

Criticism nowadays is rather too ready to take it as read that the answer to such questions is a simple, unequivocal yes. The pendulum has swung right back from the old literalism, and the subject tends to be discussed in the abstract, divorced from the living realities in which music, as a performing art, has its existence. The other day Richter was rebuked for playing the B flat Concerto K.595 without any decoration of the written notes. The assumption was that he had simply ignored an accepted truth. It is of course quite right that performers, especially the prestigious ones, should be prodded into taking account of the results of scholarly thinking and research. But the issue is not so clear-cut as such criticism implies. It has yet to be shown that extensive decoration is compatible with maximum vitality of performance. Decoration, under the impact of the Sadler's Wells' *Figaro*, has come to be thought of rather as though it were a good thing in itself regardless whether the particular decoration is suited to the music it seeks to embellish or, hardly less pertinent, to the style and technique of the performer concerned. A singer whose embellishments to a Mozart aria fail to sound spontaneous defeats his own purpose. Neglect of this basic truth was, I felt, inclined to mar the effect of Sadler's Wells' pioneering work.

The same thought struck me more forcibly when listening to K.595 and the C major Concerto K.467 as performed by Friedrich Gulda on a recently issued record. Gulda's K.595 can certainly not be reproached with Richter's offence. Throughout the work we find the melodies varied, the longer notes filled out with trills, turns, scales and arpeggios, and in the left hand the addition of octaves, extra notes to the chords, extra rhythmic beats and alberti basses. The whole thing goes well beyond the modest experiments we have lately begun to accustom ourselves to. In doing so it naturally arouses antagonism. Musical opinion may have advanced from a rigid insistence on 'the notes and nothing but the notes' to the liberating realization that there is no such thing; but prejudice remains active. What we are used to profoundly influences our way of experiencing musical performance. Because we are not used to much decoration of the solo part in Mozart's piano concertos, it is very hard to listen to it in the right spirit, even though intellectually we know that Mozart himself expected it. However much we

try, we cannot hear it merely as decoration. It sticks out:
we lose the melody in embellishments that are meant only
to intensify it. Equally, the knowledge that Mozart intended
the soloist to support the strings in a continuo capacity hardly
reconciles us emotionally to the practice. Our attitude is
still coloured by the 19th-century concerto with its Romantic
suggestion of the individualist struggling with and imposing his will on the world around him, and we think unconsciously in terms of clearly demarcated functions. The idea
that the soloist should be in action, in a subordinate capacity,
from the start, jars against deeply rooted preconceptions.
It is also unlikely to commend itself to the soloist.

Unfortunately Gulda's actual playing—unsubtle, asser-
tive, over-accented, and uncomfortably fast in the slow
movements—does not do much to forward his cause. But
if we can forget this for a moment and, as far as possible
without prejudice, try to examine what he does, we can
learn something useful about the whole question. His very
excesses may be helpful in clearing our minds and enabling
us to come to certain tentative conclusions.

Of the two concertos, K.595 comes off altogether better.
There can be no cavilling at the rapid rising scale which is
his answer to the bare G in the left hand at bar 161 in the
first movement (C at the corresponding place in the recapitulation). Gulda's addition to Mozart's brief written
cadenza also seems to me successful; and the semiquaver
turn in the last bar of the movement (neatly derived from
some passage work earlier in the movement) is a truly
inventive touch. Sometimes his zeal to decorate leads him
into altering what I take to be the character of the music.
In the larghetto the stillness of the minim which is the first
written note of the theme is replaced by a sense of activity,
the pulse being subdivided and the second crotchet beat
filled in by the left hand. Many of the decorations in this
movement seem to me to militate against what the notes are
trying to convey. I am not claiming that in such a movement
decoration is wrong *per se*. As Stanley Sadie says in his sleeve

note to the recording, 'we may be sure that in playing the work himself Mozart would have embellished the chaste melodic lines [of the larghetto] to still more powerful emotional effect.' It is only that these particular embellishments weaken the emotional effect. Yet K.595 is the more convincingly handled of the two. By contrast, K.467 is so encumbered with ornamentation as to be less a performance than an exercise in didacticism. Whereas in the gentler, more lyrical K.595 Gulda confines the piano's continuo part mainly to an accompanying role (the effect being merely to give an extra colour to the orchestra here and there), and so produces an experiment that is genuinely instructive, in the much grander C major work he takes the bit between his teeth and treats the piano as a solo instrument from the very outset. The silent upbeat to the fifth bar of the orchestral introduction is festooned with an arpeggio; so we lose the crotchet rest that, in the score, separates the first four-bar phrase of the march theme from its continuation. The effect of the soloist's first entry as soloist is spoiled by the elaborate and obtrusive figuration given to the piano in the immediately preceding bar. Throughout the movement the piano is busy embroidering the orchestral part. The result is both distracting and, paradoxically, inhibited. In the wonderful andante, the freedom with which the solo part is treated in an apparent effort to make it sound spontaneous and improvisatory—the notes of the melody being systematically delayed in such a way that they come behind the beat, with a slight but continuous effect of syncopation—succeeds only in shattering the glassy, brooding beauty of the music and putting something restless and awkward in its place. One lesson seems to be that whatever is done in the way of ornamentation, the notes already there should be the basis.

Even the embellishments that are stylistically convincing tend to sound careful and contrived, not the natural expression of a creative imagination working in harmony with the composer's. That is easily said, and perhaps it is asking a lot; but if the justification and criterion of ornamentation is what 'Mozart in playing the work himself' would have done, we should not ask for less. I am reminded of the little cadenzas that Serkin put in at pause-points in the finale of K.467 at the Edinburgh Festival last year, and the complete sense of spontaneity with which they bubbled out, as if they had come into being in that instant because he could not contain his delight in Mozart's comic invention. This surely is the spirit in which all decoration should be added—that they underline the mood of the music and say in their own way what it is saying.

There is the rub, of course, for it depends on how the artist interprets the mood of the music. Ornamentation is a personal matter. It can only express the particular performer's response, and the particular listener is free to reject it if he feels the music differently. To say that the test is whether it sounds natural oversimplifies the issue, for one must then ask, to whom? The ingrained conservatism of listening habits is such that to some people any but the most cautious ornamentation (and that is almost a contradiction in terms) will seem excessive. The listener needs to get used to it, and for that to happen it must become second nature to the performer. The difficulty at present is to find the mean between 'going too far' and introducing, in a laudable desire to avoid excess, a breath of prudence which kills ornamentation stone dead. One has also to reckon with the conservatism of performing habits. There are distinguished pianists still about who learned their Mozart in the good old days and regard ornamentation as abhorrent. Such conservatism may be a safeguard against the rise of an orthodoxy almost as wrong-headed as the one it replaced, but it is a barrier to progress as well.

The truth is, the taste of all concerned has not yet developed very far. Ornamentation will only seem natural, and therefore itself, when it has been absorbed to the point where it springs from the impulse of the moment—an impulse directed by knowledge yet spontaneous. It would be rash to predict how far the development will go. Not so far as Gulda's rewriting of K.467, I cannot help—conservatively perhaps—wishing, but certainly so far that, for example, melodic repetitions are varied as a matter of normal practice. On the other hand the continuo convention is probably too foreign ever to be revived. Besides, if the ears we listen with are not those of Mozart's day, nor are the sounds we hear. The texture and tone quality of the orchestra is different. So is the solo instrument's. Even allowing for the weakness of the 18th-century orchestra compared with the Mozart orchestra of today, the fortepiano's light, dry sound must have enabled it to play a true continuo role which the modern piano could match only by artificially inhibiting its natural character. Perhaps more important, the modern piano's command of singing tone gives it a melodic capability the lack of which obliged the fortepiano to decorate slow melodies as a means of sustaining them. Mozart concerto performances on the fortepiano are not a practical ideal. The combination of harpsichord and modern strings in performances of baroque music provides enough horrid examples of the danger that lies in mixing our centuries. Scholarship can take us only so far towards a re-creation of the past. Properly harnessed, authenticity is a force for freedom, pointing the performer's creative imagination in the right direction, never constricting it; encouraging his confidence in his own instinct. He must be made aware of the truth so far as it can be discovered. But a too precise preaching of texts and conventions may achieve literal accuracy only to smother the flair which makes performance live. The serious thought that lies behind a truly authentic account of a Mozart piano concerto is forgotten in the living moment of communication.

(1965)

Mozart's C major Quintet

The Third Programme chamber concert at the Elizabeth Hall the other day was devoted, with audacious simplicity, to Mozart's three great string quintets, in C, G minor and D. These works, above all the C major, have a good claim not only to be regarded as Mozart's supreme masterpieces but to represent the art of music in its highest form. If the fallacy of Pure Music has any substance, they provide it. Of course there is no such thing—as Wilfrid Mellers has observed, 'a more imbecile notion' never existed, 'for the simple reason that although in one sense all music is programme music, since it is concerned with human emotions, in another sense music, in so far as it *is* music, can never be anything but pure'. But in these works Mozart achieves a refinement of expression, a fusion of form and content, for which it is hard to find a parallel even in his music. There is nothing remote or cold in this refinement. The quintets are Mozart at his most personal; they are pure feeling. The very intensity of emotion raises the music to a level where the categories dissolve and melt into each other, content and form are one, and the music simply is; their perfection, as always with Mozart at his best, is suffused with the sense of longing that makes him the most human as well as the most godlike of all composers. The more you listen to them the more you discover. It is like exploring eternity.

For this reason any attempt to analyse them can only be doomed to failure. One's thoughts fly up, one's words remain below. It is possible, for example, to show how the composer exploits the presence of two violas to achieve unusual richness of inner parts and variety of harmony, texture and colour; but how to begin to do justice to the result? The suffering expressed in the G minor Quintet is re-created on so ideal a plane that to call it poignant seems not only inadequate but irrelevant, for all that one is acutely aware of its poignancy. Nothing in music is sadder than the moment when the slow movement turns from B flat minor to major (though Beethoven does something analogous in the D flat major episode near the end of the Eroica funeral march). The lilting rhythm and the sudden release of an unbearable tension are like a pathetic vision of health in a sick-room. They prefigure the finale, whose 'cheerful' G major, following the dark concentrated passion of its adagio introduction, used to be regretted on moral principles. (Mozart's humanism has always irritated the puritan mind.) Such objections at least have the merit of not underrating the seriousness of what has gone before, even if they hopelessly misconstrue the finale. But whereas it is arguable that the exuberant conclusion of the D minor Piano Concerto is an aesthetic mistake, on the grounds that it is dramatically out of keeping with the rest of the work (and not even a kind of *coup de théâtre*, like the comic-opera ending of Beethoven's F minor Quartet), the Quintet is quite untouched by such considerations: it is above drama as well as morals.

Of the three quintets, K.515 in C—placed last in Saturday's programme and rightly so, for reasons of stature as well as key sequence—is the most exalted and therefore the least susceptible to verbal description. One cannot imagine a successful impressionistic picture of it in the manner of Huxley's account of the G minor in *Antic Hay*. It is at once Mozart's most intimate music and his grandest. 'Purity' of expression is combined with the largeness of design, architectural splendour and regal bearing that are associated with the key of C major in Mozart's works. The Olympian first movement has a spaciousness that is more often characteristic of Beethoven's chamber music—though perhaps only the first movement of the F major Rasoumovsky

Quartet matches its combination of majestic breadth and unflagging forward momentum. Having proposed his unusually expansive, and unusually asymmetrical, theme (a mixture of imperial arpeggios and lyrical phrases which establishes the character of the work), Mozart immediately proceeds to develop it before moving on to new matters; the dominant is not reached until the 86th bar. This 'development' is omitted in the recapitulation, which exceeds the length of the exposition by only a dozen bars and creates its sense of expansion by small and subtle means; the quiet finality of the end only adds the culminating touch. Even in this movement Mozart's formal processes and purposes are quite different from Haydn's or Beethoven's. The superbly urgent and powerful development section is short by their standards; the moment of return, though very exciting, is not dramatic—it conveys an irresistible feeling of homecoming, and the freedom it gives the music is a freedom not to set off on fresh adventures but to be more triumphantly itself.

The gentle, half-teasing, wholly serious Minuet which follows (enclosing an equally muted and ambiguous Trio in which persistent, questioning sevenths and strange chromatic probings alternate with more expansive and extrovert themes) is only superficially a foil to the first movement and the succeeding andante. It belongs to their world (as well as being thematically related to them). Its mild glow reflects the same vital energy that produced their grandeurs and intensities. Though the music, from the first, exerts a spell that will not let us go, we do not become fully aware of the tensions it has generated—through stepwise melodic movement, chromatic inflexions and varying phraselengths—until they are resolved at the end, when the main four-bar melody, now harmonically enriched by what it has passed through, finds at last the exact complementary phrase it has been searching for. Only then do we realize how much concentrated experience has been distilled to make the music's quiet but haunting gestures.

The andante, the most wonderful of all the great F major slow movements in Mozart's C major works, shows none of the obvious results of the study of Haydn which mark the never less than Mozartian andante of the 'Dissonance' Quartet. It has the same shape as the adagio slow movement of the G minor: a sustained flow of passionate song (here mainly in the form of a dialogue between first violin and first viola) played twice, with the briefest linking passage. The repetition contains minor but important variations: the necessity of avoiding the dominant key becomes an excuse for further enrichments of harmony and texture; and at the climax of the movement a radiant dominant pedal is added which resolves not at first into the tonic but into the sub-mediant, with a phrase heard earlier in the movement—a breathtaking heightening of the intensity just when it seemed to have reached its crest—followed by two bars, perfectly expressive of fulfilment, whose repetition Mozart has cunningly deferred until this point.

But what use is such terminology? No more than the 'moral' approach can it touch the essence of the music. The first movement's inexhaustible simplicity and splendour is the answer to those who believe heaven would be dull. But that is really all there is to be said about it. The finale, the longest movement in number of bars that Mozart wrote, is simply the most celestial of sonata-rondos, the ideal resolution of the preceding richly wrought intensities; all other comment is superfluous. The andante is a heartfelt song—of what? One cannot even say. Its sublimity exists, defying, not needing, words.

(1967)

Heroic Melancholy:
Elgar Revalued

'I sat up and said "Whew!" I knew we had got it at last,' wrote Bernard Shaw in 1920, recalling the shock of delighted recognition at his first hearing of the Enigma Variations twenty years before. It is probable that a poll of present-day musical opinion would once again endorse his view. The passing of time has wiped away the sneers of Elgar's detractors; he has vigorously outlived the imperialistic age he was supposed to have epitomized. Edwardian heartiness and grandiosity are no longer an obscene joke, but in any case Elgar's music does not seem to reflect them, or only so ambiguously that when a modern writer accuses it of 'mutton-chop complacency' we hardly know what he is talking about. In the light of what we find in the symphonies and concertos—'the great world of nervous endeavour, noble resignation, and lost innocence', as Anthony Payne has called it—the judgment is too remote even to irritate.

With the unfairness of hindsight, it is hard now to understand how Elgar's music could have been so misjudged. The 'heroic melancholy' that Yeats recognized sounds through every strain, the resplendent as well as the gentle. It is part of its body and soul, instinct in the shape of the melodic lines, the movement of the harmonies, the whole climate of the organic orchestration. Yet even Cardus could speak of the First Symphony 'extolling Church and State'—the First Symphony, one of the most intensely personal artistic achievements of the century, a spiritual quest ending in a triumph that is hard won and, the coda clearly hints, precarious! Few if any contemporary commentators noticed the darker side. But the music, we now see, was the man; and if we are tempted to go too far the other way, the reaction was necessary. The brash, jingoistic extrovert was always a myth. It is buried once and for all by Michael Kennedy in his new biography, *Portrait of Elgar*. Mr Kennedy, basing himself on the work of Diana McVeagh and other Elgar scholars, gives us a hypersensitive, touchy, moody, at times almost suicidally unhappy genius with small, nervous hands: an English eccentric who loved fishing, Bradshaw, dogs, recondite information and bonfires, who practised chemistry and patented the Elgar Sulphuretted Hydrogen Apparatus, and who nursed within him a wound that never healed.

The book tells its fascinating story well; comment and narrative are skilfully combined. Good points are made about the music, such as that *Gerontius* shows a masterly command of a natural English melodic speech-rhythm, or that the two sides of Elgar's style cannot be separated and were not separate: the salon Elgar, Mr Kennedy insists, was not suppressed in the major works but sublimated—in the Variations especially, but also in the symphonies. I find some of Mr Kennedy's other musical opinions hard to accept. The Introduction and Allegro is cited as an example of a tendency in Elgar to spoil some of his finest tunes—in this case the beautiful 'Welsh' theme first heard, softly, on the solo viola—by giving them inappropriately grandiose treatment (later in the book, however, he gives unqualified praise to this splendid work). *Falstaff*, in which he detects a certain staleness of thematic invention, is in effect criticized for being at once not true enough, and too true, to Shakespeare: Falstaff's theme 'lacks any suggestion of coarseness', whereas Prince Hal's theme, though 'a typically Elgarian *nobilmente* theme', 'lacks the real note of nobility and, in fact, is not marked *nobilmente*'. On the other hand O'Shaughnessy's dreadful poem 'The Music Makers'— an embodiment of its age, if you like—is defended because, 'though not great verse, it is no worse than many another chosen by musicians'. In the same crypto-establishment vein we find excuses made for the sins of the critics who first wrote about *Gerontius*. Maybe only the wretched Fuller-Maitland's were mortal, but all except Arthur Johnstone of the *Manchester Guardian* obtusely discussed the work within the context of English music as represented by Parry, Stanford and Mackenzie. Of course Elgar was a being apart from such figures in background, in gifts, in mastery, in what he had to say. He said it in words too—too honestly for their taste—in the notorious lectures delivered at Birmingham University in 1905–6, and now issued for the first time, edited by Percy M. Young, under their title *A Future for English Music*. The lectures went against what was acceptable and orthodox, not only by their tactlessly frank disclosure that 'English music is white and evades everything', but in drawing attention to the deficiencies of instrumental training in music colleges, and in giving the game away about orchestral music and the folly of basing its theory and practice on keyboard values. They express the eminently sensible ideas of a practical dreamer who, like Shaw before him, looked over the heads of his contemporaries towards a society in which the prestige of music was reflected in subsidized concerts and a national opera.

It is hardly an exaggeration to see Elgar as the tragic victim of the very different society within which he had to work—and not merely in the sense that, as he half-jocularly remarked to Delius, one of the penalties of his English environment was that he had had to spend so much time writing oratorios. Academic values, whose stifling effect he had escaped as a young man by being self-taught, remained a danger. Professors demurred, critics carped and jabbed (even the devoted and perceptive Jaeger fell into Stanford's 'black-and-white' fallacy and condemned a 'crude' progression in *The Apostles* on the grounds that it didn't look right and sounded wrong on the piano). The low condition of music in England constantly threatened the livelihood, self-respect and sanity of the first major composer the country had produced for two hundred years. *Gerontius* was a near-failure at its première because of atrocious singing by the inadequately trained Birmingham Festival Chorus. Even when successful, serious music did not pay. The Variations, Elgar calculated, earned him about £8 during their first five years. One could go on giving instances. The scar left by his early struggles for acceptance was not allowed to disappear. After *Gerontius*, in 1900, he cries out that 'God is against art'. Seven years later: 'I curse the power that gave me gifts.' In 1923: 'What fools we were to have tried to do anything decent.' Is this just the self-dramatization of an exceptionally vulnerable soul, the mood of despair and self-doubt inseparable from genius? The English are curiously reluctant to admit that things can have been as bad for the great artists as they say they were. In the case of the composer, the very existence of whose work is partly dependent on the actual state of the art, truth has no need of embroidery. We cannot precisely measure the effect on Elgar's output of so much material discouragement, nor say how it compares as an inhibiting influence with the Great War or the loss, soon afterwards, of his wife; but it may well have helped to dislocate an already delicately balanced mechanism, and to cause creative ideas that might have led to masterpieces to be abandoned or put aside. I think one can exaggerate the natural depressiveness in Elgar. He had an enormous capacity for enjoyment. The boisterous high spirits that friends describe, and that come out in his letters, surely mean what they say. (Even the word-play which makes both Mr Kennedy and Dr Young wince with embarrassment is quite innocent; when Elgar spells 'score' progressively as skore, skoughre, cszquorr and skourghourore, I take it that he is not hiding an acute sense of social and educational inferiority behind a mask of fooling but simply indulging his no doubt deplorable sense of humour.) The 'Spirit of Delight' which is the Second Symphony's motto 'cometh rarely'; but it did come. The memory of happiness suffuses his music—a happiness once possessed and still sought, though increasingly in vain.

It can be argued that the tensions of his life fruitfully nourished the music he did write in that brief flowering of twenty years. Ernest Newman described the man as painfully divided between the tug of his country roots and the desire for worldly success which his wife's ambitions for him eagerly fed (indeed, it will never be known how far Alice Elgar, the exalted, efficient high priestess of his genius, fostered the flame, how far unwittingly damped it). His art is about the unease within, the discrepancy between dream and reality; the Edwardian splendour only makes it more poignant. Even *Falstaff*, for all its rich humours, is half-wistful with a sense of history pervaded by regret for the old days and the uncomplicated robustness of the English gentleman. In the symphonies and concertos Elgar seems to be struggling to recapture and hold an ideal. Nearly all his best music comes back to that. The main theme of the First Symphony at the first movement's magical end— grasped at but fading from sight on that wonderful lingering fourth; the muted trombones in the adagio; the apple-laden peace of the Gloucestershire orchard in *Falstaff* and the very touch of the past in the archaic woodwind sound that strikes across the soft string texture—such moments express a deep nostalgia for something he had seen in childhood and never forgotten, down by the river and in the hills, something that he knew to be true but doomed. Ken Russell's *Monitor* film caught this exactly with its image of the boy on a white horse riding the Malvern ridges. It was a vision of an England that Elgar felt to be passing inexorably, and it moves us because we can see that he was right.

(1968)

William Tell

There are plenty of composers who fall short of greatness for want of genius. Rossini is perhaps the only genius who does so out of sheer laziness. He is the most unprincipled of the great composers—among whom he exerted himself just enough to be numbered—because he cares so little. Page after page in his 38 operas show virtue renounced after the briefest struggle. He can't prevent his brilliant inventive gift from throwing up fine ideas, but more often than not he can't be bothered to do anything about them. Formula, empty but expertly turned, is always there to save him trouble, and to round it off there is the Rossini cadence, that cadence which in Mozart always sounds perfectly integrated into the musical flow but in Rossini tends to stick out like a gesture of bored contempt for his audience's gullibility. It is the old cynic's final jest that he forces us into the ridiculous posture of talking about integrity and the abuse of great talents and shaking our heads over the gayest, most effervescent music ever written.

In three or four operas there is incriminating evidence of sustained effort made and inspiration conscientiously attended to and worked at to produce a comic masterpiece. But to compose *William Tell* and then retire, still in his thirties, was the best joke of all. Shaw, maybe, correctly gauged the moral temperature of Rossini's art when he said that the work owed its excellence to its being written for the Paris Opéra,

where the public had been educated by Gluck to expect at least a show of seriousness in *opera seria*. He rose to the occasion as a matter of business, just as he would have sunk to it had the commission come from Venice.

But just how splendidly he rose I confess I had had no inkling until last week's concert performance, given in Fairfield Hall by the Chelsea Opera Group under John Matheson. In the light of the work's power and richness, Rossini's retirement poses tantalizing questions.

One often sees it stated that he gave up (with half his life still ahead of him) because his genius was exhausted and he had nothing more to say. Another theory has it that being by now rich, as well as worldly and congenitally idle, he lacked any further inducement to compose and could at last settle down and enjoy himself: 38 operas were enough to be going on with. But such tidy conclusions ignore the fact that Rossini was under contract—a contract too lucrative for so worldly a man lightly to consider breaking—to produce four more works for the Opéra in the coming ten years. It was the 1830 Revolution and the fall of Charles X, and no other cause, that brought to an end an arrangement which the subsequent vogue for Meyerbeer might have curtailed, but not before *William Tell* had had a successor. An opera on *Faust* was under discussion when the Bourbon regime was swept away and with it the cultural world in which Rossini felt at home; and although, remembering what he did with *Othello*, we may smile at the idea of Rossini, not to mention his Parisian librettists, tackling Goethe, a single hearing of *William Tell*, faithfully performed, is enough to make one powerfully regret the fine things that could not have failed to result from however improbable a conjunction.

The composer of *William Tell* is not so much a different Rossini as a Rossini who, under the stimulus of an exceptionally important occasion, takes the trouble to be as inventive and interesting, as sustainedly dramatic, as he always had it in him to be. To see him at such pains to construct his score and bind it together, to watch the skill with which local colour (the picture of a pastoral community at work and play in surroundings of resounding natural grandeur) is used both to provide contrast and to serve the central business of the drama, and to experience the full variety and precision of his orchestration and the thrilling sense of space that he creates with it, is to feel that his *péchés de jeunesse* were, after all, handsomely atoned for. Commentators usually claim that the outcome of such un-precedented effort is something admirable but contrived and cold. Under the fresh impact of this hugely enjoyable score, I find the criticism as demonstably untrue as the old charge of excessive length—the work is long but not abnormally so—or the scarcely more serious objection that it asks impossible things of present-day singers. (*William Tell* is a challenge, but one that Covent Garden or Sadler's Wells should not hesitate to take up.) It is no use saying that Rossini did not have it in his nature to respond to the heroic demands of Schiller's drama of patriotism and liberty, when he undeniably and magnificently does so in scenes as stirring as anything in comparable Verdi operas. It is equally irrele-vant to complain that the libretto of the third and fourth acts is static and moribund, when the music galvanizes it into such compelling life. *William Tell* can afford to lose some of its copious ballet music. For the rest it only asks, like any other great opera, to be performed for all it is worth.

The rewards are rich. Only in the first act—which is largely concerned with evoking, with great charm, the world of pasture and lake, forest and mountain, that is soon to be engulfed in the drama of the Swiss struggle against Austrian oppression—does Rossini resort, though always gracefully, to conventional devices. Once into the action, he astonishes and delights us with music of masterly dramatic invention whose range covers nearly a century of opera, forward to Bizet as well as back to Mozart. The andantino of the men's Trio ('Quand l'Helvétie est un champ de supplices') is Verdian—Verdi at his best—in its grand 12/8 pulse and harmonic movement and its large nobility of style. So are the exhortation in F minor, darkly interwoven with obbligato cellos, which Tell addresses to his son just before he transfixes the apple, and the superb oath music for the men of the Three Cantons (though the magical suggestion of their approach across the distant lake to the forest rendezvous is the kind of poetic touch that Verdi was not to achieve until quite late in his career). On a more crudely popular level, Arnold's battle cry, exploding with high Cs and spotlit by whooping horns in octaves, is as rousing as the very best of *Nabucco* or *Ernani*. Still more remarkable are the prefigurings of Wagner, which burst forth fully in the final scene, when the storm clears to reveal the Alps vast and radiant, and the Swiss people salute their newly won freedom in music that is Wagnerian in its slowly gathering splendour, the transfigured *ranz des vaches* moving majestically in a gigantic chain of alternate minor and major thirds. Perhaps Rossini was right to retire after this. Others could continue where he had left off. He had shown them how.

(1970)

Wieland Wagner and the Bayreuth Experience

It is not difficult to point to ways in which the representation of Wagner's works in his own theatre falls short of the ideal which the theatre was created to make possible. Of the two productions that I have seen this year (1964), one spends most of the time swimming energetically against the current of Wagner's music. None of the singing has been first-rate except for Nilsson's Isolde (itself marred by poor diction) and much has been pretty middling. Yet the Bayreuth experience as always exerts its spell. Partly this is because the festival, like no other, is a pilgrimage, so arranged that you live Wagner throughout your waking hours, if not in your dreams, and the sacred rule quickly imposes itself: morning, read, meditate and expound libretto; afternoon, lunch (sparingly), change, walk up hill to theatre in time for start of opera at 4; evening, opera (with two intervals of an hour each) till 10 or after. Partly it is because the present presiding genius of the festival, Wieland Wagner, is for all his perversities a genius worthy of his name. But above all it is a matter of the unique conditions of performance. The lovely austerity and purposefulness of the Festspielhaus, designed by Wagner himself, makes all other opera houses seem mere entertainment pits, just as Wagner can make all other composers for the moment secondary.

After seeing *Tristan* again in this wonderful theatre I understand the Wagner madness that swept over Europe in the last quarter of the 19th century, and how it was that intelligent people could believe that all music led up to the music-dramas, if it was not actually superseded by them, the noblest works of the past being but precursors, contributors to the great evolutionary process which culminated in Wagner. Even now, under the fresh impact of Bayreuth, I almost believe it myself.

Not that the Festspielhaus is an obvious hotbed of fanaticism. It is not a place where you can wallow in the Wagnerian sonority. On the contrary, the whole acoustical and structural character of the interior seems designed to redress the balance towards a harmony of equal forces, a drama which uses music to say, with unsurpassed eloquence, what it has to say. It is a temple of the initiated. The voices and, in theory at least, the words ride out easily into the auditorium. Compared with a normal large opera orchestra, the orchestra at Bayreuth, sunk under the stage and concealed from the spectator by a huge grey hood, produces an effect rather like that of an old EMG hand-made gramophone compared with a good radiogram of the period. It is firm, clear, compact, with the emphasis on the strings. It is capable of marvellous pianissimos and illusions of distance. The string sound is incomparable in its grainy richness, range of colour, glowing warmth and definition of parts, and in an utterly natural quality of tone, 'from the wood': the texture of divided violas and cellos in the Prelude to *Tristan* was such as I have not heard anywhere else. But the theatre never produces an engulfing fortissimo. At first indeed, as with the EMG gramophone, you wish it were possible to turn the volume up. Then you come to accept it. It may not be satisfactory in every respect—the clarinet, a vitally important instrument in the Wagnerian palette, sounds much too backward, and the brass, which are located far under the stage, have to blow too hard for the good of their tone—but it provides the right sound, in level and general character, for the experience of dramatic re-creation that Bayreuth achieves.

Everything about the theatre is concentrated towards the same purpose. The steeply raked amphitheatre seating plan (mirrored, since 1951, by the steeply raked stage), the sunken orchestra, the absence of a visible conductor, the double proscenium arch, are all calculated to make us participants—communicants, almost—in the Wagnerian mystery. The process is deliberately contradictory. The two uptilted planes throw us into exceptionally close contact with the action. At the same time the double proscenium arch seems to frame and isolate it, placing it outside time, removed from the people witnessing it. It is a theatre for the enactment of myth. As we sit, in darkness hardly challenged by the faint fringe of light that seeps from the hidden pit, hearing the Prelude coming from far off and from inside our heads, our eyes and minds are drawn down towards the grey dim curtain—which seems as we stare at it to be both impenetrable and insubstantial—and towards the drama that waits behind it. The climax breaks and drains back, unfulfilled; the double basses play their long, quiet notes. And a wind like the air from another planet stirs the curtain. The veil of the temple parts. We are ready for the production of *Tristan*.

It does not disappoint us. The austere, intense, nonemotional art of Wieland Wagner belongs in these conditions. It is as if his advent had enabled Bayreuth to be completely itself. He is of course anathema to those for whom literal representation is the beginning and end of the producer's responsibility. Such people will, and do, complain of the absence of the torch (marvellously suggested by the lighting) and of Isolde's scarf and ceremonial robe. For them, all that is required is to do what Wagner said; is it not all clearly set out in the stage directions? One could reply that Wagner himself, towards the end of his life and in the light of the experience of trying to put his music-dramas on the stage, became increasingly dissatisfied with representational staging. But the main argument is one that they are not open to, since they refuse to recognize that the art of operatic production is a wilful creative art, an art of the particular, and consists not in carrying out instructions but in running risks and taking drastic decisions which may turn out badly but which have to be taken. It means being prepared to fail on a grand scale in order to have the chance of succeeding on a grand scale. Without his insight into his grandfather's works, Wieland Wagner's capricious gifts would be an irrelevance and his liberties intolerable. He has his spectacular failures. But his positive contribution to the understanding of Wagner far outweighs them. His capacity for paring the drama to its simplest outlines and seizing its essence, and the command of momentous gesture and movement that goes with it, combined with his visual genius and his mastery of complex lighting (some of his stage pictures remain imprinted on the memory like great paintings), amount to a different kind of theatrical art, imperfectly understood but, at its best, revealing fresh truths in the music-dramas and revitalizing them for a new generation of Europeans. His productions have been accused of being anti-musical—an accusation which, it must be admitted, he sometimes seems to go out of his way to substantiate. But at their best they are the very reverse; their very spareness involves a confidence in the ability of the score to convey what the eye no longer sees.

The first act of *Tristan* as realized in Wieland Wagner's current production is an excellent example of an interpretation that occasionally goes against the letter of Wagner's directions while working in harmony with his innermost thoughts. Perhaps this is mere rationalization; yet an interpretation which makes you experience Wagner with unparalleled intensity cannot be wrong. The impact of the admirable musical performance—Nilsson in blazing form, Kerstin Meyer, a haunted, childlike Brangaene, singing with too much vibrato but with a quiveringly alive sympathy which more than compensated, Pitz's splendid chorus delivering their brief scenes to maximum effect, Windgassen's Tristan less obtrusively unimaginative than in the other two acts, and the conductor, Karl Böhm, riding the rise and swell of the sea-driven music with a certainty that he was not to recapture during the rest of the evening—comes to us redoubled when the music is set in a dramatic context of such beauty and singlemindedness. The conception appears total and indivisible from first note to last; what we see on the stage seems the inevitable embodiment of what we hear and what Wagner wrote—even to the audacious liberty that Wieland permits himself in the final seconds of the act. The cruel green sky, the black ship's prow rearing hugely against it; the red screen behind which Isolde writhes and storms; the bare deck; the nightmarish vision of Kurwenal bending forward as he jeers at Brangaene; the sailors, shadowy dream people assembled in line at the corner of the stage, who appear only when they impinge on the consciousness of the chief characters and otherwise are swallowed up in darkness; the great curve of Mark's retinue, led by a lean and wolfish Melot and culminating in the golden figure of the king which sweeps in a swift half-circle round the rim of the stage, making the finest climax to the act that I have ever seen—some of these things are not in the stage directions, but they are, you would swear it, faithful to Wagner's deepest intentions.

The revolution that Wieland Wagner accomplished was in the attitude to Wagner the myth-maker, the composer of *Parsifal*, *Tristan* and *The Ring*. It was in every way the re-interpretation that the age was waiting for. His non-representational and, in both senses, economical methods, which restored Bayreuth both politically and financially at a time when its past was in disgrace and its future in doubt, have had what will surely be a permanent influence. He stripped the staging of Wagnerian music-drama of its late-19th, and early-20th, century accretions of operatic convention (the very thing, ironically, that Wagner himself, in composing his works, had set out to destroy). In doing so he de-teutonized it. But there is one work that he has not been able to do this to. *Die Meistersinger* resists him. It is ineluctably German, with what Shaw called 'the grand calm of the ideal Germany', Teutonic in a sense that no one would wish to change, except a German of Wieland Wagner's generation; and his theories batter helplessly against it. His current production has been revised and reworked (as is normal with him), and some of the eccentricities described in the press last year have been abandoned or modified: the Nightwatchman no longer picks his unseeing way over the supine bodies of an army of *Johannisnacht* revellers. But it remains more a representation of the satire on *Tannhäuser and the Singing Contest on the Wartburg* that Wagner originally thought of writing than of the work he actually wrote twenty years later. Wieland, you feel, has set out with the fixed determination that Holy German Art is not going to get away with it this time.

He loses no time in making his point. In place of the usual front curtain we have a drop in the shape of a huge blown-up facsimile of the work's title and author in Wagner's hand on a vellum-like background; above it, while the overture pursues its heedless course, we glimpse—another alienation effect—the 16th-century gallery of the stage-within-a-stage which is to be the setting for everything except the scene in Sachs' workshop. In place of the characters as the music delineates them we have the characters as Wieland Wagner apparently thinks they ought to have been delineated.

Needless to say there is a great deal of intelligence and even of insight mixed up in the contrariness. And Wieland Wagner's first act, in particular, is such a delightful piece of staging, re-creating so brilliantly the milieu of the action and controlled in every detail, from the individual masters to the anonymous apprentices, grey medieval little creatures playing dice and larking round their elders' feet, that for the moment you are captivated. Then your admiration for the wonderfully realistic and extremely funny presentation of the masters as a bunch of pompous self-satisfied provincial trade unionists is checked when you remember to listen to the orchestra. Is there really no more than parody in the great contrapuntal flowering of the masters' entry music?

Even Pogner (splendidly played by Kurt Boehme) is made
into an old windbag who fumbles and fussily consults a
scroll, while his colleagues yawn and nudge each other. And
what are we to make of the end of the second act, when in
the final bars a drunken, swaying Nightwatchman turns
and stares at the sudden apparition of a vast orange moon
rising up behind him under the 16th-century gallery? It is a
striking idea, in its way a highly poetic moment; it even
follows, up to a point and however casuistically, the stage
directions. But the music contradicts it in every syllable and
tone.

This happens repeatedly. The production says one thing,
the music calmly and persistently says another. Some Evas
are no doubt too sweet and sentimental, mere picture-book
abstractions; you could say a corrective was needed. But
Anja Silja turns her into a ruthless redhead, hell-bent on
getting away from home with her buccaneering young
adventurer (Sandor Konya) and, in the opening scene of
Act 2, totally devoid of affection for her bumbling old
father, despite all that the music tells us to the contrary.
Where Beckmesser is often depicted too farcically, this
Marker stands out as something of a scholar among his
fellows; you can see how such a man might well have been
looked up to and made town clerk. Carlos Alexander's tall
disdainful personage, massive-headed, goat-faced, is a
clever and plausible portrait. But Wieland Wagner has to
have him stroll haughtily into Sachs' workshop for all the
world as if the stabbing offbeats in the orchestra were not
reminding him at every other painful step of the humiliations
of *Polterabend*. Realism frequently overrides musical considerations. Sachs' quill-pen is still busily recording the
words of Walther's second verse as the orchestra proclaims
the sense of the beauty and wonder of the Prize Song flood-
ing the old cobbler's soul.

Yet, despite everything, the production is never less than
stimulating. By no means all of it is wrong-headed. Most
of the long scene in Sachs' room is first-rate; the cunningly

simple Dürer-like setting is one of Wieland Wagner's most felicitous stage pictures. The conception of Sachs (gruffly sung but impressively acted by Josef Greindl) seems to me pure gain: not the self-consciously wise 'philosopher', the slightly pretentious Meister, but a stumpy craftsman, a quiet man lit from within by an intense joy, whose wisdom is intuitive. (Here indeed tradition has benefited from a discreet purification.) The extraordinary feeling of goodness, of life working out right, that irradiates the production just before the Quintet, comes straight out of the music. Only in the final scene does Wieland Wagner go hopelessly off the rails, the processional guilds being replaced by a grotesque parodistic German folk dance and no procession, and at the end facsimiles dropping from the flies like autumn leaves in Vallombrosa.

The music wins, of course; Robert Heger's masterly conducting ensures that. But even at its most perverse the production earns a kind of gratitude for purging our reactions to this incomparable work of complacency and over-familiarity. *Die Meistersinger* emerges from 'l'expérience Wieland Wagner' unscathed and in a curious way enhanced. And parts of the production are good enough to suggest that Wieland Wagner may gradually be freeing his system of deep complexes and exasperations about the work, and moving towards a *Meistersinger* that is new and true.

(1964)

Zeffirelli's Don

The first night of the new *Don Giovanni* at Covent Garden was—judged by the high standards by which this sumptuous and carefully prepared production would wish to be judged— a shambles. Amid a lovely eyeful of baroque and other settings, violence was done to the work by grievous delays between scenes, and in more than one scene the musical ensemble was reduced to confusion by the one unpardonable crime in Mozart, unrhythmical singing, in which the Don himself, who would have gone to hell (and did) before he abandoned his sense of rhythm, and who must have saluted Pluto and Proserpine in phrases of impeccable poise and exactitude, was the worst offender.

If only critics were not always invited to the opening night of a new production. I found Monday's performance far more enjoyable, although this time I stood at the back of the Stalls Circle. The orchestral playing was both more vivid and more relaxed, the characterization richer and more assured, the ensemble much more polished; the elaborate changes of scene were contrived, as far as possible, with smoothness and tact. This was an effort not unworthy of a great house, and of an opera which, with all its faults, is the supreme manifestation of the art. It is easy to prove that *Figaro* is a more homogeneous and well-made work, a complete and consistent masterpiece. But wonderfully varied and true and felicitous though *Figaro* is, for anyone who learnt *Don Giovanni* at his most impressionable age there is simply no question: the difference between the two works is the difference in range and depth, ambiguity, and sheer musical audacity between the moment in the fourth act of *Figaro* when the Countess appears in her true guise and the music expresses the general astonishment by a conventional rhythmic figure and a turn into the tonic minor (perfectly satisfactory though it is in its context), and the stunned horror of that marvellous modulation into a related *major* key when Leporello uncloaks and reveals his identity in the Sextet—that scene which, for all da Ponte's perfunctoriness, is at the heart of the mystery of the unique tragi-comic fusion that is *Don Giovanni*. Uneven though it may be in dramaturgical construction, *Don Giovanni* is supreme because in it music as a dramatic language reached its highest point.

At Covent Garden there has been every sign, once past the first night, that the work has been treated by Solti and Zeffirelli with the passionate meticulousness it demands. Yet I remain unconvinced. How should *Don Giovanni* be produced? My ideal is a performance in a plain fixed setting with costumes of great richness, and the dramatic atmosphere conveyed by the grandeur of the actors and the music's innate and abundant graphic realism. Perhaps such an ideal is not realizable on the scale of grand opera. But however you do it you must start from the character of the music, and the quality that distinguishes it above all is the sense of driving momentum with which it seems to rush forward from first note to last. The drama may falter, in its lapse into conventional buffo in the first half of Act 2 (though the way Mozart uses this buffo to uncover deeper layers in the psychology of the Don and his relationship with Leporello is typical of the work), but the music, flute-haunted, possessed, diabolically virile or sublimely frivolous, is quite consistent. It insists on an unbroken flow of scenes; delays are unacceptable to it. Zeffirelli's staging sacrifices this vital quality to visual magnificence. It is true that the delays have been reduced since the first night. But a delay of even twenty seconds between the Trio of Masks and the ballroom scene is intolerable, and we suffer it in spite of the fact that the Trio is sung before a drop curtain to the accompaniment of discreet but audible rumblings of heavy masonry.

The settings, many of them at least, may be magnificent, but in the last resort they are irrelevant. It is not only that their general character (if one may so describe decor which ranges in such splendidly cavalier fashion over a century of painting and design) strikes me as unduly soft, dense, nostalgic for this music, which wants something at once stronger and lighter. We admire the charm of the Watteau landscape used for the middle scenes of Act 1, with its distant palace and lake, its trees and idyllic peasants bathed in a golden glow. But this is not what the opera is about. It is questionable whether Zeffirelli heightens the dramatic tension or actually diminishes it by reintroducing a group of peasants in the background during the Quartet. They enter, innocent, idealized creatures, then stop on seeing a 'scene' in progress between four aristocrats; they nudge each other, point, and stare in wonderment (not surprisingly, since the aristocrats are dressed in the fashion of an earlier age). It is an interesting idea, but like so many ideas in this production it complicates and refracts where one should be content to be simple and concentrated: the dramatic tension is already amply provided for.

There are, needless to say, genuinely imaginative things in the production, like the setting of the latter part of the epilogue in the same palace park, with the characters wandering large and pale and lost in the dawn light—a highly poetic realization of the morning-after feeling of the music, the prosaic but unreal world which follows the end of the perverted genius who possessed it. I do not share the view that the painter's approach is out of place in opera. In *Don Carlo*, for instance, it is essential to set the tragedy firmly and gorgeously in its historical context. In *Lucia* it excuses an absurd work by holding up the most elegant of mirrors to its absurdities. But in *Don Giovanni* it is an intruder and worse. The direct effect, at Covent Garden, is to dissipate the drama's impact in exquisite inessentials.

What is in the end important is not that Zeffirelli has surprisingly mismanaged the ballroom scene, where the guests
are made to dance to the opening allegro, and the Don, in
the final impasse, is saved by the rapiers of his servants
instead of himself cleaving a path through his enemies by a
sudden explosion of personality; nor that Zeffirelli has
succumbed to ignoble farce in the Trio 'Ah taci, ingiusto
core'; nor, equally, that in the first 'Watteau' scene he has
arranged his figures in groupings of striking beauty; but
simply that from the start he has concentrated on the wrong
things.

Perhaps if we had a complete Don it would be different.
But Cesare Siepi, in a performance of great accomplish-
ment and (on Monday at least) musical distinction, is only
half the part. With his handsome face and figure and his
arrogant guttural r's he is truly aristocratic, as few are in the
role. The seduction of Zerlina is a masterpiece of purring,
effortless carnality. But there is too strong a touch of the
mindless animal about it. Siepi stalking Zerlina is too
casual, instinctive. When he turns aside to munch a fruit and
elegantly throw away the pip, it is like a cat suddenly distracted from the bird it is dismembering. He is the great
cat but not the fallen Lucifer, the being apart—and whatever
the musicologists may tell us, the demonic Don is a fact;
his music insists on it, with its phrases striding over the
notes of the common chord ('Ma non manca in me coraggio',
'Hò fermo il cor', 'Vanne lontan da me', 'Già la mensa è
preparata', 'Fin ch'han dal vino', 'Falle passar avanti'—
but the list is almost endless) and its obsessive repetitions.
Think of those Ds and E flats at the end of the champagne
aria, or the hysteria of 'Io mi voglio divertir' and 'Vivan le
femmine', repeated over and over again. Of course, the use
of a bass (the worst solecism in opera) helps to blunt the
force of the work. The part demands to be sung by, if
anything, a slightly lighter shade of baritone than the
Count in *Figaro* and to do otherwise is to falsify Mozart,
who had nothing essential to learn about colour.

Orchestral colour, warm, subtle and vivid, is a mark of Solti's conducting. By Monday's performance he was giving the players more scope for personal expression than on the first night and at the same time controlling the ensemble more surely. Sometimes he insists too fanatically on an accompanying figure; and he misses one or two cardinal dramatic points: those two great gunshot chords, for instance, which at the opening of the supper scene should seem to sum up everything that has gone before and is to follow, and should be slightly held back and delivered with a Beethovenian conclusiveness; or that crowning symbol of the opera, the dazzling trumpet arpeggio some twenty bars from the end, which comes like an imperious reminder of the man who has left his mark on all that came near him, but which I could not hear at all. Yet the general achievement is not to be despised.

Indeed, at its very worst the whole production is rarely less than most stimulatingly awry—if some other work than *Don Giovanni* were only involved! The cast contains two exceptional performances, Mirella Freni's Zerlina, piquantly acted and robustly and excellently sung, and Geraint Evans's scuttling, ratlike old trooper of a Leporello. The Donna Anna, Leyla Gencer, is a musical singer, but her voice, shirking the implications of those implacable high As, does not command the grand style of the part. Sena Jurinac is as always a moving Elvira; but, half-smothered in black lace at her first appearance, she never quite emerges from the luxuriance of the setting. Alas, she is not alone.

(1962)

Nature and Art

Aix, like all good festivals, is so much more than just the music it performs. It is the whole warm life and golden character of the place—the broad boulevards fronted by the stately façades and massively carved doors of the palaces of the *ancien régime* and over-arched with a vault of branches that make them cool as a cathedral in the blaze of noon, the honey-coloured side-streets ending abruptly in a sky of burning blue, the sound of the perpetual splashing of water in the courtyard fountains, the thriving time-emancipated life of the pavement cafés and, passing and repassing before them, the endless procession of students and nymphets and old bags and magnificently shambling dogs, which creates the illusion that the whole town, like oneself, is on holiday and that, except for the swifts sweeping their sky-lanes over the rose-red tiles of the housetops and the cicadas sizzling with rhythmical precision, everything in Aix is given over to constructive idleness. Above all, it is opera at night under an open sky. In the archbishop's palace—a great plane-tree branching up through the floor of the balcony—under the velvet dome, 'Vega conspicuous over-head', or later, when the moon clears the parapet of the wooden proscenium arch built in the likeness of 17th-century stone, a mediocre performance is forgiven and a good one magically enhanced.

It was a pity that the symphony concerts were not also given there, as they have been in the past, instead of in the Parc Rambot, a small pleasance within easy hooting distance of one of Aix's main through-roads, where between the

eructations of a battalion of bullfrogs (splendid in any other
context), the tireless eroticism of the ubiquitous cicada, and
the heavy lorries changing gear, art has to wait its turn; as
someone in *La grande illusion* remarks of man-made frontiers, 'la nature s'en fout'. In the concert of French Romantic
music given by the Belgian Radio Orchestra under Igor
Markevich, large parts of *La Mer* were inaudible. The bullfrogs respectfully held their fire during the opening bars of
the Fantastic Symphony, but it could not last; at times it only
lacked the 'frightened dogs who kept up a howling obbligato' during the carousals of Berlioz and his fellow-students
at the Villa Medici in Rome. From what came through,
however, it was clear that Markevich was, perhaps understandably, sacrificing classical proportion and delicacy of
timbre to histrionic effect; but nothing could excuse his
Brighton Pier approach to three numbers from the first
Arlésienne Suite.

A far more impressive concert was given there a few
evenings later by the same orchestra under the admirable
Pierre Boulez. Apart from a dully conceived and scruffily
scored Concerto for Orchestra by Hindemith, the programme was fascinating. It was also much better played and,
the sun being still up and the frogs *tacet*, more of it reached
the audience intact. Even so, there were casualties to *la
nature*; what appeared to be an excellent performance of
Webern's Six Pieces, Op. 10, was partially thrown away on
the breeze. And the first hearing of 'Rimes pour diverses
sources sonores' by the young French composer Henri
Pousseur, a work combining full orchestra, a couple of
smaller groups placed at the far end of the auditorium and
two separate loudspeakers dispensing electronic music,
was inevitably made to seem without rhyme or reason. What
with the chirping of birds, the groan of passing *camions*,
the murmurings of malcontents ('C'est original, quoi?'),
and sudden gusts of wind that had the percussion players
pursuing their music about the platform like discreetly
frantic figures in a scene from a film by René Clair, it was

impossible to relate the sounds to any kind of formal pattern and therefore to begin to assess the work; the only clear reaction was unbounded admiration for the skill with which Boulez controlled and imposed order on a situation fraught with anarchic possibilities. Indeed, both as a master of the mechanics of modern scores and as a profoundly eloquent interpreter of them, Boulez stands out, in my experience at least, among conductors of contemporary music. Though he conducts without a stick, his beat seems precise to a quaver's breadth. At the same time, within the scope of a highly economical style, he manages somehow to sketch and convey to his players the inner meaning and musicality of each phrase. So many performances of contemporary music are content if they exist from bar to bar, not daring to look beyond, and the impression spreads that the composer has proceeded in an equally ad hoc fashion. The great merit of Boulez is that, being able not only to grasp a work entirely but also to persuade an orchestra to do the same, he gives you a sense of the shape and sweep of a piece as a whole. The concert ended with a thrilling account of the suite from *Wozzeck*, sung with great intensity by Helga Pilarczyk. Berg's weightier, more solid scoring overcame most of the open-air distractions. But the Webern was a fine performance needlessly squandered.

In the week that I spent in Aix the most worthwhile events were the *Wozzeck* suite and Haydn's opera *Il mondo della luna*, conducted by Giulini (which, without proving Haydn wrong in his low estimate of his own talents as an opera composer when compared with Mozart's, thoroughly justified its disinterment). The two Mozart operas were disappointing. I saw only the dress rehearsal of *Così fan tutte*, which seemed decidedly the weaker of the two, with Teresa Stich-Randall playing Fiordiligi like a female impersonator, a blend of Goody Two-Shoes and Anna Russell, dingy sets and a strangely haphazard production.

The Magic Flute went better, yet was only spasmodically

memorable. Soundly conducted by Alberto Erede and simply and on the whole pleasingly produced by Jean-Pierre Grenier, it suffered from a fundamental imbalance, the earthy roles being much superior to the spiritual ones. Miss Stich-Randall, who used to sing delightfully (think of her Nanetta in the Toscanini recording of *Falstaff*), has evidently succumbed to the Viennese scourge which replaces singing by cooing. Her Pamina was sung as it was played, in an aura of dimpled piety and cosy, knowing archness, with hardly a natural phrase to its name. In Richard Holm's Tamino there was hardly a phrase of any sort. He hewed up the vocal line into manageable chunks of two or three notes; 'hand in hand ins Tempel geh'n', for instance, was delivered in the manner of a youth leader about to set out on a hike—it was Mozart in lederhosen. On the other hand the three Ladies (Nadine Sautereau, Jane Berbié and Hilde Rössl-Majdan) were among the best I have ever seen, both in their musical ensemble and in the quiet, telling way they took the opportunities for comedy which are often either ignored or overplayed. And as Papageno the evergreen Erich Kunz gave a lesson in artistry, intelligence, wit and unquenchable vitality that might have profited his coarser colleagues. This was what one had come for. In the two Quintets, in which Erede set ideal tempos and even the inflexible Tamino yielded to the spell, and above all in Papageno's aria 'Ein Mädchen oder Weibchen', the music matched at last the beauty of the night, and one lived for a few moments the essential Mozart, round and bright and harmonious as the full moon shining down on the enchanted theatre.

(1959)

Boom Town

Wexford, since the 1958 festival, has not only built a fine new bridge across the estuary; more seriously, it has taken down the notice which used to stand guard over the old bridge, informing the motorist that 'no vehicle of a weight not exceeding five tons may proceed over the aforementioned bridge at a speed not exceeding fifteen miles an hour'. But in every other way the festival is steadfast and unchangeable. The long, grey, meandering main street, purposefully inconsequential as an Irish conversation, is still a place where vehicles wander at their peril. The bountiful bars still do booming trade as dawn is wondering whether there is any point in bothering to bring in another morning, since no one will be up to see it. At the opera the acoustics of the pigmy Theatre Royal still assault the ear with waves of savage shock-troop fortissimo, while rubicund priests bellow like bulls at every curtain call. The imported Italian singers are chosen with nice discrimination by the local postmaster. And the search for hidden riches in the lesser-known works of Verdi continues with unabated enthusiasm.

This year, however, they have failed to strike oil. *I due Foscari*, the 1958 choice, was crude, perhaps, but it was the real thing. *Aroldo*, for Verdi, is poor stuff. Originally known as *Stiffelio* and composed immediately before *Rigoletto*, it featured the marital tribulations of a 19th-century German evangelical clergyman. Even the impervious Piave seems to have realized that this would not do. Accordingly, seven years later, he tweaked it back into that majestically vague medieval never-never-land beloved of librettists hard up for a dramatic idea, where there is always a crusade going on, and the characters bear such fine old Wessex names as Egberto, Aroldo and Godvino, the date is 1200—though friars are already thick on the ground—and the action flits effortlessly from 'Kenth' to the sunset-tinted shores of Lago di Loomondo.

I am all for a bit of fun, and in *Aroldo* one gets it. But the fact that the transformation could be accomplished so painlessly does not say much for the dramatic potency of the original. The trouble was that *Stiffelio/Aroldo* had virtually nothing to offer even the relatively undemanding Verdi of 1850. There is little of that grandly simple and universal heroism of emotion which drew such responsive fire from him in *Nabucco*, *Ernani* and *I due Foscari*. The characters go through the traditional motions; they are challenged to duels which they refuse until honour is spat on, they prowl about in graveyards, they retreat into hermits' cells only to be dragged from them by an inexorable plot. But it is all done with cardboard perfunctoriness and a manifest lack of enthusiasm for the job in hand.

There are, of course, moments: a stirring Quartet for the baffled duellists in the graveyard, and Mina's prayer, 'Salvami, tu gran Dio', in the opening scene, where the vocal line suddenly soars in phrases of superb dignity worthy of the Requiem above striking chord progressions in the woodwind and horns; the greatness of Verdi's heart could not be entirely untouched even by such puppet emotions. But plots as feebly conventional as this had struck more sparks from him. (Perhaps part of the trouble was that this one confronted him with a heroine who for once is guilty of the sexual sins with which she is charged, and he did not know quite what to make of her.) Even at a sporting level it contains nothing as joyous as the final curtain of *I due Foscari*, with the dying Doge holding up the action in order to lead the company in a great swinging 9/8.

Yet at his worst the Master is always worth reviving. In *Aroldo* there is the satisfaction of watching a superb theatrical technique ticking over. With all its pseudo-heroic simplicity, I enjoyed it more than Rossini's *La gazza ladra*, where good singing, and admirable conducting by John Pritchard, were qualified not only by Peter Potter's superficial production but by the indecisive character of the work, which straddles two different conventions, and in which, side by side with genuinely touching inventions, situations fraught with stress are reflected in music of the sort of impudence and inspired triviality that occurs in the well-known overture. The noise in *Aroldo* was of course prodigious. The Radio Eireann Light Orchestra, thrashed within an inch of its life by Charles Mackerras, galloped gamely through the score, trampling some of the finer effects underfoot but conveying, I imagine, a fairly accurate rough impression—though the slow trumpet solo in the overture quavered like the voice of Yeats himself reciting in old age 'The Lake Isle of Innisfree'. Nicola Nicolov and Mariella Angioletti, as the estranged pair who meet again on the bonnie banks in the last minutes of the opera, threw all they had into their papier-mâché roles. But the evening was dominated by a performance of baying ferocity from Aldo Protti as Egberto. Dressed as Basil Rathbone in the role of Rip van Winkle, he fairly laid back his lugs and let us have it. I admire vigour, and Signor Protti is nothing if not vigorous; but from his manner of singing he might have been standing in the middle of the amphitheatre at Verona where I left him last July. It was some compensation to see him billed in next day's paper as Waldo Trotti. The Irish typesetters are wonderful for cutting an artist down to size. On the other hand, 'the chorus sank like professionals' is hardly fair to the buoyancy and competence of that splendid body, the Wexford Festival Choir.

(1959)

Shakespe-hearean Opera

The modern revival of early 19th-century Italian opera has its spiritual home in St Pancras and its most desirable shrine at the Wexford Festival. In Wexford you drown the memory of all you were once told about opera as drama. Some towns have festivals thrust upon them. In Wexford the musical events are part of the diurnal cycle, an intensification of speech into song. Since I last visited it, the Theatre Royal has been done up, the conductor no longer has to descend a fire escape in order to reach his post, the staging has become more sophisticated, and Irish compositors seem to have lost some of their careless rapture: the days of 'Heathen Hanper' and her ilk are no more. But the spirit, and the discriminating choice of artists, are unchanged. This year the new director, Brian Dickie, successor to the great Tom Walsh, has brought off an excellent Wexford joke by presenting a festival of 'Shakespearean' operas which are enjoyable precisely in so far as one forgets Shakespeare.

I had always supposed that Rossini's *Otello* had a happy ending; it seemed only right. The work was indeed given in this form by certain Italian theatres unable to stomach its ferocities undiluted. At Wexford, however, we had the opera as Rossini and the Neapolitan dilettante Marchese Berio originally conceived it. Berio apparently knew the play, but there is excuse for doubting it. Othello's passion shrinks to outraged vanity, while Rodrigo swells into a full-blown operatic rival; the handkerchief becomes a *billet-doux*, and Iago's function is limited to giving the plot (set entirely in Venice) a shove or two in the right direction. In

Rossini's defence it must be said that on the whole he rises as high as he is encouraged to—which in the last act, where the libretto comes closest to Shakespeare, is impressively high. The opening scene of the act contains what would be a marvellous stroke in a truly dramatic context and is beautiful as it is: the voice of an unseen gondolier singing a haunting strain to—however improbably—Dante's 'Nessun maggior dolore'. The Willow Song takes up a related tune in the same sad G minor, then drifts into the relative major with no loss of poignancy, returning at the end of each verse with a downward sequence of rising thirds which Verdi clearly remembered when he wrote 'Caro nome'.

Throughout, there is evidence of an attempt to fuse the disparate parts of *opera seria* into a consistent whole that would be revolutionary if Mozart had not done it nearly 40 years before in *Idomeneo*. *Otello* is the first Rossini opera in which the recitative is entirely accompanied by orchestra.* Yet what a frustrating composer he is. Just because he can be so good when he tries, how exasperating are his lapses into perfunctoriness. How senseless, how utterly beside the point are the strings of roulades into which the vocal line is always liable to break, whatever the situation. You never know when he is not going to mock you for presuming to take him seriously. There is no guarantee that an expressive passage will not be followed immediately by a barefaced melodic cliché, usually a dotted phrase in the commonest of common time dancing up the scale from dominant to tonic. In the end, it might as well end happily. The pleasure is largely sensual. It is a considerable pleasure, because Rossini handles his clichés with the utmost brilliance. Simply as sound such things as the combination of strutting quavers on bassoons and pizzicato cellos with sparkling tremolo violins, or the florid piccolo and clarinet decorations to the delightful march which signalizes the victorious Otello's return from the wars, are irresistible, especially in a theatre

---

* Actually the second; the first is *Elisabetta, Regina d'Inghilterra*.

as small as Wexford's, where the fizz and tang of the orchestral writing strike like salt spray.

Roméo et Juliette, the other festival offering, has neither the lapses of *Otello* nor the genius. Except for a rousing marcato, with echoes of the Marseillaise, sung by Juliet to keep her spirits up before she drains the potion, the score is as impeccable in tone as it is in workmanship. Perfumed night, street brawls, friar's cell—Gounod imitates them all. The conventions of opera have never been more expertly worked in the interests of bourgeois entertainment. The big fight scene builds up, with masterly control of pace, to an almost Beethovenian adagio ensemble in C minor. The four solo cellos in the Introduction have an almost Verdian gravity and sweetness. Almost is, of course, the word. The lilting prelude to Act 2, with its glistening harps and muted strings and the pleasingly archaic flavour of its harmonies moving in whole tones, would, ideally, be better suited to Offenbach in his warmest vein than to the end of the balcony scene, where it recurs to Romeo's 'Sleep dwell upon thine eyes' (or rather 'Qu'un sourire d'enfant sur ta bouche vermeille'). But there is never any question of Shakespeare here. We realize this from the start and sit back and enjoy ourselves. The enjoyment is mild but undisturbed.

(1967)

Volpone

In a less self-consciously cultural epoch Francis Burt's *Volpone*, produced for the first time in England by the New Opera Company last week, would have been suffered to come more naturally into the world. It would have been enough for the moment that the work reveals a lively talent for the theatre, that it is skilfully devised and put together, scene by scene, and has zest, wit and variety of pace—in short, that it makes an effective evening in the opera house. What more is it politic, or just, to ask at this stage? Diplomacy is a vital part of the critic's art in an age when the new is a small power with weak defences. It is a matter not of pulling punches but of knowing where to land them, of making our standards not laxer but more flexible; not of sparing what is bad but of encouraging what may be good. Mediocrity is the compost of genius; the single great work of art is nurtured by the many ordinary but indispensable ones. With all the other modern discouragements to the writing of good music, the 20th century adds its spoilt perfectionism, the intensity of culture which forces every new creation (when it does not ignore it) to explain why it is not a masterpiece and to be summarily judged alongside not merely the accepted products of the present but also the concentrated glories of the past. A new English opera ought to be such a commonplace occurrence that we could afford to be implacably discriminating (though even then we would have no sense if we complained that it was inferior to *Don Giovanni*). But until that far-off millennium arrives, we must remember what we are aiming at and dispose our ammunition accordingly.

I do not mean to suggest that Mr Burt is a mediocrity, any more than I am claiming *Volpone* to be a work of genius. Its limitations—especially its melodic limitations—are obvious. But in some ways they are less remarkable than its achievements. For a first opera by a young composer, *Volpone* is staggeringly accomplished. In reducing Ben Jonson's play to a serviceable libretto, and in providing music that keeps the action continually moving from one contrasting scene to the next, Mr Burt never fumbles for an instant. A second hearing convinced me that there is very little really dull music in the opera. The comparative lack of striking musical invention is not, surely, as important as the cleverness and energy with which he makes use of the material he allows himself. Young composers often put, if anything, too many ideas into an opera (witness Mozart in the *Seraglio* and Berlioz in *Benvenuto Cellini*). Mr Burt, on the other hand, husbands his gold more jealously than his own Fox; but I do not feel that this is because he has little to spend and that these are the only ideas in his head. Nor is it mere fond chauvinism to believe that he has gone better than his masters Blacher and Liebermann in freshness and vigour, without falling behind them in ingenuity. When he borrows from Stravinsky he does it with a skill and full-blooded conviction that makes us accept the imitation as original. The plot does not in fact give him much scope for melodic set-pieces; its pace and violence demand something like the manic rhythms and stuttering syncopations which Mr Burt untiringly manufactures for it.

There are moments when this style mounts to a splendidly dramatic sweep and arrogant momentum: in the second trial scene, and most of all in the scene where Volpone leaps from his feigned sick-bed and, disguised in the hooded cloak of a court official, strides after his enraged suitors to taunt them in the street. We are simply not allowed to notice whether or not there is melodic poverty here. Where the formal pattern of the text asks for a tune—Mosca's Parasite speech or Volpone's superbly concupiscent seduction ballad,

'Come, my Celia, let us prove'—the answer is at least engaging. This ballad is a measure of what Mr Burt can and cannot do. The tune is memorable. It has a proud, imperious cut and gait; it expresses the conceit of the Olympian rogue. But it does not attempt the fantastic imagery through which Jonson's Volpone swells to the ecstatic 'We may so transfuse our wandering souls/Out at our lips, and score up sums of pleasures.' In general, the music captures the bustle of the action, the atmosphere of obsessive intrigue, but not the splendour and havoc of the verse nor, for the most part, its pungency of characterization; the savage, encrusted richness of Ben Jonson's exposure of avarice, corruption and inhumanity hardly lends itself to Mr Burt's neo-Stravinskian idiom. His *Volpone* is seen from without, but it is seen with a sharp eye and drawn with a devilishly cool hand.

Mr Burt, in fact, is an operatic talent worth investing in. It would be splendid if Sadler's Wells would nerve themselves to take the risk and bring *Volpone* into their repertory. The NOC's production, very capably conducted by Leon Lovett, needs only a few changes. Jacqueline Delman's Celia was a dim impersonation, colourless in voice, obscure in diction, and I thought Edward Byles miscast as the Parasite; he toiled hard, but his stage persona is that of a plump good-natured fellow, more honest belly than scheming brain. John Holmes, on the other hand, relished the rich opportunities of Volpone with a hungry competence that was as impressive as anything I have seen on the Sadler's Wells stage for a long time. His powerful bass-baritone voice is not yet fully rounded and firm, but his phrasing and timing of the often complicated metrical writing proclaimed him a musician of parts. Best of all, he is that just man among the cities of the plain, a singer who can act. His performance had a commanding grandeur, an authority and wolfish charm and contemptuous zest, that was the product both of natural presence and of the most studied consideration of gesture, expression and make-up. Mr Holmes is a magnificent find. His success was also, of course, the producer's. Michael Geliot handled his large cast with power and intelligence. Ralph Koltai's brilliant revolving set, turned by a team of midgets, added an ideal flavour of grotesque panache.

(1961)

Old Wells and New

On Saturday Sadler's Wells gave their last performance in the old Rosebery Avenue home before the move to St Martin's Lane. The opera chosen was *Peter Grimes*, the work with which nearly a quarter of a century earlier the company had reopened after the war; but all temptation to make a great tearful exuberant showbiz occasion was firmly resisted. Sights are set on the Coliseum; the future is the thing. Even if the orchestra pit which will shortly resound to the opening chord of *Don Giovanni* (what Ernest Newman called 'the most magically evocative chord in the whole of music') is still a hole in the ground, and even if the adaptability of an opera company of the character of Sadler's Wells to an auditorium twice the size has yet to be demonstrated, the prospect of possessing a theatre in the centre of London which offers reasonable living conditions outweighs all uncertainties and anxieties, immediate and to come. They have waited a long time. It is not the new South Bank theatre they had hoped for, but it is decisively better than what they have, and it opens up intoxicating possibilities. There is no time for nostalgia.

I doubt whether many people ever really loved the old house, quite apart from the difficulty of getting there (let alone of getting away again afterwards). No redecoration could disguise its coldness and lack of atmosphere or style. No application, or subsequent removal, of scientific acoustical devices could make the sound pleasant. But the place was lovable by association, as the scene of stirring events, and landmarks in English operatic history. *Peter Grimes* was first heard there, and—almost as great a rebirth—*Gloriana* gloriously vindicated. It was Sadler's Wells that had the recklessness to put on *Idomeneo* and the faith and skill to prove that an opera previously regarded even by its admirers as fit only for festivals could hold its own on a repertory stage. Recently, there was that other famous act of belief and restitution, the Goodall *Mastersingers*, a piece of great conducting that had the unhasting, unresting natural force and broad splendours of a river flowing to the sea. The English Janáček movement began at Sadler's Wells, fathered by the enthusiasm of Norman Tucker.

My memories of the place do not go back much more than 15 years. I never saw Joan Cross or Arnold Matters. But I shall always remember the sovereign art of Anna Pollak, cool mistress of style and wit and the delicately absurd when all was vaudeville and unintentional absurdity around her; Howell Glynne's Frosch in *Die Fledermaus*, a web-footed gaoler warily bent on keeping his hernia under lock and key; Ronald Dowd setting a dull *Fidelio* alight or raising *Samson and Delilah* temporarily to epic stature by the power of his noble, tormented presence and impassioned declamation; Patricia Kern, unfailingly musical, an artist of inspiring flair and freshness, in half a dozen roles—Cinderella, Cherubino, Eurydice, Iolanthe, Hansel—that I have not seen better done anywhere; Margaret Neville's entrancingly natural Gretel; Gregory Dempsey's theatrical vitality, his profound intuitive sympathy with the sad, the deranged, the simple, the instinctively good; David Bowman's precise, pharisaical Kothner, a Beckmesser in the making; Eric Shilling, the *sine qua non* and *ne plus ultra* of Lord Chancellors, practised to the least twitch of the tapir nose sniffing trouble, the most expertly timed emphasis of dubious jaw or questioning eyebrow (in Frank Hauser's splendid production, a gauntlet flung down on the day after the expiry of the G and S copyright which, seven years later, has still to be taken up); also in *Iolanthe*, Denis Dowling's magisterial Mountararat, glassy but voracious of eye, imperturbable of bearing even when momentarily lost for words and mouthing like some great carp; the adorable dottiness and equally adorable sexuality of Joyce Blackham in *La belle Hélène*; Derek Hammond Stroud's Calchas in the same opera, huge and reproachful of head and deprecating of body, like an animated Beerbohm cartoon; Alexander Young's touchingly eager Tom Rakewell, his quizzical eye and command of urbane gesture in Anthony Besch's production of *Count Ory*.

Then, selected almost at random, Colin Davis' conducting of *Idomeneo*, *Oedipus* and *Mahagonny*; Meredith Davies's *A Village Romeo and Juliet*; Mackerras' *From a House of the Dead*; Bernardi's *Hansel and Gretel* and *Queen of Spades*; John Matheson's *Samson* and *Traviata*; Alix Stone's decor for *Gloriana* and *The Mines of Sulphur* and Jane Kingsmill's for *Hansel and Gretel*; above all, the achievements of team-work, the performances in which the united efforts of producer, designer, conductor, music staff and cast combined to produce a homogeneous and vital artistic result, as was seen in Colin Graham's productions of *Gloriana* and *From a House of the Dead* and (despite undistinguished sets) in the Byam Shaw/Blatchley *Mastersingers*.

One sometimes hears suggestions that that kind of achievement is rarer, and the general standard lower, under the present regime than it was under the previous one. This seems to me rubbish, whether sentimental or malicious, born of an unconscious resentment that Sadler's Wells are developing away from dear, patronizable little Englishry towards a higher type of music theatre, thus attracting more than the specialized 'Sadler's Wells public' and making the move to grander premises unavoidable. Whether they are too grand is a question that time will settle. Personally I have sufficient confidence in the flexibility of the talents which were responsible for the above-mentioned productions to feel optimistic. It is vernacular performances and a certain directness of approach that give the company its *Volksoper* character; the size of the theatre has nothing essentially to do with it. The company's commitments oblige it to perform works that sat awkwardly in Rosebery Avenue—*Tosca*, *Tannhäuser*, *Peter Grimes*.

Looking ahead, I think rather of how the challenge of the Coliseum will encourage Sadler's Wells to repeat the pattern of their *Mastersingers* and regularly exploit the presence of both halves of the company in London for several months of the year so as to accumulate an orchestra and chorus large enough to do such works in the style they demand. There is nothing anti-*Volksoper* in this, nor in the more spacious staging that the Coliseum will require. I see no reason why the good qualities epitomized in the current *Grimes* production should not survive when the disadvantage—a set so cramped that the inhabitants of the Borough are in constant danger of tripping over baskets and fishing tackle on their lawful progress up and down the main street—has been eliminated.

As to whether the adventurousness of repertory that has been typical of Sadler's Wells for the last ten years will survive the higher reasons of economics which, we are told, will require the theatre to be filled nightly to at least 65 per cent of the capacity of this much larger auditorium, that remains to be seen. Certainly it must be watched with a vigilant eye; the management will be judged partly by the degree of success with which it passes this test. But all in all I take it to be one of the most hopeful developments in English opera since the war.

(1968)

Towards an English Ring

If there is any justice and any sanity in our musical life, the production of *The Valkyrie* now enthralling large audiences at the Coliseum will be the first step—a giant step—towards a complete *Ring* cycle in English. To those who object that it is not necessary for Sadler's Wells to duplicate with a local cast what Covent Garden already do with an international one (as the opera committee of the Arts Council are known to have objected when the plan was put to them for approval a year or two ago), the answer is, first, that the box office does better business with Wagner than with almost anything else in the company's repertoire, and secondly that Wagner at the Royal Opera House and Wagner at the Coliseum are two separate and complementary experiences, both of them thoroughly necessary. Indeed, the word seems cold and cautious after last Friday's tremendous performance. Life without having seen it is hardly imaginable. What made it so moving was above all the fact of its being given in English and the sudden sharpening of focus and intensifying of reality that followed from that. I am sure there have been many like myself who know the work well and understand what is being said when they hear it sung in the original, yet who have found it taking on almost an extra dimension in a production in which the drama—the meaning, so to speak, of every phrase in the score—reaches them direct and is apprehended instantly, simply because it is sung in their own language.

The quality of this English is, of course, crucial. The old fustian—in which Sieglinde used to be made to question the panting fugitive prostrate on her hearth with 'A horn of foaming mead, guest, haply thou'lt not refuse?'—was clearly unacceptable. What I had not believed possible was that an English version of Wagner could reconcile the conflicting demands of accuracy, clarity, English usage versus Wagnerian inversion and alliteration, musical phrasing, and 'tone', as successfully as Andrew Porter's reconciles them. Line after line makes its point firmly and at the same time fits the music's natural shape. It is a masterpiece of subtle fidelity both to the score and to the sense of the verse, of which it preserves a surprising amount of the force while stripping it of its antique pseudo-medievalism. Mr Porter has been criticized for retaining in their German form 'Walküre' and the various symbolic names with which the work makes such play—'Wehwalt', 'Friedmund' and the rest. Criticized thoughtlessly: for 'Valkyrie' cannot be naturally stressed as Wagner's music commonly stresses 'Walküre'; and one look at the first act should tell us that if 'Wehwalt' is translated (into 'Woeful' or whatever), there is no escape from translating 'Siegmund' and 'Sieglinde'. And, as Mr Porter has observed, are we then to call them 'Victor' and 'Victoria'?

The translation is the foundation on which the joint-producers, Glen Byam Shaw and John Blatchley, and their cast have built a dramatic performance of extraordinary intensity. The sense of pity for the suffering of men (and gods) which is the glory of this marvellous work (and one reason why it is many people's favourite among the *Ring* operas), the simplicity of the saga world in which every experience is fresh and momentous to the human beings who inhabit it, the tragic irony of Wotan's relationship, seen and unseen, with the unhappy race he fathered, and the poignancy of their brief ecstatic joys, strike with a fierce immediacy that is overwhelming. When Sieglinde relives the scene at her wedding feast, or runs blindly towards Fafner's forest clutching to her the fragments of broken sword, when Wotan presides over the slaughter of his beloved son, it is as if a veil between us and the drama had been removed; the events, and the emotions they arouse, seem vivid as never before. Partly this is because of the skill of a production which, starting always from the music, takes a consistent view of the work and expresses it in a style at once austere and alive to its profound humanity; partly because of the conviction and commitment which radiate the entire cast. The humblest Valkyrie sings as if her life depended on it, as if the success of the evening depended on her. Musically as well as verbally, the meaning of the work blazes out into the theatre.

In all this the inspiration of Goodall is manifest. His mastery is, I should say, greater than ever. Orchestrally at last Friday's performance there were fewer slips than in his celebrated *Mastersingers*, and the fullness of phrasing, the beauty of tone and aptness of colour—in the falling string music as Siegmund bends over the sleeping Sieglinde, to name one of hundreds of possible examples—were quite as memorable. Some reports of the first night of this *Valkyrie* spoke of longueurs, and splendours spoiled by some inordinately slow tempos. The performance that I heard, which was the third, lasted some minutes longer than Knappertsbusch's monumental reading as measured by the Bayreuth timekeeper in 1951. But, as always, relative not absolute tempo is the thing in Wagner; and Goodall's understanding of this truth is unexcelled today. In his hands the music simply and naturally flows—though with none of the lack of variety of pace and mood that the metaphor may suggest. Unhurried though it is, Goodall's account of the score is one of the very few which achieve the violent effect of the final chord of Act 1 as Wagner has written it, not on the downbeat but a half-beat later.

For one moment I thought the closing scene of this act was going to be too serene an expression of first love. The next moment the doubt had gone, lost in the warm amplitude, the inevitability of Goodall's conducting, and the touching truthfulness with which the scene is interpreted by Alberto

Remedios and Ava June. Remedios, while equal to the heroics of Siegmund's music, draws a fine lyrical line rare among Wagner tenors, and Miss June makes up in sincerity and conviction what she lacks in purity of tone in the fortes. None of the cast needs any apology, and in Norman Bailey and Rita Hunter it has a Wotan and a Brünnhilde of splendid achievement and greater promise. Ralph Koltai's simple, gleaming black designs, all mirrors and elemental spheroids, add their own original and surprisingly effective note to a new experience of a familiar and inexhaustible work of art.

(1970)

From a House of the Dead

The Sadler's Wells production of Janáček's last and greatest opera is among the very best things the company has done. This has not prevented it from drawing small houses. Unlike *The Makropoulos Case* the work contains no big star role to catch the fashionable imagination; it is not that kind of opera. Nor is its title appealing; it suggests a gloomy work—the unpardonable sin against our right to be entertained which used to be held to spoil otherwise interesting pieces like *Don Carlo* and *Simon Boccanegra*. Yet *From a House of the Dead*, if not strictly entertaining, is profoundly exciting and not at all gloomy; nor does it fail to provide the lyrical satisfaction that people expect from opera. It is not even lacking in star attraction. The whole company is the star. Sung and played with a sense of complete commitment, the performance achieves a degree of team-work rare in the opera house.

It is also by far the most convincing that I have yet seen. The current productions by the Brno and Prague national companies are both in their different ways relentlessly abstract and symbolic. Sadler's Wells have chosen realism—not the painstaking, unimaginative realism of their *Katya Kabanova* but a spare, stripped realism in which every detail tells and the essence of the physical conditions, the drabness, the claustrophobia, the terrible unending routine, the forced association, is suggested with masterly economy. In doing so they have brought Janáček's idea intensely alive and made it a theatrical experience of overwhelming truthfulness.

The decor and the production cannot be considered apart from each other. Colin Graham handles the large cast with an almost faultless brilliance and tact. Ronald Dowd's truculent, secretly tormented Luka Kuzmich, Gregory Dempsey's radiant and pitiful Skuratov (a marvellously vital and touching performance), Emile Belcourt's ferocious Tall Prisoner, like a great tense bird, John Chorley's depraved yet childlike Cherevin, Margaret Neville's Tartar boy Aleya (completely vindicating Janáček's use of an apparently conventional 'operatic' device), David Bowman's bony, haunted Shiskov, and many others, are at once sharply delineated individuals and members of the brutalized, anonymous herd, merging with the austere lines and dun colours of the prison walls and ramps which Ralph Koltai has derived from old pictures of Siberian prison camps. From the moment when the prisoners stumble out into the winter dawn so vividly evoked in Janáček's frosty, crackling prelude, we believe what we are seeing: the insane quarrels, the flashes of sympathy, the sadistic humour; the mailbag-sewing session, the communal meal in the spring dusk, the hospital at night; the monologues, with their appalling glimpses of the degradation of Russian provincial life and their moments of piercing tenderness.

The brutality is neither minced nor overemphasized. Detail by detail the production works on us—or rather, allows the opera to do so—until we realize that these convicts are not remote beings but ourselves, and we recognize the prison camp as a central symbol of the reality and consciousness of our age, and the work as one of the great operas of the 20th century. But the symbol is—rightly, I am convinced—conveyed by semi-naturalistic means. Only occasionally does the production lose its touch. During that wonderful brief orchestral interlude in the hospital (after the mad Skuratov has been forced back to his bed), in which a long lyrical phrase, like a sudden release of pent-up pity, soars out on solo violin, then on clarinet, flute and bass clarinet, over tremolando cellos and basses, the stage should be completely still; at present, the coming and going of figures in the half-darkness is needlessly distracting. The staging of the theatricals in Act 2 is splendidly done, but the enthusiasm of the convict audience for throwing bread and fruit at the actors is in danger of getting out of hand. I also regret the absence of a backcloth suggesting the immensity of the steppe stretching away beyond the further bank of the river at the beginning of this scene (though it would hardly have fitted the style of the settings, and the imaginative lighting almost compensates for it).

These few details apart, the production seems to me beautifully faithful to the spirit and intention of the work. The fierce concentration of the tremendous first act, in which the world of the camps is created in a few short decisive strokes and an astonishing variety of feeling and incident is compressed into a bare twenty minutes' music, the contrasting mood of the second act, relaxed but elegiac, ending abruptly in violence, and the twilit third act, enclosing Shiskov's long narrative (which in unsympathetic hands can be made to seem a miscalculation on Janáček's part); the role of Alexander Petrovich, the well-born political prisoner, which it is difficult yet essential to hit off exactly, its function being at once central and peripheral (his arrival and departure defining the limits of the action, but his personality mainly serving to throw into relief the superficially very different attitudes and values of the other prisoners), and which Neil Easton plays with just the right emphasis and an air of sympathy and breadth of mind that stops safely short of the plaster saint—everything has been thought out and presented with a skill and dedication that reveal *From a House of the Dead* as a masterpiece of dramatic construction as well as a precious document of human savagery and fortitude.

It is entirely in keeping with Sadler's Wells' approach that the 'optimistic' ending, a chorus in praise of liberty, devised by Janáček's pupils after his death—the ending most commonly seen until now—has been rejected in favour of the original. As Janáček planned it, the opera has no conclusion. The life of the prison is seen as continuing, without reprieve; nothing is changed by Alexander Petrovich's departure. This is what we happen to see; but it is going on all the time.

Yet the extraordinary thing is that the work does not depress but uplifts. These creatures reduced to the lowest condition of human life still love and remember, can still respond with uncrushed imaginations to the release of the caged eagle from the squalid prison yard, and may suddenly —as Dostoevsky said of 'even the most abhorrent of them'— 'manifest a wealth of fine feeling, a keen comprehension of the sufferings of others seen in the light of the consciousness of their own'. That blinding moment of joy when Skuratov leaps to his chained feet and cries out, 'Thank God there still is life, still air to breathe,' stands for the whole. 'In every soul a spark of the divine,' wrote Janáček at the head of his score. The unblinking objectivity of his vision gives him the right to make such a claim, and the power of his music vindicates it. This is surely his supreme achievement—to have proved it true in so extreme a context, to have found a musical idiom and compositional technique which symbolize and embody that truth by creating beauty out of the most angular, unyielding fragments, out of the rejected matter, the scrapheap of music. The score—at first hearing forbiddingly spare and abrasive, all top and bottom, short stabbing motifs confined within a narrow circle of varied but unvarying rhythmic patterns, jarring harmonies, disconcertingly juxtaposed chords—is suffused with compassionate lyricism. As is often the case with operas accused of having no melody, it is all melody. The harshness and the sweetness, in Charles Mackerras' magnificent account of the score, are one.

(1965)